The
African American Roots
of Modernism

THE JOHN HOPE FRANKLIN SERIES IN AFRICAN AMERICAN HISTORY AND CULTURE

Waldo E. Martin Jr. and Patricia Sullivan, editors

The
African American Roots
of Modernism

From Reconstruction to the Harlem Renaissance

JAMES SMETHURST

The University of North Carolina Press
Chapel Hill

Designed by Jacquline Johnson
Set in Walbaum MT
by Tseng Information Systems, Inc.

The paper in this book meets the guidelines for permanence and
durability of the Committee on Production Guidelines for Book
Longevity of the Council on Library Resources.

The University of North Carolina Press has been a member of
the Green Press Initiative since 2003.

Library of Congress Cataloging-in-Publication Data
Smethurst, James Edward.
The African American roots of modernism : from Reconstruction to the
Harlem Renaissance / James Smethurst.
p. cm. — (The John Hope Franklin series in African American history and culture)
Includes bibliographical references and index.
ISBN 978-0-8078-3463-3 (cloth : alk. paper) — ISBN 978-0-8078-7185-0 (pbk. : alk. paper)
1. American literature—African American authors—History and criticism. 2. Segregation
in literature. 3. African Americans—Segregation. 4. African Americans—Intellectual life—
19th century. 5. African Americans—Intellectual life—20th century. 6. Modernism
(Literature)—United States. I. Title.
PS153.N5S555 2011
810.9'896073—dc22 2010047552

cloth   15 14 13 12 11   5 4 3 2 1
paper   15 14 13 12 11   5 4 3 2 1

Chapter 2 was published in different form as "Those Noble Sons of
Ham: Poetry, Soldiers, and Citizens at the End of Reconstruction," in
Hope and Glory: Essays on the Legacy of the Massachusetts 54th, edited by
Martin H. Blatt, Thomas J. Brown, and Donald Yacovone (Amherst: University
of Massachusetts Press, 2001), 168–87. Portions of chapter 4 were published in
different form in "Paul Laurence Dunbar and Turn of the Century African
American Dualism," *African American Review* 41.2 (Summer 2007): 377–86.
Portions of the conclusion were published in different form in "The Red Is East:
Claude McKay and the New Black Radicalism of the Twentieth Century,"
American Literary History 21.2 (Summer 2009): 355–67.

THIS BOOK WAS DIGITALLY PRINTED.

For Jacob

Contents

Acknowledgments

This book is a collective effort, even if its shortcomings and errors are strictly my own. No doubt I will forget somebody who helped me because I'm the sort of person who forgets his phone number from time to time. Still, I will do my best to acknowledge the people who made this book possible, and if I forget to mention you, just remind me later; I still owe you.

I am deeply indebted to the many people who answered questions, gave me leads, shared their research, read larger or smaller portions of the manuscript, explained things to me, and encouraged me in ways large and small while I worked on this project even if they did not always know it at the time: Shawn Alexander, Amiri Baraka, Melba Joyce Boyd, Joanne Braxton, Nick Bromell, Randall Burkett, Jules Chametsky, Margo Crawford, James Crooks, James de Jongh, Laura Doyle, Brent Edwards, Shelley Fisher Fishkin, Barbara Foley, Ernest Gibson, Gary Holcomb, George Hutchinson, Matthew Jacobson, Geoffrey Jacques, Jennifer James, Gene Jarrett, Aaron Lecklider, Allia Matta, William Maxwell, Kenneth Mostern, Bill Mullen, Aldon Nielsen, Nadia Nurhussein, Jeffrey Perry, Ousmane Power-Greene, Arnold Rampersad, Franklin Rosemont, Rachel Rubin (JWM), Sonia Sanchez, Eric Schocket, Mike Sell, Joe Skerrett, Karen Sotiropoulos, Lorenzo Thomas, Chris Vials, and Donald Yacovone.

I wish to thank Joel Martin (formerly the dean of the College of Humanities and Fine Arts and now the vice provost for academic personnel and dean of the faculty at the University of Massachusetts Amherst) and my colleagues in the W. E. B. Du Bois Department of Afro-American Studies at UMass Amherst for their material and intellectual support: Ernest Allen Jr., John Bracey Jr., Yemisi Jimoh, Kym Morrison, Amilcar Shabazz, Manisha Sinha, Nelson Stevens, William Strickland, Esther Terry, Ekwueme Michael Thelwell, Steven Tracy, and Bob Wolff. I am also deeply grateful to Tricia Loveland for answering many, many questions.

I want to acknowledge the help I received from the staffs of the W. E. B. Du Bois Library at the University of Massachusetts, especially Jim Kelly and Isabel Espinal; the Woodruff Library at Clark Atlanta University; the Woodruff Library at Emory University, especially Randall Burkett; the Butler Library at Columbia University; the Houghton Library at Harvard University; the Beinecke Library at Yale University; the Main Research Branch and the Schomburg Center for Research in Black Culture of the New York Public Library; the John Hay Library at Brown University; and the Moorland-Spingarn Research Center at Howard University.

I also want to thank the editorial, marketing, and production staff at the University of North Carolina Press, especially Sian Hunter, Chuck Grench, Beth Lassiter, Brian MacDonald, Dino Battista, and Paula Wald, for all their help. I am also grateful for the incisive comments of the anonymous reader arranged through the press as well as those of Bill Maxwell. Thanks, too, to the general editors of the John Hope Franklin Series, Waldo Martin and Patricia Sullivan, for their continued support.

As always, I am deeply indebted to my extended family: William Smethurst, Ludlow Smethurst, Richard Smethurst, Mae Smethurst, Andrew Smethurst, Alejandra Ramirez, Katie Smethurst, Tony Schlein, Silvie Schlein, Thea Schlein, Jeff Melnick, Rachel Rubin, Jesse Rubin, Merle Forney, Margaret Forney, Chris Forney, Julie Menin, Linnea Menin, Noah Menin, and my son Jacob Smethurst Rubin, to whom this book is dedicated. My deepest thanks are to Carol Forney for her love, gardening, and editing.

The
African American Roots
of Modernism

"There are great questions in my mind regarding
the forms of poetry," continued Mr. Dunbar. "Do you think
it is possible now to invent a new form? Have the old ones
completely exhausted the possible supply?"

— "Interview with Paul Laurence Dunbar,"
in Paul Laurence Dunbar, *In His Own Voice*

Where shall we look for standard English, but to the words of
a standard man? The word which is best said came nearest to
not being spoken at all, for it is cousin to a deed which the speaker
could have better done. Nay, almost it must have taken the place
of a deed by some urgent necessity, even by some misfortune, so
that the truest writer will be some captive knight, after all.

— Henry David Thoreau,
A Week on the Concord and Merrimack Rivers

Around 1900 technical reproduction had reached a standard that
not only permitted it to reproduce all transmitted works of art and thus
to cause the most profound change in their impact upon the public; it had
also captured a place of its own among the artistic processes.

— Walter Benjamin, *Illuminations*

James Smethurst,

introduction

New Forms and Captive Knights in the Age of Jim Crow and Mechanical Reproduction

There is still a general feeling that something happened in the expressive art of the United States in the early twentieth century that was different from what went before, something that we might call modernism, something that responded to U.S. modernity, often disparagingly. Following in the footsteps of such able critics and cultural historians as Michael North, Aldon Nielsen, Lorenzo Thomas, Ann Douglas, Laura Doyle, Dickson Bruce, Farah Jasmine Griffin, and Geoffrey Jacques, I am concerned here with the development of a modern African American literature and the interconnected impact of African American literary artists and intellectuals on the understanding of modernity and modernism in the United States. Unlike most scholars of African American literature and its relation to modernism, with the partial exception of Jacques and his remarkable book *A Change in the Weather*, my most intense focus is on the period from about 1890 to about 1919, by which time the system of Jim Crow segregation was firmly established and the Great Migration of African Americans from the rural South to the urban North and West (and South) was well under way.

What I hope to delineate are some of the ways that the establishment of Jim Crow as a national system, albeit with considerable regional and local variations, and the response of African American artists and intellectuals, especially Paul Laurence Dunbar, to this profound (and, for them, traumatic) ideological, political, economic, spatial, and cultural event deeply marked American notions of modernity — and, ultimately, modernism — for both African Americans and white Americans (and Americans judged neither white nor black). By looking at some of the different strands in the development of a modern African American literature between the end of Reconstruction and the onset of the New Negro Renaissance, we can discern how some black writers came to feel a need for the creation (or recognition) of a distinct African American literature representing, channeling, and serving some notion of a black "people" or "nation," while others, as the epigraph from Paul Laurence Dunbar at the beginning of this introduction suggests, sought to place their sense of African American expressive culture, experience, and subjectivity at the heart of the development of a modern "American" literature (and modern "American" citizenship) that expanded the form as well as the content of U.S. (and world) literature. Some attempted to do both. And, as the epigraph from Thoreau proposes, some white writers imagined that it might well be a "captive knight," which in Thoreau's time and the U.S. context would almost inevitably bring to mind the enslaved Africans and their descendants, who might turn out the "truest writer" in the modern and modernizing United States.

These developments are also of great interest, I argue, to those seeking to untangle the cultural strands that produced literary modernism and the line of bohemias or artistic countercultures in the United States stretching back to the turn of the twentieth century. Unlike many of the excellent studies on the enormous impact of African American culture (and the idea or "presence" of African Americans) on modern literature in the United States that have appeared since Toni Morrison's *Playing in the Dark* (1992), Shelley Fisher Fishkin's *Was Huck Black?* (1993), and Eric Sundquist's *To Wake the Nations* (1993), my emphasis is on the influence of African American literature (in the sense of a written literature) rather than of black language, music, and culture more generally.

In general, white authors in the United States have long been reluctant to acknowledge being influenced by black writers. Such a lack of acknowledgment stands in contradistinction to U.S. popular music where white artists even in such an allegedly "white" genre as country music have publicly paid tribute to black mentors since the early twentieth century. This reluctance has to a considerable extent been mirrored in the scholarship on U.S. literary modernism. Without downplaying the role of black music in a broad understanding of the modern and modernity and the creation and evolution of modernism and the avant garde in the early twentieth-century United States, a crucial objective of this book is to suggest how African American literature first raised many of the concerns, stances, and tropes associated with U.S. modernism and framed and made comprehensible to white (and Latina/Latino and Asian American) people a new urban territory of blackness (including music and venues for music) that came to have an intimate and formative relationship to emerging artistic bohemias.

There is an obvious sense in which the revolutionary democratic experiment that became the United States of America was from the start the first completely modern, capitalist, postfeudal (and even post–early modern) society where, contrary to some cynical contemporary commentators during the early republic, no hereditary aristocracy was ever established — even if one could convincingly argue that a semihereditary plutocracy came to exert undue influence and that an already existing racial caste system was further codified and solidified, persisting in different forms through all of the republic's history. So talking about modern culture and modern literature of the United States presents a problem. Is one then talking about the entire history and the complete arc of literature and culture, or of literatures and cultures, of the United States? If not, when does the United States become modern as we might understand it now? And is there a particular notion of American modernity that differs from that of other industrial nations in the late nineteenth century, a sort of exceptional modernism?

One way to think of the United States as it moved toward the Civil War is as a site of struggle over the question of what a thoroughly modern and internationally eminent, if not yet preeminent, United States might be. Many of the foundations of this modern state had already begun to take shape through the expansion of the political sovereignty of the United States across the North American continent through conquest and negotiation, the rise of the factory system beginning with the Slater Mills in Rhode Island and the Lowell and Cabot Mills in Massachusetts, the vast immigration from Europe, the growth of the United States as a force in international commerce, the development of a transportation system of railroads and canals, and the creation of the rapid communication system of the telegraph. This period also saw the beginning of a nationwide popular culture through the growth of minstrelsy and the emergence of truly popular public intellectuals, particularly Ralph Waldo Emerson, who made a sort of permanent cultural revolution the centerpiece of their ideas.

However, fundamental issues of citizenship, federal authority, state and sectional political power, the center of economic gravity, and the labor system remained in dispute. All of these issues turned on the status and destiny of African Americans and the institution of chattel slavery, ultimately producing the bloodiest war for U.S. combatants to date. The victory of the federal government over southern secessionists in this war seemed to set the stage for the resolution of how the contours of the modern United States would be shaped.

After the Civil War, the United States economy developed at an amazing rate. By the middle 1890s, the industrial production of the United States was twice that of Britain, the cradle of the industrial revolution. The late 1890s also saw the emergence of the United States as a colonial power in its own right. Before the 1890s, United States expansionism had been basically limited to the North American continent. Between 1894 and 1903, the United States seized Hawaii, Puerto Rico, Guam, Samoa, and the Philippines. During the last decade of the nineteenth century and the first two decades of twentieth, much of the Caribbean and Central America became a virtual United States protectorate, with United States armed forces frequently intervening in local politics. At the same time, the ostensibly independent nation of Liberia became increasingly dominated, economically and politically, by U.S. corporations, such as the Firestone Rubber Company. The United States also demanded, and received, a share of the semicolonial "concessions" in China, joining with European (and Japanese) forces in the suppression of the 1900 Boxer Rebellion.

Perhaps it is appropriate in the sense of the contradictory nature of modernity after the industrial revolution in which, as Marx and Engels famously said in *The Communist Manifesto*, "All that is solid melts into air," that the question of what the nature of the reassembled modern nation would consist after the Civil War was answered in two ways, with the second answer itself being a "neither-nor" proposition masquerading as a "both-and." The first answer during Reconstruction was to eliminate race, though not gender, as a fundamental yardstick for determining the quality of citizenship for people born in the United States. While prior to the Civil War the majority of African Americans were slaves, even those who were free in the sense of not being property were practically nowhere in the United States citizens with full and equal access to the ballot, the courts, education, and so on. The Thirteenth, Fourteenth, and Fifteenth Amendments outlawed slavery and guaranteed citizenship, due process and equal protection under the law, and full access to the ballot without regard to "race, color, or previous condition of servitude." (Gender, of course, remained a valid category for discrimination. And, racial categories continued to be a prominent feature of immigration and naturalization laws in the United States.) While it seems quite likely that the overwhelming majority of white Americans held and long continued to hold beliefs in the fundamental superiority of so-called Caucasians over so-called Negroes (and people of northern and western European descent over those of southern and eastern European origin, for that matter), it is true that African Americans found unprecedented political, educational, and economic opportunities, especially in the South, and could imagine a process through which they, despite much racist opposition, would be full cultural, economic, and political citizens.

However, this response to the problem of how the modern United States would be constructed was superseded in the 1880s and 1890s by the answer of Jim Crow segregation and the mass disenfranchisement of African Americans in the South—where the vast majority of black Americans still lived. This was the infamous system in which the quality of legal, political, and social citizenship from the right to vote, whom one might marry, and one's ability to testify in court down to where one could sit in a theater, out of which drinking fountain one might drink, and when (or whether) one might use the municipal swimming pool had everything to do with race. Black people were not returned to slavery. For one thing, as bad as the "Nadir" (to use Rayford Logan's familiar term for the period of the collapse of Reconstruction and the consolidation of Jim Crow) of the late nineteenth and early twentieth centuries might have been, African Americans generally, with some important exceptions (e.g., those incarcerated in prisons and on "work farms" or literally sold by the criminal justice system to private economic enterprises, such as U.S. Steel's Pratt Mines in Alabama), retained the right to migrate despite various attempts to limit that right.[1] This ability profoundly transformed the social, cultural, and political landscape of the United States with the onset of the "Great Migration" in the early twentieth century. Still, black people were hemmed in by a thicket of legal restrictions, covering virtually every aspect of social existence. These restrictions were generated by an unprecedented mania to codify the new Jim Crow regime in the South and the so-called border states (and beyond to varying degrees).

It is hard not to be struck by the fact that, during the 1880s and 1890s in the United States, Jim Crow segregation and the devices by which African Americans were disenfranchised (e.g., literacy tests and poll taxes) arise, and receive the blessing of the U.S. Supreme Court in *Plessy v. Ferguson* (1896) and *Williams v. Mississippi* (1898), at almost exactly the same time as the United States becomes the predominant industrial power of the world and an international power with colonial possessions after the securing of its North American territory. This era also marked the beginning of what Walter Benjamin famously called the "age of mechanical reproduction" with the founding of the recording industry, the embryonic film industry, the modern music publishing industry of Tin Pan Alley, the Hearst newspaper empire, and the invention and circulation of the pianola player piano (the first practical home player piano) and the box camera. As scholars of black popular culture (and of what we might think of as the "Africanist presence" in popular culture) have noted, representations, re-creations, and reproductions of black voices, black bodies, and black culture fueled the growth of many of these new mass culture industries. For example, landmark movies of each stage of the early film industry, from the silent versions of *Uncle Tom's Cabin* (which were among the first, if not actually the first, U.S. feature films) to D. W. Griffith's 1915 *Birth of Nation* to the 1927 *The Jazz Singer* (and the early all-black cast, all-talkie musicals of 1929, *Hearts in Dixie* and *Hallelujah!*) all revolved around such reproductions and re-creations.

This racialized consolidation of the modern United States society produced great economic growth and technological advance, but also enormous conflict, turmoil, and fears of fundamental and unbridgeable divisions that seem remarkable even in our own era of "red" and "blue" states. The year 1877, for example, not only saw the conclusion of the infamous political compromise between the Democrats and the Republicans that many historians consider to be the end of Reconstruction and the rise of racist violence attending the withdrawal of federal troops from the South, but also the surrender and murder of Crazy Horse, what might be thought of as the first modern American mass labor struggle sparked by strikers on the Baltimore and Ohio Railroad (leading to a general strike of railroad workers), and the formation of the first socialist party in the United States, the Socialist Labor Party.

During the last third of the nineteenth century and the first decade of the twentieth, the arrival of millions of immigrants from southern and eastern

Europe and the Middle East (and hundreds of thousands from the Philippines, Japan, and Mexico) to work in U.S. industry and agriculture led to·a heightened debate about race and immigration. This debate fed into deep anxieties about the bifurcation of the United States into capital and labor, as the trade-union movement continued to grow in the 1880s with the heyday of the Knights of Labor, the founding of the American Federation of Labor, and national agitation, demonstrations, and strikes in support of the eight-hour workday, of which the so-called Haymarket Riot of May 1, 1886, in Chicago (and the ensuing trial and execution of the leaders of that huge eight-hour-day rally)is no doubt still the best-known example.

This pattern of economic growth and consolidation accompanied by a sense of interlocking fragmentations of the body politic intensified even further in the 1890s with the rise of the Populist Party institutionalizing the wide gulf between western (and to a lesser extent southern) farmers and eastern capital, the transformation of the Socialist Labor Party into the first Marxist political party, the Homestead and Pullman strikes, and the final "Indian Wars." The period of the 1880s and 1890s, then, was decisive in the development of American modernity, both anxious and triumphal, and the fundamental elements of that modernity were the often-violent establishment and maintenance of Jim Crow and the disenfranchisement of African Americans. In fact, one might extend this line of thought further to note that the landmark 1913 New York Armory Show of modernist art took place in the same year that Woodrow Wilson extended Jim Crow to federal employment, an event of enormous symbolic importance to African Americans, and practical importance to members of the black intelligentsia, who, like James Weldon Johnson, had had access to fairly good government jobs through the patronage of previous Reconstruction and post-Reconstruction Republican administrations.

In short, there was a close connection between U.S. postbellum modernity and the new racial regime. Certainly, scholars have often asserted that the rise of the Jim Crow system was an integral part of the idea and reality of the "New South." As James Crooks has pointed out, when James Weldon Johnson's hometown of Jacksonville, Florida, was rebuilt after the devastating fire of 1901, it was as a modern commercial and industrial city on Jim Crow lines, "a one hundred per cent Cracker town" as Johnson commented, even though only a little more than a decade before it had been a relative stronghold of Reconstruction sentiment in Florida (Crooks, 85; Johnson, *Along This Way*, 44). As Johnson himself personally experienced when he was nearly lynched by the militia supervising the city in the immediate aftermath of the fire, the law often terrifyingly intersected with mob violence in the enforcement of these lines (Johnson, *Along This Way*, 165–70). One could see a similar pattern in key "New South" cities in the first decade of the twentieth century.

However, Jim Crow was a key constitutive element of modernity throughout the United States, not just in the South. This might seem obvious in the sense that racism, or "color prejudice" as it was often known in the late nineteenth century, remained rampant among white Americans North and South, East and West. Even so it is worth recalling that the rise and triumph of Jim Crow transformed the cities of the United States in novel ways, spatially as much as culturally and politically, forming one of the key elements of the new American city, North and South, even before the Great Migration of African Americans that began in the second decade of the twentieth century — though obviously that migration was of enormous importance in terms of how Jim Crow played out.

There is the old saw that white people in the South do not care how close a black person gets to them spatially just so long as he or she does not rise too high and that white people in the North do not care how high an African American rises as long as she or he does not get too close. But a marked and quite consciously intended increase in residential segregation, as well as other sorts of racial "separation," was a hallmark, too, of the modern New South cities and such "border" cities as Washington, D.C., St. Louis, and Baltimore in the first decades of the twentieth century. It is true that the new African American districts, especially the black commercial centers (e.g., Beale Street in Memphis, La Villa in Jacksonville, Fourth Avenue in Birmingham, and Auburn Avenue in Atlanta), were very often in much closer proximity to the "mainstream" commercial and political centers of southern cities than were the new ghettos and African American commercial and entertainment zones to the financial, shopping, and cultural hubs of northern and western cities in the early twentieth century (e.g., Harlem, "Bronzeville" on Chicago's South Side, and the Central Avenue area of Cleveland's East Side). Still, early twentieth-century southern and northern cities became more alike in terms of residential patterns than often has been allowed.

In both the urban North and South, the black ghetto as it came to be known in the twentieth century did not really exist before the final triumph and maturation of Jim Crow as a system — and the worldwide identification of the urban United States as the epitome of modernity from the Brooklyn Bridge of the 1880s to Ford's first assembly line in 1914. Typically in the nineteenth-century urban North, African Americans lived in mixed working-class areas, generally dominated in population by various legally "white" immigrant groups (even if their social status was, as such scholars as David Roediger, Matthew Jacobson, and Noel Ignatiev have shown, often decidedly offwhite), as in New York's Five Points and later in Greenwich Village and the neighborhoods of the middle West Side (Chelsea, Hell's Kitchen, and San Juan Hill), Pittsburgh's Hill District, South Philadelphia, Detroit's Lower East Side, Chicago's Near South Side, and the North Slope of Boston's Beacon Hill. There was tension, and often extreme violence, between African Americans and the other residents of these neighborhoods, particularly around the turn of the century. In fact, such fin de siècle violence is often cited as a major spur to the growth of the new African American ghettos, especially Harlem. And, unlike many older southern cities where African Americans were distributed comparatively evenly throughout virtually all residential districts in "yards" or "alleys," black inhabitants of northern cities found their neighborhood choices to be more restricted. Nonetheless, despite extreme racism and racial discrimination, especially in the area of employment, the presence of a black face on a block was generally not enough to send northern white working-class, and even in some places white middle-class, inhabitants into a panic leading to "white flight" or massive and often violent resistance to African American in-migration — at least not until the early twentieth century. So one might consider the legal and semilegal "separate but equal" system of segregation with its epicenter in the South to be the first wave of Jim Crow and the hypersegregation of urban space throughout the United States to be the second.

Harlem was perhaps the original, and certainly the most celebrated, case of early twentieth-century white flight. In 1903 central Harlem was a basically affluent, heavily German American neighborhood in upper Manhattan with some dispersed pockets of black residents. In a real estate boom that went bust, the neighborhood was overdeveloped with new apartment buildings and townhouses that landlords were unable to fill when the expected demand for new housing never materialized. Some astute African American realtors led by Phillip Payton convinced landlords and developers to rent or sell their empty housing units to African Americans. At that time, much of the black community in Manhattan was scattered in tenement slums along the middle West Side, an area dominated by extremely violent white street gangs. African Americans moved from the West Side to Harlem in search of decent housing and to escape endemic racial violence, ranging from individual assaults by the police or the street gangs to full-blown riots in 1900 and 1905.[2]

Strangely, the appearance of these new black faces in a community that had long had some African American residents provoked a hysteria in which white Harlemites fled block after block after ineffectual attempts to halt the black move uptown. By 1920, swelled by migration from the South and the Caribbean, Harlem had a black population of about 73,000; by 1930, 164,000 (and some thought more like 200,000–250,000). As the African American community moved uptown, so did such black institutions as churches, fraternal orders, civil rights groups, and even bars and nightclubs.

The story of Harlem's growth as an African American community has been told many, many times and has become a sort of landmark of revisionist accounts of modernism in the United States. Yet, again, one should note, as does Gilbert Osofsky, that "a substantial Negro population lived in Harlem at the turn of the century" (84) before Payton and his associates made their proposal in 1903. In fact, an 1899 "coon song," "You Can Take Your Trunk and Go to Harlem," describes a fight in which a black woman tells her two-timing lover to leave and "go to Harlem with your friends," suggesting that the idea of Harlem as a black destination was culturally recognizable some years before 1903.[3] Similarly, Countee Cullen's foster father, Frederick Asbury Cullen, began the Salem Methodist Episcopal Church in a Harlem storefront with a handful of members in 1902 as part of an effort by the downtown St. Marks Methodist Episcopal Church to reach the growing black community of Harlem still scattered in small pockets across the neighborhood (Osofsky, 84–85). By the time Countee Cullen was adopted by Frederick Cullen (or at least changed his surname from Porter to Cullen since the details of his early life are often unclear) in 1918, Harlem's African American residents numbered in the several tens of thousands, replacing white Harlemites, who, again, fled what they frequently described as a black "invasion" (Osofsky, 109).

To take another example, when Langston Hughes and his mother joined his stepfather in Cleveland in 1916, they lived in a basement apartment in the emerging ghetto on the East Side. This period saw not only the black population of Cleveland swell exponentially (308 percent between 1910 and 1920) but also a dramatic increase in segregation in the city. For example, despite the rapid growth of the African American community since the 1910 census, the number of census tracts reporting no Negro inhabitants more than doubled from seventeen to thirty-eight in 1920. During this same period, the number of Cleveland's 112 elementary schools that were all white went from seventeen to thirty. Whereas in 1910 no census tract reported a Negro population greater than 25 percent, by 1920 ten were recorded as a quarter or more Negro with two more than 50 percent (Kusmer, 158–64). As Hughes later noted, the World War I period also saw a concomitant local increase in Jim Crow practices in public accommodations, despite Cleveland's history as a liberal city that frequently elected Socialists to office—and hired black teachers (including Charles Chesnutt's daughter) to teach in integrated public schools (Hughes, *Big Sea*, 51). Beyond the personal histories of Cullen and Hughes, Woodrow Wilson's increasing segregation of federal jobs, the increasing number and intensity of violent racist incidents in the North and the South, and the reemergence of the Ku Klux Klan as a mass organization of millions that by the 1920s essentially ran governments of many southern and northern cities and states attested to the growth of Jim Crow as a national phenomenon.

In short, by the time Hughes was in Central High School in Cleveland and Cullen in DeWitt Clinton High School in New York, Jim Crow was in many respects intensifying and reaching the North in ways that went beyond the long-standing patterns of discrimination in employment, housing, education, and so on. Both, especially Hughes, credited white teachers and students at their predominately white high schools with doing much to introduce them to a larger artistic and intellectual life beyond the increasingly rigid boundaries of the ghetto. Yet even in Hughes's 1940 account of his days at Central High, there is a sense that his experience took place in a short moment of a school in transition during which such relations were possible. Within ten years of his graduation, Hughes notes, only 3 percent of Central High's student body was white (*Big Sea*, 29–30). In other words, there seems to have been some change in the first decades of the twentieth century causing African Americans to be seen by white inhabitants of Cleveland's East Side and of Harlem as an "invasion" to be resisted or fled to a degree that had not been the case before.

Yet after the original panic and flight, the geographic expansion of black Harlem and Cleveland slowed considerably, even as the actual African American population of uptown Manhattan and the East Side skyrocketed. The combined phenomenon of white flight and ghetto formation was generally replaced by an intense resistance to an expansion of the boundaries of the ghetto commensurate with the rate of black population increase. After the initial "white flight," the proximity of black people, as long as they were contained within a clearly defined zone, was generally no longer enough to provoke the sort of panicked retreat of white urban residents seen in the first decades of the century—at least not until the suburbanization and blockbusting of the post–World War II era. One might say that once urban spatial

Jim Crow had been established, a certain rough equilibrium was achieved. The result of this hardening of boundaries along with the continued migration north of African Americans was the emergence of the mature black ghetto, characterized by an overcrowding, hypersegregation, and sense of racial confinement unprecedented in the history of the urban United States. Again, this was a feature of cities in both the North and the South.

In short, the hard distinction still sometimes drawn between racial attitudes (and racist practice) in the South and the North in the early twentieth century needs further nuancing — though black radicals, such as Malcolm X, have long suggested that the U.S. South starts at the Canadian border. One might note that there was even a certain political Reconstruction in the North in the postbellum era, especially in New England and heavily New England–influenced northern Ohio, where African Americans were elected to state legislatures, judgeships, and city councils from overwhelmingly white urban districts — something that would be almost unthinkable in the early twentieth century (and even now in many predominantly white northern urban neighborhoods). Interestingly, many of these northern black office-holders were elected in the immediate post-1877 period, complicating the notion that rank-and-file Republicans, at least in former abolitionist strongholds, simply wished to forget about the "Negro problem" after the infamous compromise.

Unquestionably, considerable differences remained between conditions in the North and the wellspring of Jim Crow in the South. The relatively free access to the ballot and to better living conditions, including a somewhat more equitable education, greater economic opportunities, and less discrimination in public services, of the North certainly cannot be discounted — though, as the twentieth century wore on, education, public services, and often employment became increasingly segregated in many northern cities. The millions of African Americans who moved North and West (and generally remained there) between 1914 and 1970 were not delusional. Lynching largely, though not entirely, remained a phenomenon of the South and the border states, even if extreme racial violence (as well as more legalistic or quasi-legalistic actions as a means of policing spatial boundaries) was long a national phenomenon — as seen perhaps most dramatically in the wave of racial pogroms that swept many cities in the United States, North and South, in the period immediately after World War I. While modern black authors wrote of the symbolic descent South to the folk by the deracinated and/or alienated African American intellectual, few lived and worked there during the first half of the twentieth century unless they taught at a historically black college or university—and even then the tenure tended to be relatively short.

Still, the point here is the relatively simple one that the spatial dimensions of Jim Crow were important parts of a basically national system and crucial elements of modern American northern and southern commercial and industrial cities, cities that resembled each other racially in important dimensions as the twentieth century progressed. One might say that urban territory was racialized in new and more intense ways, even if the motor that drove the establishment of Jim Crow may have been the eventually successful efforts in the South to destroy Reconstruction and overwrite what I called the first answer to the question of the basis on which the modern United States would be organized. This territorial racialization of the city gave modernity and the experience of modernity, and modernism, a different cast, so to speak, from the commercial and cultural centers of the industrial world outside the United States in the first decades of the twentieth century—though eventually the results of this new geography of race would have an enormous impact on the sense of modernity and modernism internationally.[4]

One thing that Jim Crow and this territorial racialization did was give people in the United States (and, ultimately, beyond) new ways of thinking about, making sense of, figuring, coherently experiencing, and temporarily bridging the various sorts of profound divisions or senses of alienation that famously attended U.S. society after the industrial revolution (e.g., divisions of nature/civilization, unconscious mind/conscious mind, country/city, craft/mass production, owning class/working class, native/alien, heterosexual/homosexual, male/female, East/West, North/South, and so on). It both engaged and contained, for a while, the pleasures, anxieties, and discontents of modernity in the so-called West. After all, for white Americans the ghetto became not only a place in which African Americans could be separated from them for the public good but also a strangely glamorous place that one could visit, where one might be separated from one's self, so to speak.

These visits were often described (and are described) in the rhetoric of slumming, but they were not slumming in the sense of, say, Shakespeare's Prince Hal living the lowlife with John Falstaff in the dives of London. Duke Ellington and his ensemble, say, did not wear "primitive" costumes at the Cotton Club—though, of course, the dancers did. Even if we allow for the "jungle" themes of music, dance, and décor at many New Negro Renaissance–era clubs in black neighborhoods catering to a largely white (and sometimes almost entirely white) clientele, the trip to Harlem, Black Bottom, the Hill, or the South Side was one where visitors expected to encounter skilled and stylish musicians and, sometimes, dancers and waiters as well as the staging of more "primitive" forms of exoticism and eroticism. Then the visitors were able to go home. For the dancers, musicians, and serving staff (and perhaps the management in some cases), Harlem (or its counterparts in other urban centers) was often home — though one might have to step outside of the club or cabaret to get there. In fact, one could think of the creation of these black territories as part of the root of an intensified sense of dualism encountered in the work of early twentieth-century black artists and intellectuals as it was possible to be in the new and to a large extent officially designated black homeland and still find that one had to go outside to be inside.

The early Jim Crow era also saw the first more or less successful African American literary professionals, most notably Paul Laurence Dunbar, but also Charles Chesnutt, Fenton Johnson, Pauline Hopkins, and William Stanley Braithwaite — though, as for Langston Hughes after them, this professional success was often possible only through ceaseless efforts in a wide range of genres and media — and, even then, some of these writers, such as Hopkins and Chesnutt, cannot be said to have made a living by their writing. These writers all had a complex relationship to high and popular literature, to the so-called genteel, dialect, local color, romance, gothic, realist, and naturalist forms circulating in the United States in the late nineteenth and early twentieth centuries, a relationship in which the universalist nationalism or internationalism of such forms provided a counterpoint to Jim Crow color prejudice and yet in which the writers frequently foregrounded the impossibility of ever being able to rest easily in any of these forms, always remaining betwixt and between.

There are two waves of black artists and intellectuals in which I am particularly interested. One is the generation of the 1890s, including Dunbar, Du Bois, Hopkins, Chesnutt, and Booker T. Washington, the generation that grew up after emancipation and was in many respects the product of Reconstruction and its institutions, but which also came to intellectual and artistic maturity as Jim Crow triumphed over the remnants of Reconstruction and Reconstruction ideals.

The other wave is that of the first two decades of the twentieth century and includes Braithwaite, James Weldon Johnson, Hubert Harrison, and Fenton Johnson, whose careers were launched as Jim Crow reorganized modern urban life, North and South. The latter group came of age as the center (or centers) of gravity for African American literary culture began to shift from Boston, Philadelphia, and Washington, D.C., to New York and Chicago, which were also the two most dynamic locales of U.S. modernism and bohemia. As always, such notions of periods and artistic or intellectual generations or waves are complicated. In many cases what I am calling the second wave is actually of the same age cohort as the first wave—James Weldon Johnson was actually born a year before Dunbar. And what I am calling the racial redefining of urban territory in the United States that began in earnest during the first decade of the twentieth century developed unevenly in different locations over the next twenty years or so. As noted earlier, Langston Hughes and many of the younger artists and intellectuals of the New Negro Renaissance grew up during this process of territorial redefinition rather than, as with the younger artists of the Popular Front era, when the boundaries of the urban ghettos, such as Robert Hayden's Paradise Valley and Gwendolyn Brooks's Bronzeville, were much more clearly set. Still, like the generation of the 1890s before *Plessy* and *Williams* with respect to the first wave of Jim Crow, black writers during the second wave could see what was coming even if the system had not completely matured and hardened everywhere.

The chapters of this book are basically thematic and organized in a rough chronological order, though there is inevitably a considerable overlap in time. In chapter 1, I outline the rise and shape of the early Jim Crow system, politically and culturally, and some of its ideological and aesthetic impact on black literature. Because the political story is better known and has been the subject of a large body of scholarly literature, I concentrate more intensely on the cultural side.

As many commentators have noted, this era, while generally dismal for African Americans, is full of contradictions. The central contradiction is the enactment and eventual legitimization by the U.S. Supreme Court of the legal system of Jim Crow and African American disenfranchisement in the South (and a considerable portion of the rest of the United States), while the Thirteenth, Fourteenth, and Fifteenth Amendments to the Constitution remain in effect. That this counterrevolution could triumph was disheartening but perhaps not so mind-boggling to African American artists and intellectuals as the fact that its legal edifice was laid over that of the failed revolution and judged consonant. It is this sense of failed possibility remaining present alongside increasing oppression that led black writers to judge the new Jim Crow era to be as bad as (or even worse than) the slave era, when, on most scales of practical conditions and effects, it clearly was not. Again, for one thing, African Americans, excepting the not inconsiderable category of prisoners, generally retained the right to move. For another, formal education through college or university for black people in the South was still a viable possibility. In fact, the historically black colleges and universities of the South and the border states remained the most likely option for African Americans anywhere in the United States (and the Anglophone Caribbean) seeking postsecondary education during most, if not all, of the Jim Crow era.

Yet Paul Laurence Dunbar, whose parents had been slaves, wrote of the "new slavery" and suggested in "Douglass," a tributary sonnet to his former patron and employer Frederick Douglass, that even the ex-slave who had so powerfully written of, in Douglass's words, "the hell of slavery" had not known times as "dark" as that of a clearly triumphant Jim Crow system. Obviously, these were claims of a deeply bitter and angry man, echoing similar moments in the work of W. E. B. Du Bois, James Weldon Johnson, Pauline Hopkins, Fenton Johnson, and other black writers of that era.

This contradictory and divided polity found an echo in the "high" and popular cultures of the time. One aspect of the culture of the United States in the nineteenth century that the now somewhat dated but still widely circulated models of artistic center and periphery, of "mainstream" and "margins," do not adequately address is that the central problem for African American artists was not a struggle to write (and compose and sing and dance and act and draw and paint) the African American subject into U.S. culture. As contemporary observers noted, and such recent writers, historians, and cultural critics as Eric Lott, W. T. Lhamon, Toni Morrison, and David Roediger, to mention only a few, have demonstrated, versions of the black subject, the black body, and the black voice had long saturated the high and popular culture of the United States — and in fact formed a great deal of the basis of a truly national popular culture.

However, as James F. Dormon notes, with the rise of the "coon song" and the related phenomenon of ragtime in the late nineteenth century (not to mention "coon"-inflected works in other media, such as the widely circulated "Darktown" prints of Currier and Ives and "Blackville" illustrations of *Harper's Weekly*), a different, more threatening version of African Americans was promoted (Dormon, 466–67). Though the "coon song" was clearly indebted to earlier minstrel performance practices, tropes, and so on, the basic types of the early minstrel show, the happy-go-lucky tramp and the ridiculous dandy, were relatively harmless comic figures threatening only the chicken coop, the watermelon patch, work productivity, sartorial taste, and English syntax. While these types, along with the faithful-old-soul-type retainers of plantation literature, continued to exist, and even thrive, in high and popular culture, they were joined by a far more frightening (and exciting) hypersexual, gambling, criminal (in a deeper sense than the chicken- and watermelon-stealing tramp), razor-wielding, and pistol-packing, though often humorous black male (and sometimes female) of the "coon song."

The humorous or semihumorous figure of the "coon" was a bridge between the types of minstrelsy and the trope of the violent and degenerate black rapist unable to control his various appetites that was such a large feature of postbellum attacks on Reconstruction and of the ideological underpinning of the need for racial separation. Of course, the figuration of the black subject, especially the black male subject, as the embodiment of unrepressed desire and primal urges in the "coon song," intensifying earlier renderings of the Negro as a natural, instinctual being, made that figure available as a powerful modernist trope. This began a transformation of popular culture visions of African American men from a sort of feminization or demasculinization to an exaggerated hypermasculinity that might be more familiar to consumers of U.S. popular culture in our time. In other words, acting "black" or "Negro" came to take on a new meaning in popular culture from what it had in the antebellum minstrel era—though the older meanings and images continued to linger, especially on the stage and in the new medium of film. And, by the late 1910s, the "coon song" not only presented versions of black bodies, voices, actions, and tastes but also increasingly portrayed public urban or quasi-urban black spaces, especially bars, clubs, and dance halls, in African American districts as places one could, and would, desire to visit.

One complication of the "coon" craze is that many of the performers and writers of "coon songs," ragtime songs, and the African American musical comedy of the era (including Dunbar and James Weldon Johnson) were black. One could argue that such performers, lyricists, and composers took part in their own degradation for narrow and short-term self-interest along the lines proposed in Spike Lee's 2000 film *Bamboozled*. However, this craze also produced black vaudeville and a black comic musical tradition that was tremendously popular among African American audiences (which in the urban theaters of Dunbar's time generally sat in the balcony above the white patrons in the orchestra seats) at least until the 1960s, when the last of the blackface African American comics, such as Eddie "Pigmeat" Markham, finally stopping blacking up—prompting in Markham at least a sort of identity crisis as he felt that he was no longer funny without his makeup. Not only was this form popular among black audiences, but the performers, composers, and writers of it (as well as some black critics) saw it as a genuine outlet for black artistry and, even, a critique of Jim Crow politics and culture. Many of these performers, composers, and writers, such as Dunbar and James Weldon Johnson, anxiously saw the form and the other genres it influenced simultaneously as an opportunity to live as an artist and to critique Jim Crow and as a sort of artistic prison (Forbes, 78). In short, this was an enormously (and necessarily, given the racial bifurcation of audiences in vaudeville theaters) ambivalent form that, as critics have noted, exerted a fascination on black and white modernists, from Williams to Hughes to Eliot.

Yet this period also saw the wide circulation within U.S. "high" culture and popular culture of versions of African American music, dance, and literature in which the act of unmasking of a faux Negro and/or the performance of an allegedly unmediated "authentic" racial or national expression was crucial to their success. The success of the Fisk Jubilee Singers in presenting the spirituals to an international audience is a key example of this new fascination, on the part of both black and white Americans, with the authentic African American folk culture and the "real" black voice—however mediated the actual cultural practices, such as George L. White's rearrangement of the spirituals in a light "classical" style for the Fisk group, may have been.

Chapter 1 also takes up the various expressions of African American dualism most famously associated with Du Bois's notion of "double consciousness" and his metaphor of "the veil." I have a couple of purposes here in looking at Paul Laurence Dunbar, Frederick Douglass, Booker T. Washington, James Weldon Johnson, and Fenton Johnson with and against Du Bois and the notion of double consciousness. One purpose is to approach how Du Bois's notion of racial dualism was a concrete response to the particular political and cultural situation in the United States at the end of the nineteenth century and the beginning of the twentieth with the establishment of Jim Crow, the collapse of the old abolitionist leadership and ideology, and the increasingly central (and contradictory) figure of the black speaking subject in the burgeoning popular culture industries. Here I suggest how Du Bois's concept of double consciousness and "the veil" was one of a set of notions of dualism, generally linked to tropes of sight and concealment, that circulated among African American artists and intellectuals, including Du Bois, Dunbar, James Weldon Johnson, Charles Chesnutt, and Fenton Johnson, as well as in black popular culture.

The other purpose is to suggest not only that these other dualisms engaged in a sort of cultural conversation with that of the more widely examined notion of Du Bois but that they continued to speak, as it were. It is a commonplace, for example, that Du Bois's version of dualism had a huge impact on Ralph Ellison's *Invisible Man*, but the continuing influence of Dunbar's construction of dualism on post–World War II work by such poets as Langston Hughes, Sonia Sanchez, and Amiri Baraka is far less considered. Though invoking an antiracist universalism that anticipates Du Bois's positing of a relationship with Shakespeare, Dumas, and Balzac (not to mention Schiller and Goethe) on a higher level in *The Souls of Black Folk*, Dunbar's most famous "standard poems," such as "We Wear the Mask," "Sympathy," and "The Poet," protest the impossibility of the black poet working comfortably within the genteel tradition, however one might desire it. In this, one might say that Dunbar at the turn of the century and many of the African American poets of the next few decades located themselves both within and against the so-called genteel and Romantic traditions. Dunbar's poetry, too, anticipated the foregrounding of the inexorable invasion of "high" culture by mass culture that one sees in U.S. modernism from the verse of T. S. Eliot to Nathanael West's *Miss Lonelyhearts*.

Chapter 2 traces the development of the trope of the black Civil War soldier, particularly those members of the Massachusetts Fifty-fourth who led the assault on Battery Wagner during the Civil War (a unit prominently memorialized in the twentieth century by the 1989 movie *Glory* and revived as part of the Massachusetts National Guard by Governor Deval Patrick in 2009). The trope was used by black writers, most notably and successfully Paul Laurence Dunbar, to engage both the Reconstruction answer and the Jim Crow answer to the question of how the modern United States, especially the New South, would be ordered. In many respects, the trope of the black Civil War soldier during Reconstruction marked a unique period in African American literary history. Indeed, it marked a unique period in African American social history, that is, an era in which black citizenship in the United States seemed an actualizing probability, if not an actuality— something that had never happened before and would not happen again until, at least, the mid-1960s. So the postbellum figure of the black Civil War veteran was initially one of black modernity in which African American citizenship would be a key constituent of the new reconstructed nation.

The poetry invoking the Massachusetts Fifty-fourth and the black Civil War soldiers is something of a departure from the much-discussed narratives of literacy and freedom. Tropes of freedom and literacy often appear in these poems. But generally, as in Dunbar's early work, there is a transcending of both categories: it is citizenship that these soldiers have earned with their blood, not simply freedom (which quite a few could be said to have possessed as they were already legally "free" in many, if not most, cases), and it is manhood, not literacy, which they have attained through sacrifice in the cause of a divinely sanctioned civic duty. Again, these poems do not oppose freedom to citizenship but are arguments against a notion of "freedom" that would not include full citizenship, deferring it until some future date when African Americans are "ready." Similarly, they are clearly not opposed to literacy (they are poems, after all) but are implicitly opposed to a concept of "literacy" that might serve as a bar to African American citizenship—as such a concept did in fact.

The symbolic geography of these poems bridged that of the slave narratives and the early black migration narratives. If the protagonists of the slave narratives ascended North to freedom, the soldiers of the Fifty-fourth "returned" to the South (though many were seeing it for the first time) heroically and, ultimately, triumphantly. Though they returned to the folk, they generally neither embraced nor rejected a folk identity. Their identity as citizens and Americans (and African Americans) was not represented, generally, as dependent on the adoption or rejection of a particular cultural identity but on their actions in the defense of the Republic and in attacking the institution of slavery.

With the ascendancy of the Jim Crow system, the black Civil War veteran, particularly in the poetry of Dunbar, takes on a different valence. This valence is one of a betrayal or a debt not paid, of a willful forgetfulness on the part of white Americans as Jim Crow becomes a defining feature of the nation during its ascendance as the premier global industrial power and an increasingly significant international political player. It also served as an existential validation of African American humanity adrift in the fogs of an American political limbo that can be seen as a counterpoint to Dunbar's famous metaphor of the mask—and is much closer in tone to the melancholy displayed in the early migration novel. That is to say that the figure of the soldier is the black man unmasked, whose essential integrity remains even if there is no place for him in the official cultural memory, whether in literature, the prints of Currier and Ives, or, as David Blight notes about the famous 1913 Blue-Gray reunion at Gettysburg, the reunions of white Union and Confederate Civil War veterans (Blight, *Race and Reunion*, 383–90). .

Dunbar's later work was also in conversation, even debate, with the use of the black Civil War soldier by white protomodernist writers, notably William Vaughn Moody in "An Ode in Time of Hesitation," especially after the dedication of the Saint-Gaudens monument to Robert Gould Shaw and the Fifty-fourth on Boston Common in 1897, to meditate on a new and, in their view, disturbing era of the modern imperialist United States without making much reference to the cause in which the soldiers fought or the Jim Crow system under which many of the surviving veterans and their kin now lived. If not precisely modernist, Moody's poem certainly engaged a North American version of what Richard Terdiman called the "memory crisis" that attends modern bourgeois, industrial society.

However, Dunbar's sonnet "Robert Gould Shaw" pointedly turns on a double forgetfulness in Moody's vision that complains of a general lack of recall of the true or original America while leaving out the black subject/ citizen, serving as a poignant critique of the sort of white dualism that would take not only the black body and voice but also black history and, indeed, the literature of black authors that had done much to keep the memory of the Fifty-fourth alive, to mark or warn of the emergence of a new "America," while somehow eliding or eliminating black people, culture, and literature. The chapter closes with a short discussion of the disappearance of the trope of the black Civil War veteran and its replacement by other sorts of African American war veterans, particularly the black World War I soldier, a replacement that is not simply due to the passage of time, as the World War I veteran would remain an important trope of black literature throughout the twentieth century. Thus, this chapter serves as a sort of cautionary tale about keeping in mind how black influences on the emergence of a modern and even modernist U.S. literature (and sensibility) are refracted in peculiar and often not benign ways, as well as marking a sort of black literary exhaustion of the assumption of (as opposed to the demand for) citizenship, that exhaustion lending itself to various notions of a black national literature.

Chapter 3 considers the relationship of Dunbar and the immediate post-Dunbar generation of black writers, critics, and editors of poetry, especially Fenton Johnson and William Stanley Braithwaite, to the rise of the "new poetry" and the development of the character of artistic bohemia in the United States. Such scholars as Aldon Nielsen, Michael North, Carla Peterson, and Geoffrey Jacques have noted that many of the "high" modernist writers, such as T. S. Eliot, Gertrude Stein, Ezra Pound, Wallace Stevens, and William Carlos Williams, have a deep, if ambivalent, relationship to minstrelsy, ragtime, the "coon song," and forms of popular culture that presented a stylized black body and sounded the black voice. As North and Ann Douglas have pointed out with respect to Eliot (and which might also be extended to Stevens, Williams, and Pound, among others), the flip side of this attraction to black masks and ventriloquisms was a deep anxiety about the stability of one's racial status and identity, which is to say the status of one's political, cultural, and even existential citizenship in the Jim Crow United States—an anxiety that could lead to terror and madness, as seen in William Faulkner's *Light in August* and Nella Larsen's *Quicksand*.

Some scholars, particularly Lorenzo Thomas, have looked at the participation of Fenton Johnson and William Stanley Braithwaite in early "new poetry" circles. Few, however, other than Jacques, have considered the work of Dunbar and the immediate post-Dunbar generation of African American poets and its place in American poetry in the first two decades of the twentieth century. Interestingly, there was a strange dialectical relationship between African American poets and the "new poetry." On one hand, there was an assumption by nascent black nationalists and radical black democrats (and some white critics) that the path toward full cultural and political citizenship for black Americans involved African American poetry becoming truly "modern," an assumption that in part rested on the notion that black poetry, and literature generally, was "backward" or a weak imitation of "traditional" Euro-American verse.

At the same time, not only did the "new poetry" find formal and thematic inspiration in popular culture versions of the African American subject, the black voice, and African American expressive culture, but the participation of black artists and intellectuals in new bohemian circles, and the representation of those at least nominally integrated circles, became a hallmark of a countercultural break with the mainstream, especially in the bohemias of Greenwich Village in New York, of Towertown on the near North Side in Chicago, and of Beacon Hill in Boston. The work of black writers, especially Dunbar and James Weldon Johnson, formed some of the earliest and most sustained commentary on the idea of an "American" bohemia (white, black, and black and white). Such representations of interracial American bohemia became an even more pronounced feature of the New Negro or Harlem Renaissance. Not only did black artists and intellectuals of the 1920s see the black artistic "renaissance" as joining the general "poetry renaissance" and rise of modern "American" art, but they also believed (correctly, I argue) that black writers and editors, particularly Fenton Johnson and Braithwaite, had been instrumental in the creation of the broader American renaissance.

Chapter 4 looks at the migration narrative and the new racialization of space in the modern city of the early Jim Crow era in the North and in the New South. While these works are clearly indebted to earlier narratives, they differ in that public black spaces deeply tied to popular culture are crucial to the movement of the narratives in ways that were not true of the earlier narratives, where distinctly African American spaces were largely restricted to home and family. Such family sites are still present in the Jim Crow narrative and are often set in opposition to the public, commercial spaces that are seen as inimical to family in many respects. Interestingly, in many of these later stories the very designation of these public spaces as black makes them unusually vulnerable to invasion by white seekers of blackness in ways that are perhaps analogous to the depiction of the intrusion of racist violence into black family spaces (particularly during the "New Slavery" of the post-Reconstruction period) that was long a staple of African American literature dating back to Phillis Wheatley's "To the Right Honourable William, Earl of Dartmouth" with its autobiographical description of division of an African family by the slave trade. In part, the urban rootlessness that is often seen attending this displacement of family rootedness identified with the rural South by the transitory and often commercial ties of the public space is marked by this paradoxical susceptibility of the public space to white invasion within the context of rigid residential hypersegregation.

At the same time, it is often suggested in the migration narrative that this new urban racial spatialization provides the basis of what might be a distinct national or quasi-national culture as it at least partially shifted the notion of "home" from the rural South to the urban black neighborhood, North and South. The frequently invoked trope of the "city within a city" and the related notion of the "black metropolis," as the destination of the African American provincial in many migration narratives, at least implicitly, if sometimes ironically, draw on a utopian vision of black self-determination. Such territorialization had much to do with the vast migration of African Americans from the countryside to the city and from the South to the North, beginning in the second decade of the twentieth century, greatly swelling the new urban ghettos. Still, the formation of the modern ghettos, North and South, and the increasing location of interracial vice districts in these ghettos, antedated the Great Migration.

Chapter 5 takes up the question of feminism, sexuality, race, modernity, modernism, and African American writing. It takes particular note of the mixed-race figure. I employ the term "mixed race" so as to avoid the dehumanizing connotation of "mulatta/mulatto." Modernism, at least "high" modernism, like black nationalism, has been frequently described, not without reason, as powered by masculinist discourses of manhood, effeminacy, and emasculation in which a debased and threatening popular bourgeois (or would-be bourgeois) consumer culture is linked with women and a feminization of life in the industrial world, from Madame Bovary to the chattering women of *The Wasteland* (Huyssen, 45–62). However, as Christine Stansell has noted, early bohemia (and some of the most important institutions of modernism in the United States) distinguished itself from its European counterparts by its close relationship with feminism and organized radicalism, perhaps most clearly embodied in the figure of the anarchist Emma Goldman, with her mixture of radical politics and culture. Similarly, black women deeply, if sometimes ambivalently, engaged with feminism, as both organization and ideology. Building on the many valuable new studies about the "Women's Era" and early twentieth-century black feminism, this chapter investigates African American women's participation in and representation of feminist-inflected bohemia and modernist literature.

Chapter 5 also considers how struggles for sexual freedom, heterosexual, homosexual, and polysexual, within the racist and homophobic atmosphere of the United States then were crucial constituents of bohemia and the avant-garde in the United States. Much like the preceding chapter, and building on the work of earlier scholars, particularly Siobhan Somerville, chapter 5 considers how black writers, particularly Pauline Hopkins, Paul Laurence Dunbar, and James Weldon Johnson were among the earliest U.S. writers to push the hardening boundaries of a normative heterosexuality, significantly "queering" the representation of bohemia in ways in which the linkage of queerness and even open homosexuality with race, too, becomes a mark of representations of bohemia in the United States as well as crucial modernist ur-texts, such as Gertrude Stein's "Melanctha," which is considered at some length in this chapter with regard to its relation to black literature.[5] My argument here is that while considerable attention has been paid to the formal and thematic connection of Stein's story to black music, not enough (or really any) effort has been made to think about its links to the work of African American writers, which seem to me to be deeper.

The conclusion returns to the question, What was modernism? (or, perhaps, What were modernisms?), and considers some of the ways the work of black writers between the end of Reconstruction and the beginning of the New Negro Renaissance informed the corpus of interwar modernism.

Particular attention is paid to the poetry of T. S. Eliot and William Carlos Williams and to F. Scott Fitzgerald's *The Great Gatsby* and William Faulkner's *Light in August*, as well as to the work of Jessie Fauset, Rudolph Fisher, Nella Larsen, Claude McKay, Wallace Thurman, and Jean Toomer, not only demonstrating structural, tonal, and thematic resonances between the work of the black writers of the Nadir and the modernists but also locating, in an extreme anxiety about racial identity primarily, but not solely, on the part of white (or, in the case of Williams perhaps, offwhite) writers, a paradoxical adoption and adaptation of the dualism of their black predecessors.

Perhaps a note about my use of modernism and modernity is in order here before concluding this introduction. It is not my intention to play the old game of "find the modernism" so as to prove the worth of such writers as Dunbar, James Weldon Johnson, Georgia Douglas Johnson, Fenton Johnson, and William Stanley Braithwaite. As someone who was an undergraduate at what might be seen as a third-tier public university where, for the most part, news about structuralism and poststructuralism was very late in arriving, my early training in literary studies was largely according to New Critical precepts, even though I vaguely heard that such people as Derrida, Foucault, Bakhtin, and Althusser existed. So I have no doubt I still have some residual reverence for the restrictive "high modernist" canon that the New Critics promoted — or at least I still feel the pull of the notion that "modernist," however defined, equals superior literary value. However, this is a pull that I try (and have long tried) to resist for a variety of intellectual, aesthetic, and ideological reasons.

My project here, then, is not to prove that black literature at the turn of the century is worth reading because it is "modernist" in the senses that the New Critics and the New York Intellectuals defined it but to rethink the relationship of black literature during the early Jim Crow era, North and South, to a broad sense of "American" artistic modernity as well to the development of significant "American" artistic avant gardes or countercultures anchored territorially or geographically. These countercultures were largely new at the turn of the century but have been a major feature of artistic life in the United States ever since.

However, I also want to make clear that I am not trying to claim that these writers are important simply because they directly or indirectly influenced "major" white (or arguably white) artists or even some multiracial, multiethnic version of "modernism." In fact, one enormously significant impact of the work of these black Nadir artists and intellectuals on literary modernity, as opposed, perhaps, to ideas of the formations of "modernism," is that much of this work puts forward various models of a distinct modern "Negro" literature issuing from and speaking to and for some sort of black nation (or black international), creating cultural fields from which issued some of the most powerful literary works of the twentieth and twenty-first centuries. In this sense I am not so much arguing against the line of thought associated most prominently, perhaps, with Houston Baker's *Modernism and the Harlem Renaissance* (1987) that there was a black modernism in the first half of the twentieth century distinct from what he calls "Anglo-American" modernism—though many of those "Anglos," at least from the United States, owed much more to black Nadir literature than they (with the partial exception of William Carlos Williams) would allow.

If I have any ulterior motive in this project, it is to use it as an occasion to write extensively about the work of Paul Laurence Dunbar. I have long loved Dunbar's poetry. In the course of writing my first book, *The New Red Negro*, I became convinced that he was the towering figure of black poetry who cast a huge literary shadow on all African American poets who followed him—and white, Asian American, and Latino poets, for that matter. My feeling is that Dunbar and his work have been generally very poorly served by scholarship—at least until relatively recently with the appearance of new work on Dunbar, and new editions of Dunbar's writings, by such scholars as Marcellus Blount, Shelley Fisher Fishkin, Geoffrey Jacques, Jennifer James, Gene Jarrett, and Gavin Jones. However, my own scholarly inclination as someone who hovers between literary critic and intellectual historian is not for studies of individual figures (however much I love to read them) but for larger comparative works that seek to, in the much-repeated words of Fredric Jameson, "always historicize." Beyond my desire to pay homage to Dunbar as well as to scholarly guides who helped me think about modernism and African American literature, especially the late Lorenzo Thomas, who taught me so much about this subject (and many others), I wish this project to be seen as part of an ongoing and growing intellectual conversation about the nature of African American literature and culture between Reconstruction and the Harlem Renaissance and its impact on the production and reception of art generally in the United States.

chapter one

Dueling Banjos

African American Dualism and Strategies for
Black Representation at the Turn of the Century

Paul Gilroy has powerfully claimed that the notion of double consciousness in which the black subject "ever feels his twoness" was used by W. E. B. Du Bois to figure a diasporic and sometimes transatlantic black modernity expressing the ambivalent location of people of African descent simultaneously within and beyond what is known as "the West" (Gilroy, 111–45). Certainly, Du Bois's articulation of dualism, largely drawing on the language of William James and early U.S. psychology, has remained a powerful trope available to a wide range of artists and intellectuals both inside and outside the United States down to the present.[1]

To understand why Du Bois's formulation of the concept had such force, however, one has to examine the relationship of his formulation to similar expressions of African American dualism, within the political and cultural context in which these various articulations appeared. As Ernest Allen Jr. points out, Du Bois's notion of double consciousness in *The Souls of Black Folk* as an appropriate description of the literally divided spiritual, psychological, and even cultural conditions of individual black artists and intellectuals at the turn of the century is dubious at best in an empirical sense — however powerful the metaphor seemed to later generations (Ernest Allen, 217–53). However, as a figuration of the divided political status of African Americans, and their ambivalent position in what might be thought of as the consciousness of the nation as expressed in law, historiography, literature, art, popular culture, and so on, the concept of double consciousness and other tropes of African American dualism were convincingly apt.

Du Bois's book is often rightly seen as sounding a note of dissent within what is frequently termed the age of Booker T. Washington in African American politics, thought, and letters — though, to extend the musical metaphor, one can see *Souls* in many respects as a variation on Washington's theme or a revision of a Washington riff. Yet it is worth recalling that it was also the age of Paul Laurence Dunbar, whose critical and professional success as a literary artist among black and white readers was unprecedented for an African American author. Of course, Phillis Wheatley attained a considerable notoriety among many of the political and intellectual leaders of her time at home and abroad (as well as a position of historical note as only the third woman from what would become the United States to publish a book of poetry in English), and Frances E. W. Harper sold thousands of volumes of her poetry, perhaps even outstripping Dunbar in that regard (Boyd, 15).

But, as Countee Cullen claimed in the introduction to the 1927 anthology of black poetry *Caroling Dusk*, black and white readers assigned Dunbar a "uniquity as the first Negro to attain to and maintain a distinguished place among American poets, a place fairly merited by the most acceptable standards of criticism" (x–xi). Dunbar, in fact, was among the most successful poets, arguably the most successful, of his era. James Weldon Johnson, recalling an extended visit that Dunbar paid his family in Jacksonville in 1901, noted that when Dunbar sent off poems to the leading literary journals of the era, acceptance notes (and checks) followed almost immediately. Dunbar's work also inspired black literary societies devoted to the reading of his poetry, both "high literary" and "dialect" (James Weldon Johnson, *Along This Way*, 160; Knupfer, 223–24).

The age of Dunbar, Washington, and the early Du Bois is a paradoxical one. The paradox is that Dunbar (born 1872) and Du Bois (born 1868), and their African American age cohort, including James Weldon Johnson (born 1871) and even the older Washington (born 1856), Anna Julia Cooper (born 1858) and Charles Chesnutt (born 1858), were members of the first generation to grow up after Emancipation. Unlike his parents, who had been slaves, Dunbar was born free after the passage of the Thirteenth, Fourteenth, and Fifteenth Amendments. Yet the hopes and promises of Reconstruction were clearly fading with the increasing advance of Jim Crow segregation and black disenfranchisement in the South (and elsewhere) in the early 1890s despite the fact that those amendments remained part of the Constitution. One might say that Reconstruction, like Prohibition later, was essentially overturned. However, unlike the case of Prohibition and the Eighteenth Amendment that underwrote it, the portions of the amended Constitution that undergirded Reconstruction were left intact — providing, eventually, the legal basis for the 1954 *Brown* decision by the U.S. Supreme Court. There was no anti-Reconstruction equivalent of the Twenty-First Amendment that eliminated Prohibition. Thus, the dualistic fig leaf of "separate, but equal" was required in order to square Jim Crow with the highest law of the land.

Again, the advance of Jim Crow and black disenfranchisement happened, not coincidentally, while the United States became the predominant economic power in the world and, increasingly, a political world power. I say not coincidentally because this participation in international politics, particularly colonialism, was in no small part authorized by an ideology of racial superiority and was primarily promoted by a Republican Party that had, after all, arisen largely in opposition to the institution of slavery—though by the time the United States became a colonial power at the turn of the century, the GOP in the North had made its peace with Jim Crow and in the South was increasingly dominated by its pro–Jim Crow "lily white" faction (Meier, 164–65). This legal and political dualism was mirrored by a similarly double and ambivalent position in the simultaneous emergence of a relatively distinct African American transregional popular culture and of a linked and similarly national "mainstream" popular culture. As one might imagine, this could produce a sense of contradiction or doubleness in someone who was told in word, deed, and law that he or she was a citizen and yet not a citizen. And, by the early twentieth century, the problem of, in Du Bois's words, "the color line," of where and of what one might be a citizen or a potential citizen took on a new urgency and international (and internationalist) dimension for African Americans, perhaps most clearly seen in the establishment of the ur-modern black nationalist organization, the Universal Negro Improvement Association, by Marcus Garvey (a great admirer of Booker T. Washington), especially with his move to the United States in 1916, and his founding of a New York branch in 1917.

The problem of dualism, whether in Du Bois's semipsychological proposition of two more or less unintegrated consciousnesses existing simultaneously in one body, Paul Laurence Dunbar's notion of the masking of one's true nature (with the proto-Althusserian dilemma that Du Bois identifies as seeing one's self only through the eyes of others who see only the mask), or a more strictly legalistic sense of post-Reconstruction Jim Crow segregation, is the problem of being a citizen and yet not a citizen (and, by extension, of being simultaneously human and not quite human legally, socially, and culturally) in an increasingly urbanized, industrialized, and imperialist United States. How does one respond? Through integration or separatism—or through a sort of separate development of a group culture and politics that would enable the group to force itself into the "mainstream" of culture and power in the United States? By proving oneself to be worthy or by withdrawing? Or through a sort of integration through self-determination in which African Americans force their recognition as full citizens through political, educational, economic, and cultural self-development? And, if one tries to represent what one might consider the distinctly African (American) portion of black subjectivity, what might that be? The folk culture? Who then defines or constitutes the folk, and how does one allow the folk subject to speak? How does one represent or re-create his or her culture without seeming to participate in minstrelsy, "coon songs," and plantation literature — and the reflections of these genres in other forms of popular and "high" culture? How does one deal with the doubleness of popular culture as seen in minstrelsy, the cakewalk, the "coon song," ragtime, and the ambivalence of African American minstrel-influenced vaudeville?

The Poet and His Song: Reading Paul Laurence Dunbar; Paul Laurence Dunbar Reading

Paul Laurence Dunbar engaged these questions most directly in verse written in what William Dean Howells described as "literary English" (introduction, *Lyrics of Lowly Life*, xix). "The Poet and His Song," apparently among the most consistently performed "literary English" poems in Dunbar's readings to African American audiences, is second to appear in *Lyrics of Lowly Life*.[2] The familiar pastoral conceit of the poem is that the artist is a sort of arborist who sings as he works. But after an initial stanza that sets the scene, the following three stanzas each feature a problem causing the poet disappointment, dissatisfaction, and, eventually, anger and feelings of rebellion: no one acknowledges or praises his songs; he works hard while "others dream within the dell" (*Collected*, 5); his garden suffers from a strangely malignant drought or rapacious blight. The poet appears able to quell these feelings with a certain stoicism that many of Dunbar's contemporaries, particularly those working in the plantation tradition, said was a defining feature of African American folk psychology, declaring "And so I sing, and all is well." Still, each time the feelings rise higher and the tone of the poet's transition to the calming refrain seems more strained and, by the end, near hysterical, so that the reader wonders if the next rise of passion will overwhelm him entirely, much like the speaker of Cullen's "Heritage" — or tear him apart to invoke Du Bois's image in *The Souls of Black Folk*.[3] That the poet submerges or hides these emotions in cheerful song recalls Frederick Douglass's famous comments in his autobiographies about the hidden meanings and frequent misreadings of slave music — passages that are taken up at more length later in this chapter.

Douglass's remarks about the meaning and reception of slave music are addressed even more directly in Dunbar's "A Corn-Song," which sets the musical expression of exhausted slaves returning to their quarters after a long day of labor in the fields against the music's reception by "the master in his seat," who is moved to tears listening to the "mellow minor music" as his slaves trudge by. Where the master perceives a moving sweetness, the poem suggests another interpretation on the part of the slaves, a complicated combination of sorrow, endurance, and protest. Like Charles Chesnutt's stories in the 1898 *The Conjure Woman*, Dunbar's poem directly engages the sort of plantation literature claim made by Joel Chandler Harris in the introduction to *Uncle Remus: His Songs and Sayings* that the songs and stories of the black folk are "a part of the domestic history of every Southern family" (4) — and, one might add, the domestic history of every American family through literary efforts of Harris, Thomas Nelson Page, and others in the plantation tradition, including to some extent Dunbar himself. Dunbar's poem allows that Harris may be correct, that the song the master hears (like the stories Uncle Remus tells the boy in the first part of *Uncles Remus: His Songs and Sayings*) is no doubt part of the domestic history of the master and his family as well as part of that of the slaves. However, the poem also expresses what should be the obvious point that Douglass, too, makes: there are different communities of meaning based on different histories — or perhaps different class and racial locations in the same historical space. Both "The Poet and His Song" and "The Corn-Song" raise the complicated masking of the black artist working in the minstrelsy-influenced tradition of the popular stage as well as the intersecting popular culture variations of plantation literature that are foregrounded in ways strangely more direct and more oblique in "We Wear the Mask."

The "mellow minor music" also points to how these complications are embedded in the title of the 1895 collection *Majors and Minors. Majors and Minors* is organized into two sections: one of poems in "literary English" and the other of poems of "Humor and Dialect." One might take the first section to be the "Majors" and the second to be the "Minors" — though, typically, that is not directly stated by Dunbar. As "A Corn-Song" (included among the "literary" poems despite its description of a moment on the plantation and the interpolation of black folk voices) suggests, Negro music was, and had long been, associated with "minor music" as the nearest approximation of the tonality of African American vernacular music on traditional diatonic European scales. One sees, then, a certain linking of African American culture to the "Minors." However, the apparent "Majors" include not only such allegedly raceless poems (which many commentators have read as faux white) as "Ere Sleep Comes Down to Soothe the Weary Eyes" but also some of Dunbar's most militant lyrics of race pride, such as "Frederick Douglass," "Ode to Ethiopia," and "The Colored Soldiers." Likewise, the poems of the "Humor and Dialect" section include not only such clearly "Negro" dialect pieces as "A Negro Love Song" and "The Party" but also rural midwestern dialect poems, such as "Spellin' Bee" and "The Ol' Tunes," in which the race of the speaker is impossible to determine.

One might see a similar sort of complication of the racial (and class and regional) associations of different poetic (and musical) modes in the title of Dunbar's next volume of poetry (the first issued by a major commercial publisher, Dodd, Mead), *Lyrics of Lowly Life*, which includes the "Majors" and "Minors" of the previous volume along with some additional poems. Unlike *Major and Minors*, *Lyrics of Lowly Life* is not organized into sections but mixes "literary English" poems with "dialect pieces," suggesting that "Ere Sleep Comes Down to Soothe the Weary Eyes" is as much a lyric describing the "lowly life" as "When Malindy Sings" or "The Party."

As noted earlier, "We Wear the Mask," first collected in *Majors and Minors*, is the collections' most obvious invocation of African American dualism and the most influential literary expression of this sort of dualism after *The Souls of Black Folk* (and, insofar as poetry is concerned, perhaps the most influential, period). With the possible exception of "Sympathy" (and its famous dualistic line "I know why the caged bird sings!"), "We Wear the Mask" is almost certainly Dunbar's best-known and most anthologized poem today. Formally, it is a fairly straightforward rondeau — an old French lyric that enjoyed a vogue among such English poets as Swinburne, Dobson, and Dowson in the late nineteenth century. This straightforwardness is actually relatively unusual in Dunbar's "standard" poetry because he loved to play with the meter and rhyme scheme of received European poetic forms in a variety of ways that challenge the still much repeated notion of his "standard" poetry as conservative in any simple manner.

Geoffrey Jacques has provocatively argued that Dunbar's poem is a "rewriting and recasting" of Thomas Wyatt's rondeau, "What 'vaileth trouth? Or, by it, to take payn?" However, as Jacques points out, Dunbar "modernizes" Wyatt's work in a manner that is akin to symbolist poetry, and the melancholy symbolist-influenced poetry of Dunbar's English contemporary Ernest Dowson, in a sort of linguistic tour de force that reminds the reader that Dunbar's literary competency stretches, at least, from Petrarch (and the earliest English adaptations of the Petrarchan lyric) through to Swinburne, Symons, Dowson, a wide range of local color and dialect poetry, the "coon song," and the popular black theater of his cultural present. This sort of range and a back-to-the-future linking of medieval and early Renaissance verse to a racialized contemporary popular culture would, as scholars such as Jacques, Michael North, Ann Douglas, and Aldon Nielsen in their various ways note, become standard operating procedure of many of the "high" modernists (Jacques, 101–3).

The most arresting and most remembered aspect of the poem is Dunbar's metaphor of the mask. It may seem obvious, but, appropriately enough, this metaphor (and its relation to the logic of the poem) is more complicated than it might first appear. After all, the speaker of the poem identifies with a "we" who feel compelled to mask "our" true identities and true emotions from "the world." Yet there is a sort of game of doubling in this revelation of concealment. The speaker weirdly stands outside himself or herself, describing the existence and something of the nature of "the mask" that he or she as part of the "we" wears. Or does he or she really stand outside? How is that possible? On the other hand, is it not a contradiction for the speaker to proclaim that "the world" never really sees "us," only the disguise "we" put on because this naked exposure would seem to involve a lowering of the mask—unless the revelation about the mask is a mask? Is "the mask" something willingly assumed as a sort of camouflage protection, or is it imposed from the outside—or both?

Given the inescapable connection of the metaphor to the masking practices of minstrelsy and the vaudeville stage (and the traditional doubled opposites of the comic and tragic masks of the European stage), then is "the mask" a stylization of Negroes assumed by white people that is, in turn, adopted by African Americans in the era of the "coon song" and then consumed by white (and black) Americans, shaping the "horizon of expectations" for the representation and re-creation of black bodies, voices, and culture that challenges and constrains African American artists, and on and on? In other words, there is an endless regress, a sort of funhouse mirror stage in which the possibility of a double consciousness is asserted, but without the comfort of any absolutely stable features or "natural" boundaries, despite the persistence of certain popular representations of African Americans and African American culture, some of which remain remarkably recognizable even today.

This contradiction between concealment and revelation resembles that of Du Bois's notion of "the veil" and a "double consciousness" that prevents or inhibits genuine African American self-reflection and self-consciousness, while provoking endless introspection about the nature of the self and identity. In many respects, Dunbar's version of double consciousness here may be more active than Du Bois's metaphor of the veil. It allows Dunbar to indirectly assert his superiority of understanding to white readers — it signifies on them, so to speak. As in Langston Hughes's clearly Dunbarian opening in his 1951 lyric sequence, *Montage of a Dream Deferred*, the metaphor of masking makes obvious the act of concealment and its coerced motivation, underpinning militant and historically pointed social criticism — in Dunbar's case aimed at the rise of Jim Crow; in Hughes's at the rise of McCarthyism.[4]

Also, as Gavin Jones points out about Hughes's "Jazz Band in a Parisian Cabaret," "the vacillation between voices in Hughes's poem, like the wider oscillation between vernacular and 'standard' English in Johnson's *Fifty Years and Other Poems* (1917), Hughes's *The Weary Blues* (1926), and Brown's *Southern Road* (1932), was in fact a continuation of work already begun by Dunbar" (Jones, 186). Dunbar suggests a new way of reading African American minstrelsy and other forms of African American popular culture as well as his own work. After all, even to this day, there is a strong tendency to read most of Dunbar's dialect poetry as sentimental productions that issue uncritically from the local color and plantation traditions addressed primarily to a white audience. Exceptions are sometimes made for such pointedly topical dialect poems as "An Ante-Bellum Sermon" and "When Dey 'Listed Colored Soldiers," but these poems are seen as just that, exceptions — and even these exceptions are rarely considered with respect to the contemporary issues of Reconstruction and its demise with the triumph of Jim Crow segregation. However, the metaphor of the mask invites (or challenges) us to change the way we read the "unexceptional" dialect poems, say, "The Party." Again, the recessive nature of masking in the minstrel and minstrel-derived theatrical tradition lends itself to this sort of reading. The familiar minstrel figure of the ridiculous black dandy is, again, in its origin a white artist who adopts the mask of a black man attempting unsuccessfully to don the mask of high white fashion and diction. Whether consciously understood by a particular artist or audience or not, the ironies of a white artist taking on a stylized African American persona for the purposes of a comic routine based on a version of black misreadings and misperformances of high white fashion, language, and expressive culture are legion. The ironies of such humorous double maskings obviously present enormous possibilities for African American minstrel, "coon song," and vaudeville performers — though an inherent slippage or instability about where the joke might rest gave such performances an uneasy charge. Might not such a double parody implicitly carry an essential claim to human equality, if not moral superiority?

Some critics, such as Gavin Jones and Marcellus Blount, have argued that one interpretive possibility suggested by the foregrounding of the mask is that we might take many of the dialect poems more or less straightforwardly. In this way, again, the pointedly political "An Ante-Bellum Sermon" can be seen as an intermediate poem between Dunbar's "high" poetry and the more apparently typical dialect poems. As Blount, notes, "An Ante-Bellum Sermon," too, foregrounds masking and interpretation as Dunbar comments on the "new slavery" of the emergent Jim Crow system (a link that Dunbar made directly in the title of another poem "To the South on Its New Slavery") through the conceit of a southern antebellum black preacher commenting on slavery in the United States through a sermon on the deliverance of the Jews from bondage in Egypt. While the preacher weakly denies that his sermon has any application to the present, claiming "Dat I'm still a-preachin' ancient, / I ain't talkin' 'bout to-day," his intention, if not Dunbar's, is so clear that the reader is forced to take his sermon straightforwardly despite his transparently false disclaimers (Blount, 590).[5] Again, this offers a strategy for reading other dialect poems and, perhaps, Dunbar implies, much of the corpus of African American dialect poetry written by black authors. One way, then, of reading "The Party" is that beneath what might seem to be an inherently humorous depiction of a fancy dress dance in which the participants say things like, "Pass dat possume, ef you please!" is a litany of the skilled and stylish manner of black dress, dance, cooking, and conversation with a distinctly African American accent, not an imitation of "white" balls or cotillions:

> Jim, de fiddlah, chuned his fiddle, put some rosum on his bow,
> Set a pine box on de table, mounted it an' let huh go!
> He's a fiddlah, now I tell you, an' he made dat fiddle ring,
> 'Twell de ol'est an' de lamest had to give deir feet a fling.
> Jigs, cotillions, reels an' breakdowns, cordrills an' a waltz er two;
> Bless yo' soul, dat music winged 'em an' dem people lak to flew.
>   (*Collected*, 83)

One finds here the notion, stated more clearly in what is likely Dunbar's best-known dialect poem, "When Malindy Sings," which he often read before black audiences, that the African American musical tradition is superior to that of Europe ("the music of an edicated band"), speaking of acquired skills and cultural traditions, not simply inherent abilities or humorous mimicry.[6]

Also, Dunbar's black dialect poetry often suggests one possible, if strange, attribute of masking—as Bigger Thomas notes about the blindness of white (and black) people in Richard Wright's *Native Son* (*Early Works*, 542–43)—

is that it paradoxically creates a space where the black individual might be himself or herself, or at least something other than what the mask apparently suggests, at least if one were self-conscious enough. Thus, Dunbar's mask is an antecedent of the protagonist Clay's statement about the hidden (to white people) transcript of black music in Amiri Baraka's play *Dutchman*, "They say, 'I love Bessie Smith.' And don't even understand that Bessie Smith is saying, 'Kiss my ass, kiss my black unruly ass'" (Baraka, *Selected Plays and Prose*, 94).[7]

Also, what happens to Dunbar the "high" poet if we eliminate Dunbar the "dialect" or "popular" poet? Many readers are no doubt familiar with Dunbar's chafing at the limitations of the dialect genre and his characterization of his black dialect poetry (or what is assumed to be black dialect poetry) in "The Poet" as "a jingle in a broken tongue" written to please a white audience at the expense of his "real," more literarily "high" work. But would one generic body of Dunbar's work succeed as well without the other? If the "low" or popular work did not exist, wouldn't the "high" poetry be less powerful, less defined? And, without the "high" poetry and the split proposed between "real" and "mask," between "art" and box office rooted in a representation and/or re-creation of the African American voice, wouldn't the dialect poetry seem far shallower and much more easily conflated with the plantation tradition and the minstrel tradition in some uncomplicated way? In other words, the Dunbarian split here is one in which "high" and "low," "standard" literary and "dialect" are inextricably linked and opposed. This strategy allowed Dunbar both to affirm himself as a poet and to re-create the black speaking subject on the page in a way that acknowledged the problems popular culture posed for the representation of the African American folk subject while at least partially circumventing those problems. And, as I have suggested with my mentions of Hughes and Baraka, Dunbar's metaphor of the mask (and the model of identity it implies) retained its power far beyond the New Negro Renaissance — though, by the end of the 1920s, new paradigms arose that challenged without completely displacing earlier dualist models.

Dunbar's split between "real" and "mask" (and his vision of a consciousness that is doubled and redoubled practically ad infinitum in the sort of appropriations, reappropriations, re-reappropriations, and so on, of African American culture and the black subject that lie at the heart of American popular [and "high"] culture, all under the sign of "authenticity") remained a potent paradigm for the New Negro era with its concern for representing "authentically" the racial (or national) self without being imprisoned by the implicitly or explicitly racist expectations of white readers, actual or potential, or of variously accommodationist black readers. As James Weldon Johnson remarked in his autobiography when reflecting on the difference between Dunbar's dialect poetry and the work of later writers (whom Johnson termed "the folk artists"), say Langston Hughes, Waring Cuney, and Sterling Brown, drawing on versions of African American vernacular English, Dunbar's foregrounded but subversive use of what Johnson called "the stereotyped properties of minstrel-stage dialect" (*Along This Way*, 159) not only suggested ways of rereading "high" and popular culture but also provided a sort of baseline of artistic representation of the black folk and black culture against which the new "folk artists" could demonstrate their greater authenticity:

> I could see that the poet writing in the conventionalized dialect, no matter how sincere he might be, was dominated by his audience; that his audience was a section of the white American reading public; that when he wrote he was expressing what often bore little relation, sometimes no relation at all, to actual Negro life; that he was really expressing only certain conceptions about Negro life that his audience was willing to accept and ready to enjoy; that, in fact, he wrote mainly for the delectation of an audience that was an outside group. And I could discern that it was on this line that the psychological attitude of the poets writing in the dialect and that of the folk artists faced in different directions: because the latter, although working in the dialect, sought only to express themselves for themselves, and to their *own group*. (*Along This Way*, 159)

In other words, Dunbar's presentation and framing of his dialect poetry in a strangely negative way helped later African American poets imagine a distinctly and more "authentic" vernacular "Negro" literature aimed at a black audience. One could argue that this appeal to black insider authenticity goes back at least as far as the entrance of African American performers onto the minstrel stage with the superior veracity of their renditions of African American culture relative to the offering of blacked up white artists being one of their selling points—a phenomenon that can be seen in Dunbar's time in the billing of the renowned music and comedy team George Walker and Bert Williams as "two real coons."[8] One might also see such an appeal to authenticity as a form of advertisement in William Dean Howell's claim in his review of Dunbar's 1895 *Majors and Minors* and in the introduction of *Lyrics of Lowly Life*, which was adapted from the review, that Dunbar's "brilliant and unique achievement was to have studied the American negro [*sic*] objectively, and to have represented him as he found him to be, with humor, with sympathy, and yet with what the reader must instinctively feel to be entire truthfulness" (xvi–xvii). It is interesting, and perhaps typical of the era, that Howells suggests that Dunbar needed "to have studied the American negro objectively" in order to produce a representation that the white reader can somehow instinctively verify. One might also object that much of Dunbar's dialect poetry, as Gene Jarrett points out, is not attributable to a particular racial group, but is more closely related to conventions of regional or local color literature. In that case, perhaps, it shows more an objective study of the work of James Whitcomb Riley (Jarrett, 45–46).[9] Still, Dunbar himself may have had something of this notion in mind when he claimed to Johnson that he began writing black dialect poetry because he believed that he "could write it as well, if not better, than anybody else" (*Along This Way*, 160).

However, as Johnson observed, the notion of writing a black literature that made the declaration of a break with minstrelsy and "coonery" a prominent feature, expressing an authentic self to a black audience rooted in that authentic black culture, is something different from the vision of Howells, even if we might find it problematic. One might say that this notion of the relation of African American writing to black culture, and of black culture to mass culture visions of black culture (even if the idea of an actual black audience might in part be a sort of selling point to a white audience that wishes to consume African American culture and "Negroness," so to speak, even more directly), proposed a dialectic in which the work of black writers would be continuously posed against existing representations of the black folk and their alleged speech and culture, constantly striving for greater (and new) authenticity even against their earlier work. In this regard, Langston Hughes's frequent revision of his poetry (e.g., eliminating the locution "gwine") so as to, apparently, correct work that had once seemed an acceptable rendering of African American vernacular speech but now seemed too close to mass culture misappropriations (and misrepresentations) of that speech is instructive.

So much space here has been devoted to Dunbar because the implications of his take on African American dualism are less well known than those of Du Bois's double consciousness, despite the fame of "We Wear the Mask" and "Sympathy." The relatively simple point is that, though Du Bois's *The Souls of Black Folk* is perhaps the most widely recognized exposition of African American dualism at the turn of the century, it is but one of a number of such expressions, including some, such as Dunbar's, that antedate the publication of Du Bois's book. This is not to question Du Bois's influence but to suggest that *The Souls of Black Folk* was part of a larger social conversation in which his voice was crucial but not singular. In this, I am arguing with a continuing tendency to overemphasize the relative novelty of Du Bois's notion of double consciousness as a groundbreaking articulation of the political and cultural moment of the Nadir.[10] If one is familiar with this larger literary conversation, then an understanding of why Du Bois's highly figurative formulation of dualism and black existential experience in the Nadir in *The Souls of Black Folk* was so arresting becomes deeper and clearer. In other words, it is worth not only using, as is often done, Du Bois's formulations and metaphors of dualism as lenses to examine how the work of such authors as Dunbar or Charles Chesnutt expresses "double consciousness" but also examining how the work of those authors, whose early literary efforts obviously did not derive from *The Souls of Black Folk*, might throw a light on the work of Du Bois and on the larger body of African American literature at the turn of the century.

Black Reconciliation: Booker T. Washington and the Opportunities and Responsibilities of Jim Crow

Even Du Bois's sometime antagonist Booker T. Washington put forward a dualist argument in his work that had enormous impact on Du Bois's own model of dualism, both negatively and positively. In fact, one could argue that it is precisely Washington's unreconciled and irreconcilable dualist vision found beneath the surface optimism of *Up from Slavery* that Du Bois is writing against in *The Souls of Black Folk*. That is to say that for Du Bois, dualism was a political, social, and even psychological condition that black folk should openly acknowledge, struggle against, and transcend, while for Washington, it was a sort of strategy as well as a condition.

In *Invisible Man*, Ralph Ellison famously advanced a Du Boisian critique, writing of a thinly disguised version of the statue depicting Booker T. Washington "lifting the veil" from the eyes of an iconic figure of the southern black folk that stands in the center of the equally thinly camouflaged recreation of his alma mater, Tuskegee Institute: "I am standing puzzled, unable to decide whether the veil is really being lifted, or lowered more firmly in place; whether I am witnessing a revelation or a more efficient blinding" (36).

In Ellison's novel, the school's president, Dr. Bledsoe, is presented both as a successor of the Founder (again, a barely disguised Washington) and as an embodiment (or, as the Reverend Homer A. Barbee says, the "living agent" and the "physical presence" [132]) of the Founder himself. Bledsoe is a trickster Machiavelli manipulating the Jim Crow system, including the southern white political establishment and northern white patrons, for his own "confident, self-assuring, self-starting and self-stopping, self-warming and self-justifying" power (142). However, like Rinehart, the trickster hipster of the final section of the book, Bledsoe lacks a real core. He is much like an onion in which there are only layers, no heart. And his power, like the power of Rinehart, rests entirely on the given of Jim Crow and the peculiar disposition of white eyes — though one might argue that Bledsoe is more self-hating than Rinehart ever dreamed of being to the degree that we can tell what Rinehart dreams.

Yet the actual statue, completed by the white sculptor Charles T. Keck in 1922, might be read differently from the alternatives of revelation or blinding presented by Ellison's protagonist. There is almost a Baron Munchausen aspect of the statue as Booker T. Washington, an ex-slave and a product of the plantation, the coal and salt industries of West Virginia, free-labor service, and black Reconstruction higher-education institutions, now in suit and bowtie lifts the veil from a black man apparently clothed only in the folds of the veil. The seminaked figure stares out, seated on a blacksmith's anvil with a large book in his lap. A caption reads, "Booker T. Washington 1856 1915 He lifted the veil of ignorance from his people and pointed the way to progress through education and industry."

The observer is certainly struck by the contrast between Washington in a suit and the seated seminaked figure, who is often understood to be, like Washington, a former slave. That observer might find that the anvil and the book present a bifurcated, if not contradictory, image. Washington disapprovingly described in the famous (or infamous) 1896 *Atlantic Monthly* essay "The Awakening of the Negro" a young black man in a filthy cabin studying a French grammar and a young woman playing what is presumably European art music that she had learned in boarding school on a rented piano in the poverty-stricken home of her sharecropper family. Perhaps the book of the statue is a French grammar or a volume of music theory.

Yet Washington himself also makes clear in his autobiography that he was in many respects like the young man and woman he criticizes in the essay. The distinction he implicitly draws between himself and those figures before going on to defend the Tuskegee program was that he learned the value of labor and thrift and ultimately the value of himself as a human being while studying under the vocational curriculum of Samuel Chapman Armstrong at Hampton Institute; the young man and woman attended schools that focused too much on abstract liberal arts curricula without much practical application. However, it was not as a carpenter, farmer, or blacksmith that Washington made his mark, but as an educator, orator, writer, and race leader — not surprising given Hampton's orientation as a teachers' college.

In short, the two figures of the statue are opposites and doubles, products of the success and failure of Reconstruction, of citizen and subaltern, to use a now slightly dated term. This sort of doubleness can be seen, too, in the caption, in which education and industry, like the book and the anvil, are linked, and yet not quite consonant in the way that that use of the term much associated with Tuskegee, "industrial education," might have made them. While it is hard to know what was in Keck's head, the use of a term so prominently associated with Du Bois's notion of dualism, "veil," raises the possibility of a parallel doubleness on Washington's part.

Keck's uneasy pairing, even twinning, of the folk and Washington is not (or not primarily) an indirect dig at Washington but captures an essential aspect of Washington's writing, particularly in *Up from Slavery* (1901). I am not going to enter into the old and complicated debate of whether Washington was an accommodationist with or trickster guerrilla against Jim Crow, or, most likely, both.[11] As Waldo Martin points out, Washington was "an exceedingly complicated personality with many, at times conflicting, sides" (41), whose essential character still remains an open and much debated question among scholars. What interests me is how, like so many of his contemporaries, he expresses a sort of dualistic vision.

The early chapters of *Up from Slavery* draw somewhat parodically on the archetypal slave narrative in which Washington rises from slave plantation and industrial labor to literacy, self-naming, self-reliance, self-respect, and so on. Washington is cagey about the curriculum that he studied at Hampton Institute other than the Bible and relatively oblique references to the greater emphasis on industrial education at Hampton than at other historically black colleges and universities. Instead, he foregrounds the development of his skills (and later his successes) as a reader, writer, and public orator even as he (the former slave, coal miner, and salt furnace worker) learns his "trade" as a janitor. Though he may well have been entirely sincere about his education in the value of labor and thrift (values that had already been at least partly inculcated in him, he claims, by his time as a "house boy" to Viola Ruffner, the wife of a former Union general, in West Virginia), it is worth noting that his trade was one that had been performed by African Americans in the South long before and long after his sojourn at Hampton Institute and was, in fact, a job that white Americans, North and South, would see as a natural "black" job. In other words, Washington juxtaposes some opposing, in fact dualist, visions of himself at the turn of the twentieth century: the potential dignity of labor and his (and his family's) experience of labor in a mining community; his "trade" as a janitor and his actual life work as educator, public speaker, writer, and community leader; the students of Hampton (including the young Washington) "who had had enough actual contact with the world to teach them the need for education" and an allusion to the earlier essay with its famous image of the young man in the dirty cabin.

In *Up from Slavery*, too, Washington, like Du Bois, seems ever to feel his twoness. In it, the fragmented political subjectivity of African Americans during the early Jim Crow era is thematically and stylistically rendered more clearly than in perhaps any other text of its time. As Washington himself reflects in *Up from Slavery* when he sets up his presentation of his famous 1895 Atlanta Cotton States and International Exposition speech (included in its entirety within the memoir), this sort of fragmentation is not surprising and is, perhaps, even inevitable, given its diverse sources and audiences. After all, Washington's autobiography deeply engages, among other things, the abolitionist antebellum slave narrative as well as the generally more conciliatory postbellum slave narrative to address three distinct and, to a large extent, hostile audiences crucial to the success of Washington's educational and political projects. These were an African American audience that encompassed both the increasingly disenfranchised black masses and the intelligentsia (North and South); a southern white one that combined the remnants of the old southern landowning class and the recently ascendant power brokers of the Jim Crow New South (many of whom had been of middle class or poor backgrounds before the New South/Jim Crow realignment of southern politics and economy) rooted in the Democratic Party; and a northern white one consisting largely of the industrialist and mercantile philanthropic class whose members often had some personal or family tie to abolitionism and who formed much of the backbone of the Republican Party.

While it is possible, as Robert Stepto argued, that *Up from Slavery* does not entirely fit into the genre of slave narrative, nonetheless, its very title invites such a comparison. Its title also resonates with what Stepto provocatively saw as one of the deep structures of early African American literature, the ascent North to freedom, a notion that is taken up at more length in chapter 3 (Stepto, 32–51). Also, as discussed later in this chapter, while Washington's book broke in certain ways from the antebellum narrative, it closely resembles the postbellum slave narrative, particularly Douglass's *The Life and Times* in some important respects.

Another text that loomed large in the composition of *Up from Slavery*, albeit largely negatively perhaps, was the other autobiography assigned to Washington, *The Story of My Life and Work* (1900). As Louis Harlan reminds us, Washington's two autobiographies have a complicated relationship to each other. Washington worked with ghostwriters in the production of both books. However, the earlier autobiography was aimed primarily at a black audience, while the later one was written and produced with northern and southern white audiences in mind — although clearly Washington and his publisher expected (and realized) a considerable sale to African Americans. The busy Washington delegated virtually all writing and editorial duties on *The Story of My Life* to the ghostwriter, Edgar Webber, a promising young black journalist. Webber apparently turned out to be an inefficient and largely incompetent writer and editor, producing a work filled with stylistic, typographical, and factual errors with only minimal oversight by Washington. A hurried and slapdash production job by the publisher, J. L. Nichols & Co., compounded the problems (including several blank pages) that the last-minute efforts on the page proofs of Washington's friend and sometime political ally, the newspaper editor, poet, and political militant T. Thomas Fortune, were able only partially to patch up. Though Fortune labored to fix the most egregious of the earlier autobiography's problems, Washington remained dissatisfied with the book and Webber's job.[12] One result of this debacle was that when the opportunity arose for the commissioning of a series of autobiographical articles by Washington with the view of collecting them into a new volume to be published by Doubleday, Page and Company, Washington took a far more active role in the writing and editing — though again he worked with a ghostwriter, Max Bennett Thrasher (Harlan, *"Up from Slavery,"* 21–23).

Up from Slavery particularly echoed, and contested with, Douglass's three autobiographies. One can see the detailed accounts of Washington's appointments and meetings with leading political, social, and intellectual dignitaries, North and South, domestic and foreign, that dominate the latter part of the book as a move to position himself on the same level as Douglass, who, too, devoted much of the last twenty chapters of the revised version of *The Life and Times* to descriptions of his work as a leading politician and diplomat, ending with his appointment as resident minister and consul general to Haiti — though Washington denied that he had ever had such an intention except to the extent it was thrust on him by public demand. This move was a maneuver not simply to fill a space left by the death of Douglass in 1895 but also to come to grips with the moment of Jim Crow. Washington later suggested in the 1911 *My Larger Education* that Douglass was a heroic abolitionist leader who was never able to produce a workable vision for African Americans in the post-Emancipation era:

> Mr. Douglass's great life-work had been in the political agitation that led to the destruction of slavery. He had been the great defender of the race, and in the struggle to win from Congress and from the country at large the recognition of the Negro's rights as a man and a citizen he had played an important part. But the long and bitter political struggle in which he had engaged against slavery had not prepared Mr. Douglass to take up the equally difficult task of fitting the Negro for the opportunities and responsibilities of freedom. (423–24)

Yet what Washington is talking about here is perhaps not so much the problem of fitting African Americans for "the opportunities and responsibilities of freedom" but rather the negotiating of the restrictions and limitations of the ascendant (and by 1911 triumphant) Jim Crow system after the collapse of the Reconstruction era with which Douglass was also much linked.

It is worth noting here that Dunbar, too, used the figure of Douglass in a surprisingly similar manner to that of Washington, especially in the later of Dunbar's two tributary poems, "Frederick Douglass" and "Douglass."[13] One might trace the evolution of Jim Crow (and the often violent manner of its triumph) and a recognition of the final collapse of Reconstruction ideals by the late 1890s in these poems. In the elegy "Frederick Douglass," written immediately after Douglass's death in 1895 and collected in *Majors and Minors* in that same year (and reprinted in *Lyrics of Lowly Life* the next year), the speaker takes note of the gloomy and desperate political situation of African Americans, but predicts their ultimate triumph (and the triumph of the militant and unrelenting hope for justice and citizenship that Dunbar attributes to Douglass), claiming that Douglass's message is still being heard, still relevant:

> Oh, Douglass, thou hast passed beyond the shore,
>   But still thy voice is ringing o'er the gale!
> Thou'st taught thy race how high her hopes may soar,
>   And bade her seek the heights, nor faint, nor fail.
> She will not fail, she heeds thy stirring cry. (*Collected*, 7)

In a sort of postelegiac sonnet, "Douglass," which appeared in the misleadingly titled 1903 collection *Lyrics of Love and Laughter* (misleading because it contains some of Dunbar's most bitterly angry poetic comments on the post-Reconstruction Jim Crow South, including "Douglass," "To the South on Its New Slavery," "The Haunted Oak," and "Robert Gould Shaw"), once again African Americans are shown as enduring a storm, "a tempest of dispraise" that both threatens and isolates them. Now, however, the storm is so fierce, and Douglass so far away, that they are unable to hear his voice:

> Oh, for thy voice high-sounding o'er the storm,
> For thy strong arm to guide the shivering bark,
> The blast-defying power of thy form,
> To give us comfort through the lonely dark. (*Collected*, 208)

Dunbar here differs from Washington in his claim that if Douglass were still alive, he could help steer and comfort African Americans through the "lonely dark" of the Nadir—though he does make the amazingly biting claim that even Douglass, a former slave whose mistreatment was powerfully represented in his autobiographies, never knew times as evil as the Jim Crow, post–*Plessy v. Ferguson*, post–*Williams v. Mississippi*, post–Wilmington Riot present. Still, his bitter despair does echo Washington in the suggestion that Douglass is no longer here and that Douglass's message can no longer carry over the storm of the "New Slavery," and that consolation through the triumph of the principles for which the lost one (and the Reconstruction era to which he was tied) stood is no longer really possible in the foreseeable future. In other words, if the poem is an elegy, it is for Reconstruction and its promises, not Douglass as such.

Of course, such direct bitterness is rarely evidenced in *Up from Slavery*. Many, many critics of Washington's book have noted its conciliatory and relatively mild statements about slavery, lynching, and Jim Crow, and have often compared it unfavorably not only to antebellum slave narratives but, in some cases, to *The Story of My Life and Work*.[14] Indeed, the earlier book tells many of the same incidents without the sort of humorous invocations of popular culture tropes drawn from minstrelsy, "coon songs," and so on, which characterize the later work. *The Story* also utilizes figures typical of the abolitionist antebellum slave narrative that are left out of *Up from Slavery*. For example, one feature common in the antebellum slave narrative is a childhood incident of dramatic violence, cruelty, and/or depravity, often to a relative of the narrator, that stands as the young narrator's cross-

ing of the threshold into slavery from a state of relatively unconscious innocence. In Douglass's autobiographies, this incident is the whipping of "Aunt
Hester" ("Aunt Esther" in *The Life and Times*), which Douglass describes
in *Narrative* as "the blood-stained gate, the entrance to the hell of slavery,
through which I was about to pass" (*Autobiographies*, 18). There is a similar
moment in *The Story of My Life and Work*: "The thing in connection with
slavery that has left the deepest impression on me was the instance of seeing
a grown man, my uncle, tied to a tree early one morning, stripped naked, and
someone whipping him with a cowhide. As each blow touched his back the
cry, 'Pray, master! Pray, master!' came from his lips, and made an impression
upon my boyish heart that I shall carry with me to my grave" (18–19).

That incident of the initiation into the hell of slavery does not appear in
Up from Slavery. However, as is discussed at length later in this chapter, the
second Washington autobiography does engage the antebellum slave narrative, especially those of Douglass, in complicated and sometimes, though
not always, adversarial ways. It might also be worth recalling that those
earlier narratives were also intended for a dual but largely white audience.
The genre of the antebellum slave autobiography (along with novels informed by its tropes and conventions) was enormously popular, particularly
through Harriet Beecher Stowe's adaptation of it in *Uncle Tom's Cabin* —
an adaptation that, as Eric Sundquist notes, became further entwined, both
positively and negatively, with later antebellum narratives by black authors
who both echoed and critiqued Stowe's novel.[15] The popularity of the slave
narrative, and pseudo–slave narrative fiction, remained considerable in the
postbellum period, though perhaps more as children's literature than among
adults, even as it became ever more deeply entangled with blackface minstrelsy, African American or "Ethiopian" minstrelsy, and the popular comic
musical theater, as well as, ironically, the plantation literature genre that
had in many respects emerged as a negative response to the initial publication and success of Stowe's novel. In fact, *Uncle Tom's Cabin* became a main-
stay of the silent movie industry with Edwin Porter's 1903 adaptation of the
novel being arguably the first feature film created in the United States.[16]

Washington's autobiography also drew on the genre or subgenre of the
postbellum slave narrative, especially Douglass's *The Life and Times*. As
William Andrews has shown, one common feature of such postbellum slave
narratives as *The Life and Times* and Elizabeth Keckley's 1868 *Behind the
Scenes* is a moment of encounter and, generally, reconciliation between the
former slave and the former slave master. As Andrews also points out, these

meetings frequently display a reversal of fortune in which the former slave stands above the often impoverished and/or sickly former master, as does Frederick Douglass when he visits Thomas Auld as Auld lay on his death-bed (Andrews, *To Tell a Free Story*, 5–6). The sense of forgiveness by the ex–slave for the ex–slave owner is pronounced. Douglass's attitude toward Auld is much like Washington's toward his unknown and quite possibly white father. Both Auld and the father are described as the victims of the system of slavery. Douglass's account does differ in that Auld in essence apologizes to Douglass and owns up to the immorality of slavery, saying that in his place he would have behaved exactly as did Douglass, where Washington's father, and the other white "victims" of the slave system, are pardoned without such a confession (Andrews, *To Tell a Free Story*, 9–10).

One way of thinking about this sort of reconciliation (not unlike, perhaps, the idea behind the Truth and Reconciliation Commission in present-day South Africa) is that if Douglass is a sort of representative former slave em-bodying the African American capacity for self-development, then Auld is a southern white counterpart epitomizing the capacity for mental and moral regeneration and transformation on the part of the former slave-owning class and its supporters. In other words, it is a sort of alternative reconcilia-tion or reunion that includes African Americans as equal partners with northern and southern white Americans, not only condemning slavery but defending Reconstruction and its institutions and ideals, which is opposed to the sort of reconciliation promoted by, among other people and organiza-tions, Horace Greeley (a former abolitionist) and the Democratic Party in the 1870s. Greeley's sort of reconciliation sought to recast Reconstruction as a time of political horror and social degradation in the South, proposing essentially a reunion between former white supporters of the Union and of the Confederacy that left out African Americans as a permanent subordi-nate and basically disenfranchised caste.[17] In this way, though Washington was perhaps too young during the slave era to have this sort of dramatic en-counter, the feeling of reconciliation and forgiveness that pervades *Up from Slavery* is not unusual in the postbellum narrative, even that of Douglass. One can see the remark about the tripartite audience in his prefacing of his Atlanta Exposition speech and his triumphant recounting of his speech be-fore a black and white audience (including, apparently, most of the political leadership of the Commonwealth of Virginia and the leading white citizens of the city of Richmond) in Richmond's Academy of Music, as a variation on the alternative reconciliation that includes African Americans as partners rather than subalterns—even as the speeches themselves deny any desire for "social equality."

The echoes of antebellum slave narratives, particularly those of Douglass, are legion in *Up from Slavery*. It opens with the standard beginning, including the locution "I was born" that was the "Once upon a time" of the antebellum slave narrative, used by Douglass in *Narrative of the Life* (though not his other two autobiographies). The passage that follows describing the allegedly uncertain facts of Washington's birth echo and parody the opening of Douglass's first narrative. As Robert Stepto points out, where Douglass's uncertainty about the precise date of his birth was a matter of considerable anguish that emblematized the stealing of his human birthright, Washington typically jokes, turning it into a matter of no great account, saying that he suspects that he "must have been born somewhere and at some time." Stepto also notes that it is almost certain that, in fact, Washington did know his date of birth (because his older brother John knew it). Consequently, this echo seems a deliberate strategy on Washington's part rather than some accidental coincidence of biographical detail. And, if one goes through the first two chapters of *Up from Slavery*, one is struck by the parallelism of details between Washington's work and the narratives of Douglass, including the mention of the possibility of an unknown (or at least uncertain) white father, the comparison of the meals of slave children to the feeding of animals, and the self-naming or renaming by the narrator.

However, perhaps the most striking parallel between *Up from Slavery* and Douglass's texts has to do with the description and interpretation of the music of the slaves. Douglass famously told and retold his story of the formal duality of slave music ("They would sometimes sing the most pathetic sentiment in the most rapturous tone, and the most rapturous sentiment in the most pathetic tone" [*Autobiographies*, 23]), as well as intersecting circles of interpretation, misinterpretation, and incomprehension:

This they would sing, as a chorus, to words which to many would seem unmeaning jargon, but which, nevertheless, were full of meaning to themselves. I have sometimes thought that the mere hearing of those songs would do more to impress some minds with the horrible character of slavery, than the reading of whole volumes of philosophy on the subject could do.

I did not, when a slave, understand the deep meaning of those rude and apparently incoherent songs. I was myself within the circle; so that I neither saw nor heard as those without might see and hear. They told a tale of woe which was then altogether beyond my feeble comprehension; they were tones loud, long, and deep; they breathed the prayer and complaint of souls boiling over with the bitterest anguish. (*Autobiographies*, 23–24)

Typically, Douglass treats this folk music and various circles of auditors with considerable ambivalence. He suggests that one needed to be outside the slave culture, to be self-conscious in a way that only a truly free person could, in order to accurately and completely read the music. At the same time, he claims that his first insight into the slave system, even before he "was outside the circle," came from listening to this music. Though a considerable portion of Douglass's narratives details his journey away from the culture of the southern folk, he does say, that "those songs still follow me, to deepen my hatred of slavery, and quicken my sympathies for my brethren in bonds" (*Autobiographies*, 24).

In fact, those songs continue to haunt and affect him to such an extent, he tells the reader, that he is actually weeping as he writes — though one might suspect that is as much for all he had to give up to become Frederick Douglass as for the folk in bondage. In what might be a similar paradox, he notes that many of those outside the circle in the North have formed an idea of black song as indicating the "contentment and happiness" of the slave. It is hard to believe, in this reference to the North, that Douglass in 1845 does not have the versions of black song, black bodies, and black voices presented by blackface minstrelsy (with its northern origins) in mind. Interestingly, his later autobiographies also add a more regionally specific note, pointing out a southern white predilection for reading cheerfulness in black music and, in fact, demanding (to paraphrase Bob Dylan's "Maggie's Farm") that they "sing as they slave," perhaps reflecting the rise of the plantation literature that grew exponentially in response to *Uncle Tom's Cabin* and that was far more associated with southern white writers than minstrelsy.

There is a similar moment in *Up from Slavery* where Washington recalls a change in the atmosphere of the slave quarters as the Union army approached his plantation:

As the great day drew nearer, there was more singing in the slave quarters than usual. It was bolder, had more ring, and lasted later into the night. Most of the verses of the plantation songs had some reference to freedom. True, they had sung those same verses before, but they had been careful to explain that the "freedom" in these songs referred to the next world, and had no connection with life in this world. Now they gradually threw off the mask, and were not afraid to let it be known that the "freedom" in their songs meant freedom of the body in this world. (19–20)

This passage recalls not only the passages about the doubleness of slave music in Douglass's autobiographies but also the poetry of Dunbar, particularly "A Corn-Song," "We Wear the Mask," and "An Ante-Bellum Sermon." Like Dunbar's poetry, it assigns to the black subject, and the southern black folk, a self-consciousness that is lacking in Douglass for the most part. Washington's employment of the metaphor of the mask, particularly in connection to music, also calls to mind the performance associated both with blackface minstrelsy and with the black writers, composers, and performers (including Dunbar and James Weldon Johnson) associated with the popular music and musical theater industries.

In fact, one of the major ways in which *Up from Slavery* diverges from Douglass's early autobiographies (and, indeed, *My Life and Work*) is the way in which it utilizes stock figures and routines of minstrelsy, the "coon song," and the plantation tradition of literature, visual arts, and drama (and, soon, film) and then inverts, demystifies, or pairs them with a contradictory image or figure. Such scholars as Waldo Martin, Adolph Reed Jr., and Houston Baker Jr. have, with varying degrees of sympathy or condemnation, called our attention to the moment in *Up from Slavery* where Washington employs the archetypal image of the chicken-stealing "coon" when he describes his mother cooking what some might consider a stolen chicken before Emancipation (Martin, 45–46; Reed, 31; Baker, *Modernism*, 33, 36). At first the scene threatens to become humorous in a way that it does not in the drier recollection in *The Story of My Life and Work*, that his mother regularly took the master's eggs and chickens without permission when her children were hungry. However, Washington immediately undercuts the stereotypical "coon" image with his assertion that to call this act "theft" within the context of slavery was meaningless.

Perhaps the most famous invocation and disruption of a familiar minstrel or plantation literature dream in Washington's second autobiography occurs in his 1895 Atlanta Exposition speech. In that speech Washington invokes the "faithful old soul" figure of plantation literature: "While doing this, you can be sure in the future, as in the past, that you and your families will be surrounded by the most patient, faithful, law-abiding, and unresentful people that the world has seen. As we have proved our loyalty to you in the past, in nursing your children, watching by the sick-bed of your mothers and fathers, and often following them with tear-dimmed eyes to their graves, so in the future, in our humble way . . ." (221). This plantation vision is followed by Washington's famous and weird metaphor of the five fingers and the hand. The metaphor makes a certain dramatic sense. One can imagine how effective it was in performance. But on closer inspection the detached hand with "black" and "white" fingers that are strangely divided from each other and from the whole seems akin to the tropes of gothic literature, particularly those of Poe (and weirdly anticipates W. F. Fryer's Poe-esque short story "The Beast of Five Fingers"), as well as resembling Du Bois's gothic notion of two souls warring within a single body, rather than any comforting dream of racial harmony through the eschewal of "social equality." In fact, Washington touches on a series of modern anxieties about splits, between black and white, labor and capital, immigrant and native-born that threaten to tear the body politic of the United States apart.

Similarly, at times Washington represents the custom of the ex-slaves of assuming new names and giving themselves middle initials that signify nothing except their "entitles" as a variant of "Zip Coon" linguistic dandyism and then speaks with a certain sense of irony of how he had "the privilege" of naming himself (35)—a privilege he now claims to be rare even though only a few pages earlier he had claimed it was a common and somewhat comic practice among the former slaves. This sort of humorous minstrelsy-"coon song" incongruity that coexists with contradictory images of the folk characterizes a great deal of *Up from Slavery*. There is much description of various students (including a reference to Washington's picture of the boy with a French grammar in a dirty cabin that he first mentioned in "The Awakening of the Negro" [1896]) learning the "rules" of Greek, Latin, and French and their utter inability to apply the knowledge to any practical purpose. In short, it is not far from the stock comic image of the black dandy who imitates high fashion, diction, and intellectual discourse without developing real taste or understanding.

One can also see something like this type of minstrelesque humor when Washington describes his visit to Alabama to scout out property for his new school:

At the time I went to Alabama the coloured people were taking considerable interest in politics, and they were very anxious that I should become one of them politically, in every respect. They seemed to have a little distrust of strangers in this regard. I recall that one man, who seemed to have been designated by the others to look after my political destiny, came to me on several occasions and said, with a good deal of earnestness: "We wants you to be sure to vote jes' like we votes. We can't read de newspapers very much, but we knows how to vote, an' we wants you to vote jes' like we votes." He added: "We watches de white man, and we keeps watching de white man till we finds out which way de white man's gwine to vote; an' when we finds out which way de white man's gwine to vote, den we votes 'xactly de other way. Den we knows we's right." (110–11)

Washington here sets himself up as a straight man in a comic routine. However, he immediately complicates the routine when he hastens to add after this passage that this humorously presented racial knee-jerk approach to politics by African Americans in the past is being currently replaced by the practice of voting according to principle rather than according to the race of the candidate. This recasts the meaning of the preceding passage in that such racialized balloting (and the restriction of the franchise so that the African American voting population in much of the southern Black Belt was being reduced to near zero) was in fact being practiced in the present by the great majority of the white electorate—1900 was, after all, the year in which white Democratic North Carolina voters passed an amendment to the state constitution effectively disenfranchising black voters, capping a racist and extraordinarily violent campaign to break the interracial Republican-Populist coalition that took office in the state in 1896.

In addition to the implied critique of Jim Crow, it is worth remembering that in the first chapter of the narrative, Washington recalls how the slaves were able to gather the news about the events and great issues of the day through the "grapevine," allowing them to discuss the political situation of the United States in considerable detail. In fact, Washington claims, the slaves were generally better informed about current events than the white people of the plantations in his part of Virginia. Again, this picture of a slave population able to intelligently discuss the burning political issues of the antebellum United States exists alongside Washington's comic routine based on the conceit of an allegedly illiterate and uninformed free black electorate in the postbellum era.

It may be true, as Houston Baker has argued, that Washington offered "*domestic immobility* as the regimen for the black body of the 'country districts'" (*Turning South*, 60) while arrogating to himself the mobility and privileges of the flaneur, the urban watcher, walker, loafer, and dandy that Walter Benjamin made such a powerful critical figure of modernity and modernism in his discussions of the work of Charles Baudelaire. However, it should be recalled, as is taken up at more length in chapter 3, that Washington made his interlocking physical, social, and intellectual travels, both up from slavery and in the service of Tuskegee (and, perhaps as Stepto, Baker, and others have suggested, of the uplift myth embodied by Tuskegee) such a large part of his narrative that it is hard to see how his mobility prohibits or precludes that of others — quite the opposite because Washington offers himself as both singular individual and inspiration. In other words, immobility and extreme mobility exist side by side. Washington seeks to negotiate the problem that, rather than seeming the opposite of the flaneur, the African American male by the early Jim Crow era in the familiar forms of vaudeville and the "coon song" — the tramp and the dandy cut loose from the plantation (to which the black dandy always had a somewhat tenuous connection) and joined by the sexually rapacious, razor-wielding, pistol-packing brute — became the ur-model (often in strangely recombined forms) of the American flaneur in the twentieth century. He is, though, a flaneur radically restricted in his geographic range by the new spatialization of race in the urban United States during the early twentieth century.

The notion of Washington as a sort of political and literary trickster, though not entirely inapt (as shown in the scene where he tampers with the clock at the salt furnace where he works to enable him to get to school on time), does not completely capture the spirit of *Up from Slavery*. Rather, over and over Washington contradicts himself without true reconciliation, threatening to tear apart the text over which intense authorial and editorial care has been expended after what was perceived as the stylistic disaster of *The Story of My Life and Work*. One might consider *Up from Slavery* as the text in which the political and cultural splits of the Jim Crow United States are most clearly laid bare, resulting in profound textual contradictions of style and theme. The ending is upbeat, as Washington speaks before an interracial though no doubt segregated audience at Richmond's Academy of Music in the former capital of the Confederacy, spreading a message of "hope and cheer." Still, he has just before drawn the reader's attention, however mildly, "to the evil habit of lynching," and notes that his optimism runs counter to "superficial and temporary signs which might lead one to entertain a contrary opinion" (318–19). If the United States is seen as a sort of text, then, Washington asks the reader to look beneath its apparent meaning, the "superficial and temporary signs," to find the deeper optimism he discerns. In short, his message, like the United States, and his text, is profoundly divided — an unavoidable existential state for African Americans, one might infer, in the Jim Crow, post-Reconstruction, post-Douglass era.

Again, then, Du Bois's problem with Washington is not simply his industrial education philosophy but Washington's indirection and his seeming acceptance of dualism as a permanent state.

"Seriously Considering the Possibility of a Man's Being Turned into a Tree": Charles Chesnutt and the Black Vaudeville Theory of Slavery

An even more ambiguous dualism is found in the conjure stories of Charles Chesnutt, published between 1887 and 1898. Scholars have remarked, as has Chesnutt himself, on the obvious connections between the secondary folk narrator of the stories, Julius McAdoo, and Joel Chandler Harris's Uncle Remus. However, Chesnutt also noted that Harris's character was only a starting point and that his project with the Julius stories was quite different from that of Harris (Chesnutt, *Stories, Novels, and Essays*, 907). Julius is a sort of revision of Remus and the plantation literature tradition, drawing on such African American folktales as the stories of Master and John in which the slave John almost inevitably gets the better of Master while fulfilling Master's commands to the letter (if not the spirit). However, this revision is even more in the vein of African American minstrelsy and vaudeville, particularly the stories of plantation life told by Bert Williams, than that of Harris's Remus (Sundquist, 330–32).

As mentioned earlier, this sort of minstrelsy or black vaudeville was a radically ambivalent form. The humorous exchanges between Julius and the pretentious John, the self-satisfied but not terribly perceptive primary narrator of the stories who never uses a nickel word when a dollar one will do, recall somewhat those between John and Master in the old folktales (as well as the back-and-forth between Uncle Remus and the young boy in *Uncle Remus: His Songs and Sayings* [1881] and the interplay between various white adult narrators and black former slave secondary narrators in many of the plantation stories of Thomas Nelson Page). However, John's and Julius's dialogue (like the encounter between Booker T. Washington and his political minder in Alabama) more closely resembles the give-and-take between a stiff "straight man" (usually straight in demeanor *and* diction) and a comic and often emphatically non-"standard"-speaking "funnyman" that has long been a staple of comic theater and a particular hallmark of the popular variety theater that developed out of minstrelsy.[18]

Obviously, one divergence from the model of Harris's Remus stories is that Chesnutt's straight man is an adult white man (though, interestingly, the racial identity of John and his wife Annie is rarely raised in a straight-forward manner, especially in the earlier stories) addressed directly by the black folk subnarrator as opposed to Harris's interactions between a white child and a black adult (whether Remus or another black subnarrator) witnessed by a white adult narrator, "Miss Sally" (the boy's mother), who is a sort of voyeur or spy, however benign. In Harris's "Legends of the Old Plantation," one might see the white reader as doubly placed in the position of "Miss Sally," peering into a cabin window from a point of superiority (even if she is a woman) and as the child gazing raptly at the elderly Uncle Remus as he tells his stories. Harris proposes an almost maternal relationship, a sort of love (to take from Eric Lott), between the white boy and the black man located in an idealized past. Harris's plantation literature visions of the antebellum past become paradoxically "Negro" (though he says in his introduction that few southern African Americans will admit knowing the tales to a "stranger"), and black folk culture becomes "a part of the domestic history of every Southern family" (4), presumably equating (as many do to this day) "Southern" with "white." One might see this double location of black and white, of author (and author as part of his own audience) and subject, as both inside and outside, adult and child, slave past and post-Reconstruction present, both of which are opposed to a nightmare vision of Reconstruction more directly attacked in the section, "A Story of the War," which concludes the book. (Of course, the origins of these tales in slave culture give them meanings with respect to slavery of which Harris is apparently unaware or, more likely, cannot completely control or contain within the reconfiguration of the plantation genre.) Perhaps Harris, too, in his comment about the refusal of black people to tell their stories to strangers indicates not only the familiar plantation literature story of the fading away of the old-time Negro and old-time Negro culture, replaced by a troubling and often troublesome "New Negro" (a critical label that T. Thomas Fortune and others would turn into a badge of pride), but also an anxiety about the emergence of a new black culture (and a new black audience) on which he might have no claim — even on the bifurcated level of Dunbar's "A Corn-Song."

Chesnutt situates the white reader in a far more unsettling location in which he or she (but especially he) is much more likely to be the "butt" of the joke — though, again, as with the comedy of black vaudeville, the target of the humor shifts rapidly. In a sense, what Chesnutt does with Julius is much like what Dunbar does in "We Wear the Mask," offering an interpretive guide for African American culture, particularly African American popular culture. Chesnutt allows the reader to see both John's awareness of Julius's transparent and apparently unsuccessful attempts to manipulate him (and his wife) through storytelling and John's unawareness of Julius's successful efforts to achieve his aims on a deeper level. While Julius's aims include quite practical objectives (e.g., a good job, lumber for his church, and the reinstatement of his grandson in John's employ), they also include, among other things, a vivid and figurative narration of the horrors of slavery in which people are changed into things, often commercial property, such as a work mule, a tree that is eventually milled into lumber, and a sort of human grapevine. John is unaware, or at best only dimly aware, of this symbolic level, though his wife Anne is able to perceive and understand the true horror underlying Julius's transformation stories:

> "What a system it was," she exclaimed, when Julius had finished, "under which such things were possible!"
> "What things?" I asked, in amazement. "Are you seriously considering the possibility of a man's being turned into a tree?"
> "Oh, no," she replied quickly, "not that"; and then she murmured absently, and with a dim look in her fine eyes, "Poor Tenie!" (53)

Thus, the reader is given a glimpse into not only what might be considered the spiritual dimension of the slave system but also something of the depths of Julius's dualist storytelling — again, a dualism that has even more in common in many respects with the ambivalent humor of the black popular musical theater of the late nineteenth century, performed for both black and white audiences, than with that of Joel Chandler Harris or even the antebellum black folk tradition (Sundquist, 276–346).

Among the topics that Julius's stories do not and perhaps cannot really address, even through the indirect manner of Julius (except, ironically, through pointed omission), is the Civil War and Reconstruction and their meaning. The reader does find out through Julius that the old master of the McAdoo plantation was killed in the war and that the McAdoo family abandoned the old plantation after his death. But, except for the speculation of the narrator John that does not seem based in any actual testimony of Julius, what Julius did during and immediately after the war is untold. Was he a soldier or scout in the Union army, forced, as was the grandfather of the narrator of *Invisible Man*, to give up his gun after Reconstruction? Is he truly literate? If so, did he learn to read in one of Reconstruction's literacy classes — or could he read before the war? The reader discovers that Julius is a pillar of one of the local black churches, but not whether he can actually read the Bible. John asserts that Julius remained in the area of the old McAdoo plantation because he could not rid himself of "the habit of being owned" (55). Yet the reader also observes that Julius has set himself up as a small-time entrepreneur, selling the grapes (or perhaps wine made from the grapes) of the vineyard that John proposes to buy at the beginning of the tales. As in *Up from Slavery*, such omissions and incongruities are left hanging without any real resolution—much as are the endings of Chesnutt's more bitter, and more melancholy, novels about the violent crushing of the hopes of Reconstruction, *The Marrow of Tradition* (1901) and *The Colonel's Dream* (1905).

W. E. B. Du Bois's *The Souls of Black Folk* famously elaborates the concept of African American dualism, particularly echoing Dunbar's open bitterness. However, while there are moments that recall the indirection of Washington and the melancholy of Chesnutt, Du Bois differs from and critiques them, especially Washington, suggesting that it is a state that cannot and should not stand. His notion of individual double consciousness had a metonymic relation to the development of a broad African American self-consciousness that in turn was related to the location of African Americans within American culture. Du Bois argues that, as Douglass and other partisans of Reconstruction feared, the sort of reconciliation between white southerners and northerners had taken place in a way that fundamentally excluded black people. When Du Bois speaks of "the strange meaning of being black here at the dawning of the Twentieth Century" (5) in "The Forethought" of *Souls* and goes on to say in perhaps his most quoted statement that "the problem of the Twentieth Century is the problem of the color line" (5), the white people of the North and the South have, in the main, embraced each other before the altar of Mammon (embodied most clearly in the New South city of Atlanta and the northern capital that animates the post-Reconstruction economy of the South), becoming simply white Americans. These now reunified white Americans are veiled from a resubjugated caste of African Americans for whom the categories of "Negro" and "American" are set at odds in a way that threatens to tear them apart.

As David Blight points out, for Du Bois the sectional reconciliation of white people into more or less a single group leaves untouched (or, in fact, deepens) the chasm between the former slave owner and his or her offspring and the former slave and her or his descendants, a chasm that through the reunion of white northerners and southerners becomes a national rather than sectional divide. This divide, Du Bois argues, is ultimately as intolerable for the nation as it is for African Americans and the black subject. The internal process of the struggle to accommodate and/or to integrate two disjunct consciousnesses is seen as analogous to the group movement from the unconsciousness of slavery to the self-consciousness developing in the post-slavery era and, in turn, to the relationship between black and white within the body politic of the United States. In all three instances, there is a certain optimism as to the possibility (if not inevitability) of the successful integration of the disparate parts. Even if Du Bois's notion of a possible resolution of the problem of double consciousness is one in which the "Negro" and the "American" selves will not completely merge but rather coexist in a sort of multicultural state that does not threaten to split the black subject, nonetheless a sort of integration, if not assimilation, is posited. By contrast, Dunbar's (and Chesnutt's and, to some degree, Washington's) dualism is pessimistic and increasingly bleak, filled with a bitterness that Du Bois would not match until the McCarthy era fifty years later—though even Du Bois's model was amenable to a more pessimistic reading (e.g., the failure of the black subject to integrate his or her own split consciousness could be seen as analogous to a larger political failure of the American republic).

The relative optimism of *The Souls of Black Folk* should not be overstated. The three chapters preceding the final chapter of the book, "Of the Passing of the First Born," "Of Alexander Crummell," and "Of the Coming of John," are by turns melancholy, horrified, uncertain, elegiac, loving, angry, proud, despairing, and outraged, but none of them are optimistic. The voice inside Du Bois that whispers, "not dead, but escaped" (133) about the death of his young son in "Of the Passing of the First Born" can hardly be said to be confident about the rending of "the veil" in this life. The elegy to Crummell mourns the passing of the public memory of Crummell as well as his life. The bitter tone of Du Bois's chapter on Crummell resembles that of Dunbar's "Douglass," which, again, compares the present moment of the establishment of Jim Crow and the final dashing of Reconstruction hopes unfavorably with even those of slavery, and "Robert Gould Shaw," which suggests that Shaw and the martyred members of the Fifty-fourth Massachusetts Regiment would have been better off staying home given to what the country has come.[19] "Of the Coming of John" describes a victim of the veil and double consciousness whose body is literally torn asunder or mutilated by a lynch mob.

The final chapter, "Of the Sorrow Songs," ends on a note of measured optimism: "Even so is the hope that sang in the songs of my fathers well sung. If somewhere in this whirl and chaos of things there dwells Eternal Good, pitiful yet masterful, then anon in His good time America shall rend the Veil and the prisoned shall go free" (163). The final words of hope that close the chapter are not those of Du Bois but of the spiritual "Let Us Cheer the Weary

Traveller." The words preceding the song seen above are full of hedging and doubt — uncertain if there is an "Eternal Good," whether God or some other sort of transcendent force or principle that could impose justice or rational meaning that could make coherent a fragmented world. Du Bois's text here resembles Marx's opposing possibilities of socialist revolution or barbarism as the ultimate destiny of humankind. Still, it is the folk and their measured optimism in the end that have the last word in the chapter, not the represented voice of Du Bois.

This is another revision of *Up from Slavery*, of the parallel closing moment where Washington brings "hope and cheer" to the audience at the Academy of Music. In *Souls*, the divided intellectual cannot bring himself to wholehearted optimism except through the adoption or ventriloquizing of the folk voice. One might say that there is both cheer and threat here — a sort of multilayered jeremiad. One way or another the split will have to be healed through citizenship, whether in the contemporary United States or in some other sort of polity, possibly a black nation or some revolutionized multiracial, multinational state organized on principles fundamentally different from that of the United States. While the first choice would no doubt be less shocking for white Americans in the long run, Du Bois's apocalyptic close to the chapter suggests that, as was the case in Exodus (and, indeed, the slave-owning class before the Civil War), social cataclysm is more likely than a rational relinquishment. In an embryonic form one can perhaps discern the alternative to dualism that became dominant largely with the engagement of African American artists and intellectuals with the Communist Left in the late 1920s and beyond — that is, a national identity and expressive culture that is not divided but rooted in some notion of the culture of the African American folk and, later, working class with some sort of right to the determination of its own definition and destiny, whether inside or outside the polity of the United States.

In other words, this forerunner of that U.S. Left model of expression sees the task of the artist not as the transmutation of folk elements into a new high culture that would eliminate the contradictions of the dual cultural identity of African Americans but as a sort of channeling of the folk or common people whose culture is essentially the culture of the "Negro nation." As noted earlier, variations of earlier dualistic notions of black identity and culture would continue to exert powerful influences — even on the work of individuals, such as Hughes and Baraka (and Ralph Ellison, for that matter), much engaged with various forms and combinations of Marxism and nationalism.

A similarly bifurcated Dunbarian bleakness set in opposition to apparently upbeat dialect or vernacular poetry with a Du Boisian sense of the need for the solution of an unbearable divide invoking popular culture representations of the black folk, now transposed to the urban North, can be found in Fenton Johnson's early verse collected in the 1915 *Visions of the Dusk* and the 1916 *Songs of the Soil*. In *Visions of the Dusk*, one finds dialect poems juxtaposed with "Negro Spirituals" that anticipate James Weldon Johnson's verse renderings of the African American folk sermon (the first of which, "The Creation," was published a few years later in 1919) that were eventually collected in the 1927 *God's Trombones*. Like James Weldon Johnson, Fenton Johnson does not attempt to literally reproduce vernacular speech in his spirituals but instead gives the flavor of folk cadences, imagery, idiomatic sayings, and so on:

> Let me not go there by fiddle tune or harp,
> Down by Beulahland,
> Play no banjo on my journey to the King,
> Down by Beulahland,
> Let me fight my battles in the way I choose
> I alone must win the crown of Righteousness,
> Let me be a soldier with my armor on,
> Down by Beulahland. (37)

The diction and imagery of the spirituals is in marked contrast to the dialect pieces, most pointedly in the poem "De Ban'," which follows the "spiritual" "The Song of Beulahland":

> Don't you heah de ban', Miss Mandy Lee?
> Don't you see de leadah wave to me?
> How dose da'kies ma'ch if to wo',
> Fo'teen strong, all bright wid music's glow;
> Daih is Eph un Jackson, drummah boy,
> Wid dose sticks he's beatin' scrumptious joy,
> Daih is Trombone Pete in suit o' raid,
> Holdin' high wid pride his wooly haid,
> (Hum! Ti! Tum! Tum! Boom! Ti-Boom! Boom! Boom!
> Git away an' gib dose anguls room!) (37–38)

Johnson's "De Ban'" is a rewriting of Dunbar's "The Colored Band" (first collected in the 1903 *When Malindy Sings*). Both poems take the "coon"/ plantation genres in their more jovial aspects to an extreme (with Johnson's "da'kies" and "wooly haid" echoing Dunbar's "Rastus on parade" and "picka-ninnies"), while proclaiming the superiority of African American music to the "high-toned music" of the white bands so that, as Johnson's speaker says with considerable irony, the black band "sholy owns de livin' Souf" (38). Much as the diction and imagery of Dunbar's poem forms a contradictorily meaningful pair with the dignity, elegance, and precision of the bands and bandleaders pictured in the accompanying photographs by the Hampton In-stitute Camera Club, "De Ban'" sits side by side with a "spiritual" with a distinctly African American cast, but which pointedly avoids, and even the-matizes the avoidance of, dialect and late minstrel/"coon song"/plantation conventions. For example, the line "play no banjo on my way to the King" takes on a particular significance, suggesting the encounter with God and judgment involves the dropping of all masks and the healing of all divisions in a way that invokes and rejects minstrelsy.

This sort of dualist opposition between authentic black core and popular culture mask in an even more Dunbarian mode characterizes *Songs of the Soil*. "Harlem: The Black City" is possibly the first literary work positing Harlem as an archetypal African American landscape (de Jongh, 15):

We ask for life, men give us wine,
We ask for rest, men give us death;
We long for Pan and Phoebus harp.
But Bacchus blows on us his breath.
O, Harlem, weary are thy sons
Of living that they never chose;
Give not to them the lotus leaf,
But Mary's wreath and England's rose. (6)

After the manner of Dunbar's early collections of poetry, Johnson sets this revelation of the split between African American self-consciousness and the horizon of expectations for African American identity and expressive cul-ture within the broader culture of the United States against an apparently straightforward fulfillment of those expectations — at least for those unable or unwilling to look deeper. And, as in much of Dunbar's poetry that promi-nently foregrounds this split (e.g., "We Wear the Mask" and "The Poet"), the "literary" diction, iambic tetrameter rhythm, classical allusions, and other apparently conservative elements of Johnson's poem heighten the sense of an unwilling and imprisoning dualism. "Harlem: The Black City" is im-mediately followed by "De Music Call," which appears to fit the mold of what James Weldon Johnson criticized as the limited range of sentimental "dialect" literature ("W'en de music plays Ah pats de feet"), often, as in "De Music Call," drawing a direct connection to the minstrel-influenced stages. However, as with Dunbar's "We Wear the Mask," "Harlem" suggests the possibility of rereading "De Music Call" and other dialect poems in the volume, while using the dialect poetry as a sort of "exhibit A" illustrating and supporting the argument about the nature of African American dualism made in the "standard" poem.

James Weldon Johnson's use of the familiar African American literary trope of the mixed-race individual to embody a sort of dualism in *Autobiography of an Ex-Colored Man* (1912) has a similarly bleak ending. Johnson's unnamed narrator-protagonist fails in his project of reconciling his disparate cultural selves through the creation of a new African American "high" music synthesizing the folk culture in the form of the spirituals and the popular culture in the form of ragtime within a "high" frame derived from the European art music tradition. His project comes to an end after he flees the horror, humiliation, and shame of the legal and extralegal enforcement of the Jim Crow system in the South, culminating in a lynching where the victim is burned at the stake. Interestingly (and ironically), it appears that only in these moments of shame and terror is the narrator able to resolve his divided self. Even in his moments of greatest pride in the cultural achievements of the black folk, the narrator seems divided from that folk. His description of the details and effect of the spirituals sung by a rural African American congregation is more one of an engaged but alien folklorist than of an intimate insider: "How did the men who originated them manage to do it? The sentiments are easily accounted for; they are mostly taken from the Bible; but the melodies, where did they come from? Some of them so weirdly sweet, others so wonderfully strong" (*Writings*, 109–10).

This sense of being an outside observer is superseded when the narrator-artist-intellectual suddenly finds himself one with the lynch victim whom he had previously characterized as degenerate and rendered without a "single ray of thought" by terror: "A great wave of humiliation and shame swept over me. Shame that I belonged to a race that could be so dealt with; and shame for my country, that it, the great example of democracy to the world, should be the only civilized, if not the only state on earth, where a human being would be burned alive" (*Writings*, 113).

Even here, where the narrator suddenly finds himself one with somebody whom he claimed was "a man only in form and stature," a dualism is expressed over his own status as "Negro" and as "American" (carrying with it the status of full citizen and full human) that he has clearly internalized.

There is an obvious echo of Douglass's claims of how he was transformed into a brute, and his mistress into a sort of demon by slavery, when the narrator rhetorically asks, "Have you ever witnessed the transformation of human beings into savage beasts?" (Johnson, *Writings*, 113). One might also see in the lynching a kind of demonic minstrel staging, or the logic of the "coon song" taken to its furthest degree, as the burning victim, degraded by terror into the figure of a menacing and degenerate "coon" is watched with bestial cheers and yells by many (though not all) in the white audience. The narrator's identification with the victim, and his shame over that identification, recall his later comments about the limitations of dialect as a literary language due to the tendency of readers, especially white readers, to convert dialect works into the comedy or pathos seen attending the minstrel and plantation traditions.[20]

It is important to recall the obvious point that this is not the black cultural and civil rights activist James Weldon Johnson's autobiography we are reading but the fictional biography of the unnamed protagonist; the bleakness and the unresolved split personality of the narrator-intellectual-artist (who has basically ceased to be an intellectual and artist by the end of the novel) is not the inevitable fate of all who attempt to solve the problem of cultural identity figured by Johnson's version of dualism. The life of the ex-colored man does echo Johnson's at times — though often in reverse (e.g., in contrast to the ex-colored man, Johnson was a native of, not a migrant to, Jacksonville, Florida). Johnson also got some inspiration from the life of his friend and onetime law partner, J. Douglas Wetmore, who went to law school at the University of Michigan and "passed" at times for white.[21] The overall framing of Johnson's novel is more positive, ending with the protagonist's bitter regret over the failure of his project, while others followed his original path with great promise, if not yet complete realization. Nonetheless, it is the protagonist's failure to resolve his self-divide satisfactorily with which the reader is left most vividly in the end. To the degree that this is autobiographical, this failure can be seen as perhaps a figuration or displacement of Johnson's own bitterness over the failure of Reconstruction and its institutions and ideals in the South, particularly his hometown of Jacksonville, Florida.[22]

Despite their differences, the dualisms expressed by Du Bois, Dunbar, Washington, Chesnutt, James Weldon Johnson, Fenton Johnson, and other black contemporaries were products of and responses to a particular political and cultural era — that is, the era in which African Americans had a dual legal status as citizens and subcitizens. This era saw the final collapse of Reconstruction institutions and, for the most part, ideals, as well as the passing of the old abolitionist leadership. One response to this collapse was the public accommodationism with (and private opposition to) Jim Crow associated with Booker T. Washington. Du Bois's polemic against Washington is one of the most famous aspects of *The Souls of Black Folk*. A praise poem to Washington notwithstanding, Dunbar's version of dualism also contained an implicit critique of Washington. For example, "The Poet" and the opposition of true poetry and "jingles in a broken tongue" can be read as, among other things, a pointed, if pessimistic, rejection of Washington's famous passage about the boy in a filthy cabin reading a French grammar in *Up From Slavery* with its notion of utilitarian self-limitation.

These dualisms provided models for the representation of African American subjectivity, which in turn was seen to have a metonymic relationship to the development of an African American group identity and, further, an "American" national identity in which the schism of black and white that defined the United States would be reconciled (whether in some new hybrid form, some multicultural coexistence, or some combination of the two). It also provided ways for African American artists to negotiate the contradictory elements of the emerging and interconnected "mainstream" and African American popular cultures in the representation and re-creation of the speaking folk or popular subject. In other words, one of their most-lasting contributions to American culture was the way these dualisms provided models for writers to engage the divided and often contradictory elements of popular culture in ways that foregrounded those divisions and paradoxes, anticipating the representations of fragmented subjectivities that became standard operating procedure of much U.S. modernism, "high" or otherwise. If in their own ways Du Bois, Dunbar, Chesnutt, Washington, and the Johnsons did not capture, develop, or make vivid these circulating dualisms, then their models would not have had the almost instantaneous and long-lived influences that they did.

Of course, as already noted with respect to Walker and Williams and others in minstrel- and "coon"-inflected vaudeville theater and music, the popular artists themselves (including Dunbar and James Weldon Johnson at different points in their careers) and their black audiences, too, had to navigate many of the same dualist contradictions, providing not only cautionary tales or foils for black writers but also continuing examples of how one might successfully manage such contradictions and still connect to a mass African American audience. As a result, one can also find implied in the work of many of these writers a forerunner of the sort of twentieth-century radical nationalism that saw such dualisms as a trap inherent in tying African

Americans to dreams of individualist citizenship within the United States and that suggested that the resolution of these bifurcated identities lay only in the establishment of some sort of black polity. So it is not surprising that the early twentieth-century Left nationalist Hubert Harrison would early on see Dunbar as a people's poet expressing a national black identity, a position Harrison apparently held his entire adult life (Perry, 74–75; Harrison, 176, 357, 395).[23]

When the nation was in peril; when the country was rent
asunder at the center; when the rebel armies were in the field, bold,
defiant and victorious; when our recruiting sergeants were marching up
and down our streets from early morn til late at night, with drum and fife,
with banner and badge, footsore and weary; when the fate of the Republic
trembled in the balance, and the hearts of loyal men were failing them for fear;
when nearly all hope of subduing the rebellion had vanished, Abraham Lincoln
called upon the colored men of this country to reach out their iron arms and
clutch with their steel fingers the faltering banner of the Republic; and they
rallied, and they rallied, full two hundred thousand strong. Ah! then, my friends,
the claims of the Negro found the heart of the nation a little more tender and
responsive than now. But I ask Americans to remember that the arms that
were needed then may be needed again.

—Frederick Douglass, "The United States Cannot Remain Half-Slave
and Half-Free," in *Frederick Douglass: Selected Speeches and Writing*

I would sing a song heroic
Of those noble sons of Ham,
Of those gallant colored soldiers
Who fought for Uncle Sam!

—Paul Laurence Dunbar,
"The Colored Soldiers," in *Collected Poetry*

chapter two

Remembering "Those Noble Sons of Ham"

Poetry, Soldiers, and Citizens at the End of Reconstruction

Following French social historian Pierre Nora, Richard Terdiman has argued
that a particular mark of modernity in Europe—and, ultimately, a central
concern of modernism—is the "memory crisis" arising from people's sense
of "the insecurity of their culture's involvement with its past, the pertur-
bation of the link to their own inheritance" after the revolutionary period
of 1789–1815 (3–4). If this sense of the insecurity or instability of cultural
memory, if, again, "all that is solid melts into air," is a central topos of modernity and modernism, then some of the earliest literary engagements with the
"memory crisis" took place in African American literature.[1] The intertwined

issues of national, racial, and ethnic identity in black writing, from that of Phillis Wheatley and Olaudah Equiano in the eighteenth century through the autobiographies of Frederick Douglass in the nineteenth century to debates between E. Franklin Frazier and Melville Herskovits in the twentieth century to the conversation about reparations for the descendants of slaves in the United States that still continues in the twenty-first century have significantly turned on the question of cultural memory, its disruption, displacement, survival, and possible recovery.

Of course, to a certain extent the United States long prided itself on the disruption of cultural memory, as the place where the individual could fashion or refashion herself or himself, willfully repressing any collective memory of cultural origins in the Old World or, indeed, in the New — though this repression and remaking was not generally posed as a crisis. However, by the late nineteenth and early twentieth centuries, what might be thought of as a double memory crisis arose, producing twinned anxieties about ruptures in cultural memory caused by mass immigration and assimilation and mass immigration and nonassimilation, between the forced or willed forgetting of "old country" cultures and the threat to "American" cultural, moral, and political identity occasioned by "offwhite" and fundamentally (and more or less perpetually) alien nationalities.[2]

It would not be until the rise of U.S. modernism and the emergence of a significant bohemia in the United State in the second and third decades of the twentieth century that these immigrants and their offspring, especially the "new immigrants" from southern and eastern Europe and the Middle East, began to make a noticeable mark on U.S. literature in English — popular music and theater were different stories. African American authors, then, were practically the only significant group of English-language writers in the United States who were not white Christians (generally Protestants) of northern or western European descent until the twentieth century — Emma Lazarus notwithstanding. If, as various scholars have noted, African American culture provided the children of the "new immigrants" models of becoming "American," black authors provided early examples of engaging the double anxieties of cultural memory: the fear of becoming deracinated and the fear of being cast as the permanent alien who disrupts memory as well as the body politic ("How does it feel to be a problem?" Du Bois famously asked in *The Souls of Black Folk* [10]).

While the Middle Passage and its consequences have been the most durable (and, over the long term, perhaps the most significant) focus of the issue of memory addressed by black writers (seen even in the discussions over whether Barack Obama was "black" early in the 2008 presidential election campaign), the adjudication of black citizenship was arguably *the* central question in U.S. politics and culture in the period immediately preceding the rise of North American modernism in the early twentieth century. The trope of the black Civil War veteran and the recollection of the vital African American contribution to the maintenance of the Republic (and the southern white betrayal of that republic) became a staple of African American writing, especially poetry, presenting a countermemory or countermemorial to various sorts of "Lost Cause" pro-Confederate versions of the past as well as to "reconciliationist" portraits of the United States that left out African Americans as anything but devoted servants, comic relief, or bestial threats.

Though the trope was initially used by black and white writers, and more white than black, during the war, it was employed almost solely by African American authors during Reconstruction to remind white Americans of the debt owed to the African Americans who helped save the republic and served as a symbol of black pride and community in a time when political, cultural, and social citizenship was to a significant extent a genuine, if embattled, reality. As Reconstruction faded and Jim Crow segregation became ascendant, black uses of the trope of the black soldier, especially in the hands of Paul Laurence Dunbar, shifted from an argument for political and cultural citizenship to a commentary and critique of white protomodernist expressions of a perceived "memory crisis," as the United States consolidated its position as an international economic and, increasingly, political power.

Many of the earlier poets, with the exception of Frances E. W. Harper, discussed here are distinctly minor. Still, their work did create a sort of field out of which Dunbar's poems of the black veteran emerged, suggesting the possibilities both for a general modernist sensibility of alienation and the divided self and for a black modernism or modern literature that is in some senses opposed to or corrective of white modernist uses of black culture and black history. Thus, the trope of the black Civil War soldier, while largely a figure employed initially by African American authors to buttress black citizenship during Reconstruction, ultimately can be seen as a sort of literary bridge between the black literature of Reconstruction (and of an unambiguous entrance of African Americans [men anyway] into modern U.S. society as citizens) and the later genres, tropes, and stances discussed in the following chapters of this book. The argument here is not that the trope made a big impact on U.S. modernism as a whole. Rather, it is a transitional trope that vanished with the triumph of Jim Crow and was replaced by the figure of the World War I veteran, which has persisted from the Harlem Renaissance to

Toni Morrison. It emblemizes a road taken and then abandoned, profoundly altering African American notions of what the United States might be (and what it was), producing a variety of responses, from the radical democratic to the (black) nationalist.

Sidney Kaplan notes that shortly after the 1897 dedication of Augustus Saint-Gaudens's monument to Robert Gould Shaw, the martyred white commander of the Massachusetts Fifty-fourth Regiment (one of the first and the most famous of the black regiments of the Civil War), "a new generation of poets began to respond to Saint-Gaudens' monument and to the saga of the Fifty-fourth with a new sense of consecration" (118). However, this poetry, particularly that by African American writers, was also part of a body of writing considerably antedating in its beginnings the dedication of the monument on Boston Common. The writing of this greater body of poems was largely motivated by the political and cultural wars raging from the 1870s through the 1890s as the southern white segregationist reaction against the reforms and institutions of Reconstruction gradually won complete control of the South, establishing the legal and extralegal Jim Crow system and effectively disenfranchising African Americans throughout most of the region.

A wave of poetry by black authors, beginning in the late 1870s and ending in about 1900, used the Fifty-fourth and the black veteran to embody the argument for (male) African American citizenship. Or, rather, perhaps it is more accurate to say that the trope was used to demonstrate an incontrovertible authority for that citizenship, becoming, by the end of the century an indictment of a white American refusal to acknowledge, or inability to even see, that authority—and, by extension, African American human subjectivity.

African American poets in the last two decades of the nineteenth century showed far more interest in the actions of rank-and-file black soldiers than their white counterparts writing about the Fifty-fourth, who tended to focus on Shaw. The work of black poets invoking the Fifty-fourth and the black Civil War soldier generally recalled in theme, tone, and purpose what historian David Blight has termed the verbal Civil War monuments of Frederick Douglass's speeches and writings in the 1880s and 1890s, monuments memorializing black sacrifice and bravery and promoting African American citizenship.[3] The heroic journey of the black soldier to the South described explicitly or implicitly in this poetry also served as a bridge between the symbolic geography of the slave narrative with its move to the North and that of the early migration narratives, which, as discussed in the next chapter, end with a sort of melancholy, often suspending the protagonist between North and South.

By the end of the century, however, this rhetoric of citizenship was much muted in the poems written about the Fifty-fourth and the black soldier by African American writers. The later poems functioned as elegies for Reconstruction and the immediate possibility of full African American citizenship as well as for their ostensible subject, Robert Gould Shaw and the soldiers of the Fifty-fourth—and their bitterly melancholic tone was much like that of the early black migration narratives. They were also testimonies to the establishment of the modern Jim Crow regime in the South. The trope of the black Civil War veteran largely disappeared from African American poetry and fiction after the turn of the century except as a brief or oblique, if significant, reference, as when in Ralph Ellison's *Invisible Man* the narrator's grandfather alludes to his role in the war somewhat cryptically when he speaks of giving up his gun after Reconstruction. While the black veteran did not disappear as an important trope in black literature, the Civil War soldier was replaced by the veterans of other wars, particularly World War I. This could be seen as a natural consequence of the press of history. Yet the figure of the black World War I veteran would recur in African American literature for many decades after 1918, from the work of Claude McKay to that of Toni Morrison, suggesting that it was not simply historical proximity to the Civil War that motivated the usage and abandonment of the trope of the Civil War veteran.

"For Freedom He Will Strike and Strive": The Massachusetts Fifty-fourth and the Beginnings of the Trope of the Black Civil War Soldier

The first poems about Shaw and the Massachusetts Fifty-fourth, overwhelmingly by white New England writers, appeared shortly after the Union attack on Battery Wagner in South Carolina on July 18, 1863. They generally represent Shaw as an abolitionist martyr redeeming America from the stain of satanic slavery, often with Shaw literally ascending into heaven, as in Epes Sargent's "Colonel Shaw: On Hearing That the Rebels Had Buried His Body under a Pile of Twenty-five Negroes" (1863):

> There, where the smoke from Sumter's bellowing guns
> Curls o'er the grave, which no commingled dust
> Can make less sacred. Soon his monument

Shall be the old flag waving, and proclaiming
To the whole world that the great cause he died for
Has nobly triumphed, — that the hideous Power,
Hell-born, that would disgrace him, has been hurled
Into the pit it hollowed for the Nation, —
That the Republic stands redeemed and pure,
Justice enthroned, and not one child of God
Robbed of his birthright, freedom! (2)

Like many of the poems by white authors during the war, such as Elizabeth
Sedgwick's "Buried with His Niggers!" and L. H.'s "To Robert Gould Shaw,
Buried by South Carolinians under a Pile of 24 Negroes," Sargent's poem
is a sort of harrowing of hell by the Christ-like Shaw in which the notion
of Shaw's physical contact with black bodies in death presumably provides
a certain shocking intensity to the poems for contemporary white readers.

Those white writers who focused on the black soldiers tended to represent
them as agents of a deified Freedom, generally figured as a "she," as in the
case of Ralph Waldo Emerson's "Voluntaries" (1863):

She will not refuse to dwell
With the offspring of the Sun;
Foundling of the desert far,
Where palms plume, and siroccos blaze,
He roves unhurt the burning ways
In climates of the summer star.
He has avenues to God
Hid from men of Northern brain,
Far beholding, without cloud,
What these with slowest steps attain.
If once the generous chief arrive
To lead him willing to be led,
For freedom he will strike and strive,
And drain his heart til he be dead. (179)

These poems share some of the same sort of northern Protestant racialist
primitivism that is displayed in other types of antebellum and postbellum
American literature by both black and white writers in which African Americans are seen as possessing special spiritual gifts they can provide to America
in exchange for the gifts of freedom and self-consciousness.[4]

Few African Americans wrote formal poems about the Fifty-fourth Massachusetts and the assault on Battery Wagner during the 1860s. In fact, the only extant poem on the subject by a black author published during the war is "The Massachusetts Fifty-fourth" by Frances E. W. Harper, arguably the most important African American poet between Phillis Wheatley and Paul Laurence Dunbar and one of the best-selling black poets of all time. As Donald Yacovone points out, the poem "establishes a moral symmetry, following in the Christian tradition of death and rebirth" (102).[5] This use of a Protestant rhetoric of martyrdom and redemption was, as we have seen, not unlike that of most of the white writers who wrote of Shaw and the Massachusetts Fifty-fourth. However, in Harper's poem the redemptive figure of Shaw (or even the more generic "chief" of Emerson), ubiquitous in the work of these authors, is absent, replaced by a collective figure of the black troops whose blood would heal the Republic:[6]

> Oh! not in vain those heroes fell,
>   Amid those hours of fearful strife;
> Each dying heart poured out a balm
>   To heal the wounded nation's life.
>
> And from the soil drenched with their blood,
>   The fairest flowers of peace shall bloom;
> And history cull rich laurels there,
>   To deck each martyr hero's tomb.
>
> And ages yet uncrossed with life,
>   As sacred urns, do hold each mound
> Where sleep the loyal, true, and brave
>   In freedom's consecrated ground.

The replacement of Shaw with the black troops as the agents of sacrifice and redemption, and the lack of any mention of white or "northern" leadership, distinguishes Harper's poem sharply from the majority of poems about the Fifty-fourth published during the Civil War. Harper's poem also imputes to the black soldiers a self-consciousness and an agency lacking in nearly all the poems by white writers. Her work further differs from many of those by her white contemporaries in that it does not attempt to use the fact of Shaw's burial with black soldiers in a mass grave either for shock effect or to emphasize Shaw's Christ-like characteristics. Also, though Harper may in fact be linking the dead at Battery Wagner with Christ, she eschews the hymn form that one might expect, preferring instead iambic tetrameter quatrains that also set up the soldiers of the Fifty-fourth as heroic in a more "classical" sense (and it is worth noting the plural of "heroes" in the poem signifies that, unlike the case in many of the poems by white authors, Shaw is one hero among many). Nonetheless, Harper's piece shares with those other works a personification or figuration of Freedom whom the soldiers serve.

"Our Just and Equal Rights": The Black Soldier in African American Poetry of Reconstruction

In the years immediately after the Civil War, the Massachusetts Fifty-fourth and the black Civil War soldier generally almost disappear as subjects of American poetry. Those poets who do invoke the Fifty-fourth are nearly all, so far as I can tell, African American.[7] The epics of James Madison Bell, *The Progress of Liberty* (1866) and *The Triumph of Liberty* (1870), are among the few poems in which the Fifty-fourth appears before 1877.[8] In both poems, not only is slavery the civic curse that causes the Civil War, but also the black soldier is the essential component in the removal of the curse and the redemption and renewal of the Republic. In both poems, the Massachusetts Fifty-fourth assumes a particular importance as it is the only black unit actually named. As in Harper's poem, Bell's work emphasizes the agency of the black soldiers without the intercession of a white intermediary, and his focus on the African American troops themselves excludes mention of Robert Gould Shaw. Also like Harper's "The Massachusetts Fifty-fourth," Bell's poems objectify or personify "freedom" and "liberty." However, in Bell's verse black freedom is not simply defined as emancipation from slavery (in the sense of no longer being a piece of property that can be bought or sold). Instead, it is explicitly extended to a notion of citizenship, particularly in *The Triumph of Liberty*:

There is no right a freeman has
    So purely sacred as his choice.
How e'er bereft he'll cling to this,
    And in its potency rejoice;

For in its exercise he stands
    The peer of titled wealth and state,
How e'er possessed of spreading lands,
    Or gifted they in high debate —

He is their peer, however grand,
    Or much upon themselves they dote,

For there's no station in our land
　　Which ranks a man above his vote. (146)

Both poems end fulsomely praising the Republic — *The Triumph of Liberty* includes an almost ludicrous catalog of great natural resources ("And hail to thy Streamlets"), technological and economic advances ("And hail to thy Telegraph"), and governmental institutions ("And hail to thy Magistrates, Judges, and Courts") that sounds more than a bit like Roger Angell's humorous year-end poems in the *New Yorker* — and hailing the new order of Reconstruction.

Similarly, in Joshua McCarter Simpson's "Let the Banner Proudly Wave," an "air" included in *The Emancipation Car* (1874), the black soldiers figure as the redemptive agents of freedom, again in terms of a "rights of man" republicanism rather than of the northern Protestantism that characterized Harper and most of the white poets writing of Shaw and the Fifty-fourth:[9]

We've stood and fought like demons,
　　Upon the battle field;
Both slaves and Northern freemen
　　Have faced the glowing steel.
Our blood beneath this banner
　　Has mingled with the whites,
And 'neath its folds we now demand
　　Our just and equal rights. (144)

While the themes of freedom and slavery of Bell's work appear here, and elsewhere in the poem also, the notion of citizenship is considerably expanded. Simpson reminds the reader that freedom and citizenship are not interchangeable concepts legally or culturally in the United States. He makes the obvious observation that not all of the black soldiers were legally slaves — and none were practically. The Massachusetts Fifty-fourth was in fact a regiment of freemen, many of whom had been born in the North and a minority of whom had ever been slaves.[10] This observation is missing in the earlier poems that pose an opposition between slavery and freedom in which the slave fights to be free. This is as true of Harper's poem ("Bearers of a High Commission / To Break Each Brother's Chain") as it was of those by white authors. However, Simpson makes the plausible claim that to be "free" in the sense of being a "free Negro" is not the same as being a citizen with "just and equal rights."

Simpson's claim reminds the reader of an apparently simple point that is nonetheless worth recalling: though "freedom" might be a constitutive element of American citizenship, there were many categories of people in the United States (e.g., un-naturalized "white" immigrants, "nonwhite" immigrants who were prohibited from citizenship, African American "freemen" in many states, Native Americans, women in many respects) who were "free" in the sense of not being property, but who were not full-fledged citizens. Thus, for Simpson, as for later black writers, African Americans are entitled to citizenship, not merely "freedom," because they have earned their status as citizens through the sacrifice of the black Civil War soldier just as native-born white Americans are entitled to citizenship through the sacrifice of the patriots of the American Revolution. Just as the blood of the Revolutionary patriots symbolically guarantees or authorizes white citizenship in American political mythology, so does the blood of the Fifty-fourth and other black soldiers guarantee black citizenship. (Of course, such a move ignores black participation in the Revolution, but still the Civil War was the first U.S. military conflict in which black troops officially took part on behalf of the Republic in a prominent manner). These writers were not opposing "freedom" to "citizenship," the first being considered a necessary precondition for the second in the United States; rather, they noted only that the two conditions were not the same, a recognition that would gain new poignancy with the rise of Jim Crow and mass African American disenfranchisement.

Bell's poems may be "uniformly soporific," as literary scholar Joan Sherman claims, except where unintentionally humorous, and Simpson's poem slight in many respects (Sherman, 83). Nonetheless, they are important as forerunners of later poems by African Americans who use the Massachusetts Fifty-fourth and the black Civil War veteran to make a claim to citizenship and to "Americanness" that has been proved by the sacrifice of the black soldier. These poets are unlike those black and white writers and intellectuals, such as Ralph Waldo Emerson and, later, Booker T. Washington and the early W. E. B. Du Bois (as opposed to the Du Bois of *Black Reconstruction*), who in their different ways proposed a notion of freedom as a precondition for the former slaves to develop the self-consciousness necessary for citizenship. Instead, Bell and (particularly) Simpson make a demand for "citizenship now" based on the sacrifice of the black Civil War soldiers in the service of freedom *and* the republic and on a republicanism that implicitly invokes the more secular side of American Revolutionary rhetoric embodied in such documents as the Declaration of Independence. This emphasis on a particularized citizenship and Americanness, whether assumed or questioned, instead of an idealized and unspecified freedom, is perhaps the distinguishing mark of much African American literature during Reconstruction. In this sense, this Reconstruction use of the figure of the black veteran can be seen as an explicitly antidualist literary move during a period when black citizenship, while in dispute, was nonetheless enshrined in the Constitution and to a considerable extent in actual practice.[11]

Simpson's poem and Bell's epics notwithstanding, the post–Civil War wave of poems about the Fifty-fourth and the black Civil War soldier did not really begin until Reconstruction was in decline or even dead in a certain sense. As I have noted elsewhere, the precise boundaries of Reconstruction are hard to fix. Did Reconstruction essentially end, as Eric Foner and many other scholars suggest, with the Compromise of 1877 between the Republicans and the Democrats that sent Rutherford B. Hayes to the White House in exchange for a promise not to use federal power to guarantee the political rights of African Americans in the South (Foner, 564–601)? Or did it end with the final consolidation of Jim Crow and the disenfranchisement of the mass of African Americans in the South, and the legitimizing of Jim Crow and black disenfranchisement by the U.S. Supreme Court, at the end of the nineteenth century and beginning of the twentieth?[12]

If Reconstruction is taken to mean that era in which the federal government actively intervened in state and local government in the South, largely for the purpose of establishing and defending African American citizenship, then Reconstruction clearly ended in 1877. However, it is also clear that African Americans and their allies did not see Reconstruction as a lost cause, so to speak, until well after the Compromise of 1877. Black poets, much as Simpson had earlier in a time when Reconstruction was already in retreat, were particularly active in promulgating a rhetoric of citizenship that contested attempts to end the changes wrought by Reconstruction and to effectively limit the political and social rights of African Americans. The Fifty-fourth Massachusetts became an important literary embodiment of African American citizenship and Americanness earned through blood. Thus, when I write here of late Reconstruction or a late Reconstruction rhetoric, I mean it to refer to this nebulous period from the late 1870s to the early 1890s in which one could say that Reconstruction itself had died, but in which the effects and the ideals of Reconstruction still lived.

This late Reconstruction rhetoric can be seen clearly in Albery Whitman's 197-page *Not a Man, and Yet a Man* (1877). Whitman's epic is particularly interesting for its mixture of Protestant jeremiad, parable, quasi-scientific or medical rhetoric, echoes of Longfellow's *Hiawatha* and Cooper's *The Last of the Mohicans*, neomedieval romanticism, and a republican rhetoric of citizenship. It tells the story of Rodney, a slave of African and European descent (with his European "blood" predominating), who is a mixture, so to speak, of Leatherstocking, Uncas, Hiawatha, and Ivanhoe.[13]

The final section of the poem, "The End of the Whole Matter," begins with a sort of parable in which Rodney, a victorious "black" Union officer, encounters his former slave master, Aylor, wounded and dying on the battlefield. As Aylor dies, he is tormented by the memory of his torture of Rodney and his rape of Rodney's lover and, later, wife, Leoona. Seeing Rodney, Aylor begs water and forgiveness that Rodney gives as Aylor dies in his arms. This parable of forgiveness is immediately followed by a call for reconciliation, and reconstruction, that acknowledges the valor of both sides:

> And now my country let us bury all
> Our blunders sad beneath grim battle's pall.
> Gathered beneath the storm's heroic folds,
> While our dear land an aching bosom holds,
> Let us forget the wrongs of blue and grey,
> In gazing on the grandeur of the fray.
> Now the vanquished his repentant face
> Lean in the victor's merciful embrace,
> And let the victor, with his strong arm heal
> The bleeding wounds that gape beneath his steel.
> And may no partial hand attempt a lay
> Of praise, as due alone to blue or grey.
> The warrior's wreath may well by both be worn,
> For braver man than either ne'er was born. (206–7)

As in the moment of reconciliation between Frederick Douglass and Thomas Auld in Douglass's final autobiography, Whitman's plea to forget "the wrongs of blue and grey" on the battlefield does not call upon Americans to forget what he sees as the root cause or sin of the war, slavery. Rather, as in the opening parable, it is necessary for the sinners to confess and repent for their sins before they can be forgiven. For Whitman's speaker, the war was necessary, even divinely inspired:

> The war was God-sent, for the battle blade,
> Around the seething gangrene, Slavery, laid,
> By Heaven's arm, this side and that was prest,
> Until the galling shame dropt from the Nation's breast. (207)

The jeremiadic Protestantism of this passage would not have been out of place in many of the earlier poems that mentioned the Fifty-fourth, the black soldier, and Robert Gould Shaw — though the use of the metaphor of disease rather than a Christ-like figure of redemption was unusual if not completely unique.[14] However, what *is* unique is the manner in which that rhetoric merged with a rhetoric of citizenship and government with God as the divine surgeon who uses the instrument of the Union Army to heal the body politic:

> War was inevitable, for the crimes
> That stained our hands (and in the olden times
> Engendered) now were Constitutional,
> And spreading thro' the Nation's body all.
> Deep rooted where the vital currents meet
> Around the heart of government, their seat
> Evaded Legislation's keenest skill,
> Or bent the stoutest edge of human will.
> 'Twas then that God the raving Nation threw
> Upon her own war lance and from her drew,
> By accidental providence, a flood
> Of old diseases that lurked in her blood. (207)

This medicalized jeremiad is immediately preceded by a passage in which African American soldiers are represented as an integral part of the instruments through which God drew out the infection of slavery:

> And where our sons their battle lances drew,
> Fought not their sable comrades bravely too?
> Let Wagner answer 'mid the reeking storm
> That mingles with black dead proud Shaw's fair form.
> Ask it of Fisher, and a thousand more
> Brave fields that answer with their lips of gore.
> And while America's escutcheon bright,
> Is bathed in war-won Freedom's glorious light,
> Forget it not, the colored man will fight.
> More patriotism Sparta never knew,
> A lance more knightly Norman never threw,
> More courage never armed the Roman coasts,
> With blinder zeal ne'er rode the Moslem hosts,

And ne'er more stubborn stood the Muscovite,
Than stood the hated negro in the fight. (207)

The "lances" of the (presumably) white soldiers mirror those of the black troops. The medievalism of "lances" resonates with the mixture of medicine and medievalism in the following section, again suggesting that both the black and white troops are instruments of God. The new connection and equality between black and white is emphasized in the mention of Shaw. Shaw here is not so much a Christ figure as a figure of the disintegration of racial division, suggestively linked to the dead black troops with the word "mingles."

Strangely enough, the voice of Whitman's speaker identifies with white readers, the "we" whose "sons" were joined by their "sable" comrades. Yet this sort of identification fits the general recognition of the bravery of soldiers on both sides of the Civil War and the call for forgiveness and reconciliation. The poem is addressed then in large part not simply to the former abolitionists of the North and partisans of the Union but also to the former soldiers and supporters of the Confederacy.

Again, this sort of call for reconciliation that includes African Americans, white northerners, and white southerners counters white reconciliationism based on the acceptance of black subordination and the end of Reconstruction. It is closely akin to similar moves by black authors working in other genres, particularly the postbellum autobiography by former slaves, perhaps most notably the description of the postwar encounter between Douglass and the ailing Auld in *The Life and Times of Frederick Douglass*. For Whitman's speaker, as for Douglass, the reconciliation can work only if the sin of slavery—and, indeed, any other system in which citizenship is restricted on account of race, religion, or ethnicity (if not gender)—is erased after sincere repentance on the part of the sinners. This can be seen most clearly as the poem ends in a mixture of medievalism and a radical republicanism:

Free schools, free press, free speech and equal laws,
A common country and a common cause,
Are only worthy of a freeman's boasts—
Are Freedom's real and intrinsic costs.
Without these, Freedom is an empty name,
And war-worn glory is a glaring shame.
Soon where yon happy future now appears,
Where learning now her glorious temple rears,

Our country's hosts shall round one interest meet,
And her free heart with one proud impulse beat,
One common blood thro' her life's channels flow,
While one great speech her loyal tongue shall know.
And soon, whoever to our bourne shall come,
Jew, Greek or Goth, he here shall be at home.
Then Ign'rance shall forsake her crooked ways,
And poor old Caste there end her feeble days. (213–14)

Again, as in many of the early poems invoking the Fifty-fourth and the black soldier, freedom is objectified in a somewhat abstract manner, yet its objectification and abstraction are undermined with the claim to citizenship that flows both from natural rights and from the efforts of black (and white) soldiers. Any sort of restriction on the rights of people residing within the United States, whatever their race, religion or nationality, makes a mockery of America and threatens to bring another divine operation like the Civil War. Thus, Whitman is not merely commemorating the valor of black soldiers, or even reminding the reader of the evil of slavery. Rather, he is arguing for the preservation of Reconstruction and against any future system that would threaten the citizenship of African Americans, and other Americans, whether or not it was precisely the same as antebellum slavery.

"Hot Terror of a Hopeless Fight": The Figure of the Black Soldier and Jim Crow Reconciliation

As far as I know, there was a hiatus in the use of the Fifty-fourth Regiment and the black Civil War soldier by African American authors from the late 1870s until the early 1890s, when the figure returned with the related notions of memory and forgetting heavily foregrounded.[15] By the 1890s, it was obvious that in most respects black citizenship was doomed in the South (and perhaps beyond), unless there was some drastic intervention by the federal government legally and practically, as the shape of the post-Reconstruction South of segregation and African American disenfranchisement became clear. The 1881 passage of a law segregating railroad cars in Tennessee marks one possible beginning date of the Jim Crow era. Another significant date is the 1890 adoption of "literacy and understanding" tests designed to eliminate African American voters in Mississippi. This enactment of the legal infrastructure of segregation and disenfranchisement brought forth a renewed defense of Reconstruction and its legacies by African American writers. Probably the best known is Frances Harper's aggressively upbeat (in terms of the future of black citizenship) 1893 novel *Iola Leroy*, a work in which the heroism and sacrifice of black soldiers in the Civil War figures prominently—though Harper's feminism added a dimension to the discussion of Reconstruction and citizenship that is missing in the work of male African American writers who used the figure of the black soldier.

The Massachusetts Fifty-fourth and the black soldier generally also returned to African American poetry in the 1890s. One minor effort, "The Old Flag" (1890) by George Clinton Rowe, is interesting because it is one of the few poems (if not the only poem) about the Fifty-fourth by either a black or white author that names a black soldier—or any member of the Fifty-fourth other than Robert Gould Shaw (Rowe, 47–48).[16] "The Old Flag" is a brief praise poem for William H. Carney, the black sergeant wounded in the assault on Battery Wagner who bore the regimental colors back to the Union lines, where he was alleged to have exclaimed, "The dear old flag has never touched the ground, boys!" (Carney was the first African American to be awarded a Congressional Medal of Honor [Hargrove, 155–56].) Rowe celebrates not simply the bravery of "the noble hero of our race" but the patriotism and the Americanness of Carney, and, by extension, of all African Americans.

There is a strange doubleness to Rowe's poem. At times he uses the word "our" to mean the people of the United States generally ("our country—South and North"), presumably encompassing something like the reconstructed and reconciled republic of Albery Whitman. At other times, "our" seems to refer to African Americans specifically ("our race"). Thus, the "we" of the poem, by extension the imagined audience of the poem, seems indeterminate. Perhaps this doubleness or indeterminacy is intended to trouble both categories, making it an early statement of black "double consciousness" that, as noted in the previous chapter, would be shortly articulated so powerfully by Dunbar, Du Bois, James Weldon Johnson, Charles Chesnutt, and even Booker T. Washington. Interestingly, freedom does not figure directly in this poem, unlike others about the Fifty-fourth and the black soldier. Rather, it invokes bravery and patriotism, and a notion of citizenship implied by patriotism.

Undoubtedly, the poet laureate of the black Civil War soldier is Paul Laurence Dunbar—he wrote at least a half-dozen poems about the African American veterans of the Civil War, often mentioning the Massachusetts Fifty-fourth, as well as poems commemorating black soldiers in the Revolution and the Spanish-American War. In fact, one might mark the beginning of Dunbar's serious literary career from the publication of "Our Mar-tyred Soldiers," ostensibly a poem to Union soldiers generally, in a Dayton, Ohio, newspaper on June 8, 1888 (when Dunbar was sixteen). That Dunbar would write such poems seems natural insofar as his father, Joshua Dun-bar, returned from Canada after escaping from slavery on the Underground Railroad to enlist in the Fifty-fifth Massachusetts, another regiment of free African Americans, and later the Fifth Regiment of Massachusetts Volun-teer Cavalry (Gayle, 6–8). But beyond the personal connection, Dunbar was the most powerful poet who used the figure of the black soldier to mount a defense of Reconstruction. Later, when it became clear that the hopes of Reconstruction had finally failed, Dunbar reappropriated the Fifty-fourth Massachusetts, the black soldier, and, for the first time in his career, Robert Gould Shaw to bitterly elegize the passing of those hopes. As seen already, both usages derive as much from other black (and white) writers as from family history. At the same time, Dunbar became intensely engaged with the material, giving it a concreteness and specificity missing in the works of other writers, black and white. It seems likely that this intensity was linked to his father's experience.[17]

In Dunbar's early poems dealing with black soldiers, as in much of the previous poetry by other black authors treating that subject, the soldiers fight (or have fought) for citizenship, and not merely freedom:[18]

Yes, the Blacks enjoy their freedom,
    And they won it dearly, too;
For the life blood of their thousands
    Did the southern fields bedew.
In the darkness of their bondage,
    In the depths of slavery's night,
Their muskets flashed the dawning,
    And they fought their way to light.

They were comrades then and brothers,
    Are they more or less to-day?
They were good to stop a bullet
    And to front the fearful fray.
They were citizens and soldiers,
    When rebellion raised its head;
And the traits that made them worthy,—
    Ah! those virtues are not dead. (*Collected*, 51)

Here in "The Colored Soldiers," first collected in *Majors and Minors* (1895), the sacrifice of the black soldiers becomes a claim to their right and, by extension, the right of African Americans (men, anyway) to citizenship in the 1890s. While Dunbar later wrote a tribute to the "the Great Emancipator" Abraham Lincoln, he insisted in "The Colored Soldiers" that citizenship was not a gift to African Americans — and as such something that could be taken away — but a status earned. Again, as in the work of such black poets as James Madison Bell and Joshua McCarter Simpson, there is an implied connection to the patriots of the American Revolution whose sacrifice made citizenship an inalienable right, not something granted by a king or queen — or a president.

Beyond the issue of citizenship, there is, as in Simpson's "Let the Banner Proudly Wave," an essential claim to a common Americanness of black and (loyal) white through the metaphor of blood mixing on the battlefield ("And their blood with yours commingling / Has enriched the Southern soil" [*Collected*, 51]). This metaphor, as well as the other rhetorical moves of the poem, argues against a notion of citizenship and national identity based on skin color or other racialized notions, reminding northern white readers of their common sacrifice with their fellow black Unionists (not with white Confederate soldiers), creating a new bond of blood that transcended generally accepted concepts of race.[19]

"The Colored Soldiers" is, then, one of the prime examples of Dunbar's politically and poetically optimistic phase in the early and mid-1890s, "We Wear the Mask" notwithstanding. Like other Dunbar poems from this era, such as "Ode to Ethiopia" and the elegiac ode "Frederick Douglass," "The Colored Soldiers" is assertive, uplifting, proud, and commemorative while looking forward into a promising, if challenging, future as long as Americans, both black and white, stay the course of Reconstruction. These poems honor black achievement and black potential and call on all loyal Americans to do the same.

However, the tone of Dunbar's poems dealing explicitly with the politics of race in the United States changed radically as the decade wore on. The change was occasioned by events marking perhaps not so much an alteration in the course of American politics and culture as a confirmation that the movement toward segregation and African American disenfranchisement was irrevocable anytime in the near future. As noted elsewhere in this study, two events in particular signaled the final setting of this course. The first was the 1896 Supreme Court decision in *Plessy v. Ferguson* that upheld the constitutionality of Jim Crow segregation. Though it was only one in a series of retreats from Reconstruction by various branches of the federal government (e.g., the Compromise of 1877, the 1883 Supreme Court decision striking down the Civil Rights Act of 1875 that outlawed the segregation of public accommodations, and so on), the 1896 Supreme Court decision marked a final legitimizing and hardening of the legal infrastructure of segregation. It would be a decade before the establishment of the Jim Crow system was complete throughout the South, but the ruling in *Plessy* (especially when joined by the 1898 Supreme Court decision validating the various legal devices limiting black suffrage in *Williams v. Mississippi*) marked the end of any hope that Reconstruction could be reinvigorated or its remaining fragments preserved.

Ironically, the second event was the dedication of Augustus Saint-Gaudens's long-awaited Shaw Memorial on Boston Common in 1897. This event produced a flurry of poems about Shaw and the Fifty-fourth, including the first significant group of poems commemorating Shaw and the Fifty-fourth by white authors since the Civil War. Not surprisingly given the monument's highlighting of Shaw, these poems by black and white authors marked a return both to elegy and to Shaw as a central figure in poetic treatments of the Fifty-fourth. However, there remained a broad distinction between African American authors, who, like their black predecessors, put much emphasis on the black rank and file and elegized the death of Reconstruction as well as that of Shaw, and white authors, who emphasized Shaw and elegized an earlier (and often ideal) America, without reference to Reconstruction with any specificity.

As Dunbar would imply in "The Unsung Heroes," the black rank-and-file soldier is absent in most of the poems written by white authors about Shaw and the Fifty-fourth after the dedication of the monument. In these poems, such as Richard Watson Gilder's "Robert Gould Shaw" (Gilder was one of the chief editors of *The Century* magazine that played such a crucial role in the advancement of Dunbar's career, but who came more and more to a white reconciliationist view as the nineteenth century drew to a close) and Thomas Bailey Aldrich's "An Ode on the Unveiling of the Shaw Memorial on Boston Common," Shaw becomes a heroic object abstracted from historical context. In Aldrich's poem particularly, one is hard-pressed to find any reference to the historical moment in which Shaw's heroism took place or some allusion to the cause for which he fought (other than a single oblique mention of "his dusky braves"). These poems even fail to note the presence of the black troops on the monument, an aspect so striking to observers that William James would note in his speech at the dedication "one can almost hear them breathing as they march" (William James, *Memories and Studies*, 40). In an ironic sense, most of the works produced for or in response to the dedication of the Shaw Memorial might be seen as emblematic of white reconciliation and the compromises with Jim Crow and the "New South" made even in the former heartland of abolitionism at the turn of the century. These poems honor a hero without mention of the cause that virtually all the earlier poems intimately connected to Shaw, seeing abolition and U.S. "Freedom" as virtually synonymous. They also avoid the issues of Reconstruction and black citizenship that had been so large a part of black literary treatments of Shaw, the Fifty-fourth Regiment, and the black soldier generally.

The one poem by a white contemporary that was close in spirit to the later works of Dunbar on the black soldier and the end of the hopes of Reconstruction was William Vaughn Moody's 1900 "An Ode in Time of Hesitation." Unlike the poems of such other white poets as Aldrich, Gilder, and Robert Underwood Johnson, "An Ode in Time of Hesitation" links the memorial to a specific historical past in a headnote beneath the title: "(After seeing at Boston the statue of Robert Gould Shaw, killed while storming Fort Wagner, July 18, 1863, at the head of the first enlisted negro regiment, the Fifty-fourth Massachusetts)" (15).

Also, unlike Aldrich, Gilder, and Johnson, Moody describes the bronze relief of Shaw *and* the black rank and file of the Fifty-fourth in brief, but arresting detail:

This bright March morn I stand,
And hear the distant spring come up the land;
Knowing that what I hear is not unheard
Of this boy soldier and his negro band,
For all their gaze is fixed so stern ahead,
For all the fatal rhythm of their tread.
The land they died to save from death and shame
Trembles and waits, hearing the spring's great name,
And by her pangs these resolute ghosts are stirred. (15)

Moody's work is as much an elegy to a past era and a call to remember a bygone America as it is to Shaw and the Massachusetts Fifty-fourth. In some respects, it can be seen as a reworking of William James's speech at the dedication in which the heroism of Shaw and the black soldiers of the

Fifty-fourth are recalled without direct reference to current racial politics. For James, it is rather the question of war in general and the ability of the United States to solve large social questions without recourse to violence that in the end occupies the center of his speech. For Moody, too, it is not the end of Reconstruction and the emergence of Jim Crow and what Dunbar termed "the new slavery" in the South that mark a new, debased America, but the prosecution of the Spanish-American War and the rise of American overseas colonial expansion, especially in the Philippines. Moody here invokes a fear of forgetfulness and a separation from what he sees as the true heritage of the United States due to what might be thought of as a bourgeois imperialism linked to Gilded Age capitalism. The anxiety raised by Moody is close to the sorts of European fears of historical rupture due to the bourgeois revolutions of the late eighteenth and early nineteenth centuries—though perhaps it is more accurate to say that Moody portrays this forgetfulness as the product of a counterrevolution. Shaw and the Fifty-fourth are linked to an idealized American past in which force was in the righteous cause of freedom and democracy generally rather than the particular fight to end slavery and the subsequent battles over African American participation in the life of the American republic. "An Ode in Time of Hesitation" concludes on a jeremiadic note, promising that the heroic dead will return to bring disaster to the nation unless it turns from its imperialist course. Though threatening, after the manner of traditional jeremiad, still the poem holds a possibility of choice, a choice that, as in most jeremiads, turns on a recalling and returning to a true and righteous path.

Without specifically engaging the contemporary state of African American citizenship or freedom in a concrete sense (or, indeed, what it was concretely for which the soldiers of the Fifty-fourth fought), Moody uses the image of a righteous Shaw and the Fifty-fourth to figure a notion of the degradation of an ideal earlier America by an imperialist avarice and alienation from a spiritualized essence, much as the neomodernist poet Robert Lowell would do decades later in "For the Union Dead"—though Lowell's lines "When I crouch to my television set, / the drained faces of Negro school-children rise like balloons" (137) referring to the civil rights struggles in the South during the 1950s and early 1960s, might be said to indirectly allude to the failure of Reconstruction and betrayal of the Fifty-fourth's actual mission that is missing in Moody's poem.

Dunbar's later poems carry on a gloomy and often critical dialogue with those about Shaw and the Fifty-fourth by his white contemporaries. It is quite possible that Moody's poem directly influenced Dunbar's "Robert

Gould Shaw" or that, in part, Dunbar was responding to Moody because "An Ode in Time of Hesitation" appeared in the *Atlantic Monthly* a few months before the first publication of Dunbar's work in 1900. Certainly, the honored war dead who are invoked in Moody's poem are those whose dream of citizenship was subverted in the South of the United States after 1877, not Cuba, Puerto Rico or the Philippines. Even Shaw was seen as dying for black freedom, if not always citizenship, in the work of black and white authors during the Civil War. Yet that dream and its subversion is nowhere to be seen in Moody's poem. Dunbar may well have viewed this as an appropriation of the figures of Shaw and the black soldier that largely drained both of them of their original meaning.[20] Dunbar was also far more pessimistic as to the possibility of American renewal or redemption than Moody—though relatively positive as to the possibility of the survival of black intellectual, spiritual, and moral integrity.

An example of this pessimistic yet proud stance can be found in the only substantial dialect poem written directly about the black soldiers by Dunbar, "When Dey 'Listed Colored Soldiers," first published in 1899. The speaker of the poem is the black female "folk" wife or lover of an African American soldier, and former slave, Elias. The poem is an elegiac narrative in which the speaker recalls the enlistment and departure of Elias and some of the human costs of the war as well as a memorial to Elias's death in action. As in the poetry of James Madison Bell and Albery Whitman, there is a sort of reconciliation of former master and slave in which the sorrow of the speaker is linked to that of the family of her onetime master, who also suffered much loss in the war:

> Mastah Jack come home all sickly; he was broke for life, dey said;
> An' dey lef' my po' young mastah some'r's on de roadside,—dead.
> W'en de women cried an' mou'ned 'em, I could feel it thoo an' thoo,
> For I had a loved un fightin' in de way o' dangah, too.
> Den dey tol' me dey had laid him some'r's way down souf to res',
> Wid de flag dat he had fit for shinin' daih acrost his breas'.
> Well, I cried, but den I reckon dat's whut Gawd had called him for,
> W'en dey 'listed colo'ed sojers an' my 'Lias went to wah. (183–84)

A moral, one might say human, equality is implied by the parallelism of suffering in which the black speaker asserts that she feels the same emotions as her former masters. Despite the empathy of the speaker for the suffering of her former owners, she clearly retains belief in the Civil War as a holy war against the evil of slavery—again, recalling also Douglass's final autobiography in which the reconciliation of black and white is linked to an acknowledgment of the evil of slavery and the justness of abolition rather than to the effacing of the institution of slavery that characterized white reconciliationism.

Such a claim to a common humanity, the admission of a feeling of civic responsibility toward the republic on the part of Elias and the speaker, and the speaker's sorrow mitigated by a sense of a higher duty are at odds with the still-common assessment of Dunbar's dialect poems as accommodating racist plantation genre misappropriations of black culture or as being at best only indirectly critical of slavery and racism. Instead, there is a radical imputation of consciousness to the black folk, male and female. This folk consciousness is presented without the supervisory presence of the elevated, literate (often light-skinned and mixed-race) African American figure common in so many early representations of the black soldier, as in Albery Whitman's epics and Harper's *Iola Leroy*. The introduction of the uneasy issue of the civil position of women, both black and white, in the Reconstruction and the immediate post-Reconstruction republic also gives the poem a dimension that was generally missing in the poetry and prose drawing on the figure of the black soldier by African American male authors — including Dunbar's later poems, which are much concerned with notions of manhood.

Despite the imputation of a sort of equality between the former slave and the former slave owners and despite her obvious sense of civic duty, a claim to citizenship (as opposed to freedom) on the part of the speaker is not much in evidence here. No doubt, if asked by someone whom she could trust, the speaker (like Dunbar) would have said that African Americans deserved citizenship. The poem could be taken as an implicit argument for an African American capacity for and right to citizenship in all its senses. However, unlike the case of "The Colored Soldiers," here this argument remains only implicit, reminding the reader of the distance between what African Americans in the post-Reconstruction, Jim Crow South deserved and what they could expect.

This essentially pessimistic, though proud, vision can be seen in Dunbar's response to the Shaw Memorial and to the new burst of poems about Shaw and the Massachusetts Fifty-fourth by white writers. One of Dunbar's poems most frequently reprinted in periodicals during his lifetime is the elegiac Petrarchan sonnet "Robert Gould Shaw" (1900).[21] In many respects, the opening octave of the sonnet seems to have more in common with the Civil War era elegies to Shaw by white writers than to the work of earlier black poets, including Dunbar's own. The black rank and file of the Fifty-fourth is only barely present as the "unlettered and despised droves," while Shaw is seen in the familiar position of a sacrificial redeemer:

> Why was it that the thunder voice of Fate
> Should call thee, studious, from the classic groves,
> Where calm-eyed Pallas with still footstep roves,
> And charge thee seek the turmoil of the state?
> What bade thee hear the voice and rise elate,
> Leave home and kindred and thy spicy loaves,
> To lead th' unlettered and despised droves
> To manhood's home and thunder at the gate. (221)

The poem differs from most earlier elegies to Shaw in that "manhood" replaces "freedom" as the key word. In this respect, it recalls Emerson's notion of Shaw's leadership and the institution of the Fifty-fourth as a sort of rite of initiation into full humanity, although the emphasis on "manhood" also has much in common with the rhetoric of African American nationalism as it developed in the late nineteenth and early twentieth centuries.[22] This emphasis anticipates the turn into the concluding sestet: manhood achieved is something not easily taken away, unlike freedom or citizenship in the new post-Reconstruction South (and much of the North):

> Far better the slow blaze of Learning's light,
> The cool and quiet of her dearer fane,
> Than this hot terror of a hopeless fight,
> This cold endurance of the final pain,—
> Since thou and those who with thee died for right
> Have died, the Present teaches, but in vain! (221)

In short, the fulcrum of the poem is an assumed and willed forgetfulness (or misremembering) by white Americans, North and South, mirrored by an inverse black capacity for struggle and endurance with pride, if without real hope.

This turning marks the poem's shift from an elegy for Shaw to, as in his sonnet "Douglass," a more bitter one for Reconstruction and African American citizenship in the South, suggesting that it might have been better if Shaw had stayed in the Harvard College library or the Boston Athenaeum rather than dying along with the other fallen soldiers of the Fifty-fourth. Dunbar sees Shaw buried with his nameless and forgotten black troops once again. Of course, these soldiers had names, as Dunbar knows well from his own family history. Dunbar implies here, as he would state explicitly in "Unsung Heroes," that these black droves are rendered nameless through a national forgetfulness. The ending then is one of defeat — or at least a dream of citizenship deferred.

Though this bitterness and despair distinguishes Dunbar's poem from other elegies to Shaw, "Robert Gould Shaw" strikes a tone much like that of other Dunbar poems of that period, such as "The Haunted Oak" (about lynching); another angry yet pessimistic elegiac sonnet, "Douglass" (again, in contrast to the combative optimism of the 1895 "Frederick Douglass"); and "To the South: On Its New Slavery." It also is close in spirit to the one nondialect poem Dunbar wrote directly on the subject of the black Civil War soldier at the time, "The Unsung Heroes."[23] As in "Robert Gould Shaw," the black soldiers who fought and died at Battery Wagner, Fort Pillow, and Port Hudson achieve a divinely sanctioned manhood through their sacrifice — but without a white intermediary ("They fought their way on the hillside, they fought their way in the glen, / And God looked down on their sinews brown, and said, "I have made them men" [*Collected*, 197]). The poem closes with a plea to God to inspire the memory of the soldiers' sacrifice and manhood in their resistance to racial oppression in those poets who have "not the fire to smite the lyre and sing them one brief strain." The final note of the poem is one of pessimism in which the speaker sees no likelihood of such poems being written, Dunbar's efforts notwithstanding, short of divine intervention. Given the number of poems written about Robert Gould Shaw by white authors in that era or shortly before, Dunbar's criticism seems even more pointedly bitter.[24]

The works of Moody and Dunbar mark the decline of the black Civil War soldier as an important trope in American poetry. The black Civil War soldier, unlike the black abolitionist, the black slave revolt leader, and the black fugitive slave, virtually disappeared from poetry by black and white authors. Two exceptions are elegies to Shaw by African American writers, Benjamin Brawley's "My Hero" (1915) and Henrietta Cordelia Ray's "Robert G. Shaw" (1910). Both are slight poems that marked the exhaustion of a subgenre and made little effort to engage the complexities of the political situation of African Americans in a time when segregation and disenfranchisement coexisted with the Fourteenth and Fifteenth Amendments. The main significance of the poems lies in the degree to which they see the struggle waged by Shaw and the Fifty-fourth as distant and almost mythical. For example, Brawley represents the attack on Battery Wagner as a scene from Arthurian legend with Shaw as Galahad without the historical detail that marked Albery Whitman's use of a similar neomedieval rhetoric. Ray's poem is more in tune with the works commemorating Shaw written immediately after the dedication of the Saint-Gaudens monument and, indeed, seems almost to be a version of Dunbar's "Robert Gould Shaw" with an upbeat ending. Nonetheless, even in Ray's poem, the final line, "In rev'rent love we guard thy memory," suggests how distant the sacrifices of Shaw and the Fifty-fourth are temporally and spiritually from the writer's present.[25]

After 1915, the Civil War veteran is almost entirely absent from African American poetry. It is true that the African American veteran and the contradiction between the valor and sacrifice of the black soldier and the ongoing denial of full citizenship to African Americans continued to appear in African American poetry from Frederick White's *Pleas of a Negro Soldier and One Hundred Other Poems* (1908) to James Weldon Johnson's "The Color Sargeant" (1917) to Gwendolyn Brooks's "Negro Soldier" in *A Street in Bronzeville* (1945) and beyond. But those poems almost always treated recent or contemporary wars (e.g., the Spanish-American War in the case of White and World War II in that of Brooks).[26]

While there is a certain historical sense to this concentration on military conflicts chronologically close at hand, it is worth noting that the Civil War and the white veteran certainly remained a live topic for white poets, especially southern white poets, perhaps most famously (or infamously, depending on one's stance) Alan Tate's "lost cause" revision of "The Wasteland," "Ode to the Confederate Dead" (which first appeared in its final form in 1937). The 1930s and 1940s saw a renewal of historiographic interest in African American participation in the Civil War, particularly in the work of scholars influenced by Marxism and the Communist Left, such as W. E. B. Du Bois's *Black Reconstruction* (1935) and the early studies of Herbert Aptheker.[27] But there was no corresponding renewal in poetry by black or white writers, even in Popular Front–influenced, historically oriented poetry of the late 1930s and early 1940s. During this period, many black poets, including Sterling Brown, Melvin Tolson, Langston Hughes, Margaret Walker, and Robert Hayden invoked Frederick Douglass, Nat Turner, Gabriel, Harriet Tubman, Sojourner Truth, Cinqué, and Crispus Attucks, but not the soldiers who had been so significant in late nineteenth-century poetry by black authors.

Ironically, the mid-twentieth century works inspired by the Shaw Memorial that are probably best known today, John Berryman's "Boston Common" (first published in 1942) and Robert Lowell's "For the Union Dead" (1964) are by white writers and appeared decades after "Robert Gould Shaw" and "An Ode in Time of Hesitation." Lowell's and Berryman's poems meditated on the possibilities of heroism in the modern era. Both poets used Shaw and the Fifty-fourth much as Moody did, as an image of an ideal America and the difficulty, if not impossibility, of a noble act in the contemporary United States. And in both cases, the black soldiers following Shaw are seen as relatively unimportant and indistinguishable, "Negroes without name," as Berryman said without the bitter irony of Dunbar. However, these poems were themselves separated from each other by decades and were not part of a broader usage of the Massachusetts Fifty-fourth and the black soldier in a way that, as we have seen, existed from 1864 to about 1903.[28]

Perhaps the final and emphatic end of any hope of the revival of Reconstruction at the turn of the century rendered the figure of soldier-citizen so closely connected to Reconstruction obsolete, leaving it a figure of bitterness and despair in the hands of Dunbar near the end of his career. Even as a trope of bitterness, betrayal, and a knowledge of self-worth unrecognized by American society generally, its power waned as the dominant historiography of Reconstruction as well as widely circulated popular culture pieces recast the period as one of horror and corruption relieved only by a sort of vaudeville buffoonery, the relatively marginal (in terms of "mainstream" scholarship at the time) radical work of Du Bois, Aptheker, and James A. Allen notwithstanding. Undoubtedly, the most influential early twentieth-century example of the black soldier as both tool and emblem of the horror of Reconstruction is D. W. Griffith's 1915 film *Birth of a Nation* in which African American troops brutalize white southerners and their loyal black servants.

A telling popular culture instance of the black veteran as buffoon can be found in the Tin Pan Alley song, "The Yankee Doodle Negro" (1905), composed by the white songwriter Henry Arthur Blumenthal. That song recast the veteran into the "coon" stereotype, proclaiming "every coon loves his Uncle Sam." Of course, there had been earlier lampoons of the black soldier in popular song, as in the musical comedies of Irish American librettist Edward Harrigan that he wrote with Tony Hart (Anthony Cannon) and David Braham in the 1870s, 1880s, and 1890s. Those songs focused on caricatures of various ethnic types, especially Irish Americans and African Americans. However, they did not deal with the black veteran of the Civil War but the private ethnic militias that sprung up in the late nineteenth century. By contrast, not only does Blumenthal's song mention the veteran's service in the war, but the illustration on the cover of the song's sheet music presents an elderly black (or at least blacked up) man with enormous white, smiling lips, wearing a GAR uniform decorated by his service medal. One might see this song as a sort of emblem of northern and southern (white) reconciliation and abandonment of Reconstruction ideals in the early Jim Crow era.

The speaker of the song declares himself to be a "coon" "who was brought up, down in Dixie" and loves the stars and stripes and fried chicken.

In many respects, the trope of the Massachusetts Fifty-fourth and the black soldier during Reconstruction and the early post-Reconstruction period marked a unique moment in African American literary history — and a unique moment in African American history generally, at least until the mid-1960s. As literary critic Robert Stepto convincingly pointed out in his seminal study of African American narrative, *Beyond the Veil* (1979), African American literature is marked by what he called the pregeneric myths of freedom and literacy (xv). In text after text, one sees enacted an African American journey toward freedom and literacy. This journey is often a literal journey from the South to the North, from the country to the city, from the legal status of slavery to a more ambiguous (in antebellum America) status of freedom, from being a thing or brute to being human. This geographic, spiritual, and legal journey also moves away from the African American folk associated with the South toward an individualism associated with the North. There is another narrative of physical and spiritual journey common in African American literature: the journey South to the folk, a topic that is taken up at some length in the next chapter. This is a symbolic journey away from individualism, from deracination, and the separation of instinct and intellect toward community, group identity, and nature.

The poetry invoking the Massachusetts Fifty-fourth and the black Civil War soldiers is something of a departure from these narratives of literacy and freedom tied to journeys North and South. Tropes of freedom and literacy often appear in these poems. But generally, as in Dunbar's work, there is a transcending of both categories: it is citizenship that these soldiers have earned (or should have earned) with their blood, not simply freedom (which they could be said to have possessed from the start because the members of the Fifty-fourth were already practically and in most cases legally "free"), and it is manhood, not literacy, that they have attained through sacrifice in the cause of a divinely sanctioned civic duty. Again, these poems do not oppose freedom to citizenship but are arguments against a notion of "freedom" that would not include full citizenship, deferring it until some future date when African Americans are "ready." Similarly, they are clearly not opposed to literacy (they are poems, after all) but are implicitly opposed to a concept of "literacy" that might serve as a bar to African American citizenship — as did such a concept in fact.

At the same time, there is no simple return to the South and the "folk." If the protagonists of the slave narratives ascended north to freedom, the soldiers of the Fifty-fourth "returned" to the South (though many were seeing it for the first time) heroically and, ultimately, triumphantly—at least until the later poems of Dunbar. Though they returned to the folk, they generally neither embraced nor rejected a folk identity. Their identity as citizens and Americans (and African Americans) was not represented, generally, as dependent on the adoption or rejection of a particular cultural identity but on their actions in the defense of the Republic and in attacking the institution of slavery. In this, their claim to citizenship was much like that of, say, Irish American and German American soldiers, whose varying relationships to "mainstream" American culture (and to the cultures of their ancestral "homelands") did not affect their de jure (if not de facto) citizenship.

However, with the failure of Reconstruction and the triumph of Jim Crow, the figure of the Civil War veteran became available as a trope not so much of the earned citizenship of African Americans as of the broken promise of the United States to black Americans, indeed, of a break with the fundamental premises of the United States as it staked a claim to international political, economic, military, and technological eminence. Particularly in Dunbar's poetry, the veteran, then, became an early dualist trope of an African American dissatisfaction with a modernity intimately bound up with Jim Crow. At the same time, the figure of the veteran embodied the recurring failure of the United States to honor the covenant established by the sacrifices made by American soldiers in the Revolution that vouchsafed U.S. citizenship (a covenant publicly renewed by the sacrifice of black soldiers during the Civil War), a failure that was made all the more galling to African Americans as citizenship was extended to, or retained by, white betrayers of the Republic and their latter-day sympathizers. A tone of bitter melancholy pervades this poetry, as it does the early migration narratives.

The trope of the black Civil War veteran faded from use as Jim Crow was fully consolidated. However the trope of the black veteran remained as a sign of the persistent betrayal of the promises and alleged principles of American democracy, and of the long-term alienation of the African American people from the U.S. state, from Dunbar through Claude McKay's Jake in *Home to Harlem* to Gwendolyn Brooks's "Negro Hero" in *A Street in Bronzeville* to the unnamed doctor in the Golden Day episode of Ralph Ellison's *Invisible Man* to Shadrach in Toni Morrison's *Sula* (and the origins of the Seven Days group in Morrison's *Song of Solomon*) to the late twentieth- and early twentieth-first century Vietnam poems of Yusef Komunyakaa and Lamont Steptoe. The World War I veteran, who was often the spectacular victim of racist violence while still in uniform during the "Red Summer" of 1919 and who served under the leadership of a president, Woodrow Wilson, famously (or infamously) associated with both democracy and Jim Crow segregation, became a particularly persistent figure of black alienation.

Despite its virtual disappearance after the early twentieth century, African American poetry (and fiction) using the figure of the Civil War veteran can be seen as a significant bridge between black literature of the Reconstruction era and that of the Nadir, between black political, cultural, and social citizenship and the dualist thought of Jim Crow. Indeed, especially in the hands of Dunbar, it can be seen as an important vehicle of an early modernist sensibility of alienation and fragmentation as well as the root of at least the possibility of a separate black modernist tradition that not only diverged from what might be thought of as an essentially white modernism but also critiqued white modernists for their use of black people, black bodies, black voices, black culture, and even black history, while forgetting or repressing the context and the heart of what they used.

I'll be down to get you in a Taxi honey.
—Shelton Brooks, "The Darktown Strutters Ball"

chapter three

The Black City

The Early Jim Crow Migration Narrative
and the New Territory of Race

What happened when black became a place, not perhaps yet a country, as Amiri Baraka coined it, and no longer a cluster of cabins on the edge of the plantation, but an urban neighborhood, a seeming city that one could reach by foot, private car, taxi, subway, train, or streetcar? As noted before, one of the chief features structuring the growth of the modern, post-Reconstruction city in the United States, a feature that would grow more obvious as the twentieth century wore on, was the racial segregation of urban space on a new scale and the growth of the black ghetto.

As Farah Jasmine Griffin observes in her seminal *Who Set You Flowin'?*, the migration narrative describing the movement from a provincial, often rural ancestral home in the South to the northern metropolis was a dominant form of African American expressive culture in many genres and media during the twentieth century (3). On one level, that migration and urbanization should be at the center of African American writing in the twentieth century seems self-evident. One could argue that, other than racism and Jim Crow themselves, the "Great Migration" of African Americans from the rural South to the urban North and West over a period of about sixty years was the single largest fact shaping African American life in the twentieth century—and, indeed, U.S. urban (and, negatively in the post–World War II "white flight" era, suburban) life. After all, in 1890, about 90 percent of all African Americans lived in the South. In 1970, the proportion was about 52 percent. In Chicago, Detroit, Cleveland, New York, Buffalo, Newark, Philadelphia, Pittsburgh, Los Angeles, Oakland, Boston, and so on, the dramatic growth of the black population was due overwhelmingly to migration from the South—though New York, Boston, Philadelphia, and other eastern seaboard cities also saw a significant immigration from the Caribbean (often, too, a movement from the countryside to the city). The African American community nationwide, which was still very rural in the 1890s, became predominantly urban by the 1940s and overwhelmingly urban by the 1970s.

In short, this migration was enormous, in terms of both numbers and duration. It dramatically changed the landscape of African American life and American life generally. But while migration and urbanization might seem to be natural subjects for black writers in the United States, it is worth noting that their treatment by African American authors was not predetermined by the actual facts of the Great Migration in any simple way. For example, while it is true that there was a huge exodus of African Americans to northern and western cities in the twentieth century, there was also a tremendous migration of African Americans from the country to the city within the South. In fact, it is this migration that to no small extent made the growth of large southern cities possible — and ultimately made the African American population of the South nearly as urban as that of the North. Yet the movement of African Americans to Houston, New Orleans, Memphis, Birmingham, Atlanta, and so on has nowhere near the same literary resonance as the move to New York, Chicago, Detroit, Cleveland, Philadelphia, Oakland, Los Angeles, and other large northern and western cities. Why? Some reasons are obvious — since southern cities always had sizable (and sometimes majority) African American populations, the intrasouthern migration was perhaps less startling than the growth of the huge black ghettos of the urban North that seemed to emerge almost overnight even if they, in fact, had a considerable foreground. And the northern and western urban centers were economically more important, larger in population, and the home of much more of the national mass media and culture industries than the cities of the South — at least until the last few decades of the twentieth century. Still, if one were to consider the question of black migration and urbanization from a strictly numbers-crunching point of view, there does seem to be an imbalance in the cultural weight given to the migration North by African American artists in the twentieth century.

While it is true that there was a tremendous movement of African Americans from the country to the city and from the South (and the Caribbean) to the North, much the same could be said about native-born white Americans, including the migration North and West of eight million to twelve million white southerners (as opposed to about four and a half million black southerners) between 1940 and 1970. These white southerners often crowded into "hillbilly" neighborhoods, some of which still persist today (or survived until very recently) in such cities as Baltimore, Cincinnati, Chicago, and Detroit. The fact is that the population of the United States as a whole also rapidly urbanized during the years of the great African American migration. (The farm work force went from something like half the population to less than 5 percent during the twentieth century.) Chicago's population, for example, grew from about 1.7 million in 1900 to 3.4 million in 1930. Other northern industrial centers, such as Cleveland, Detroit, Indianapolis, Akron, Philadelphia, and Pittsburgh, saw similar increases. To a large extent, the internal white migration from the country to the city that significantly fed this urbanization was masked by the arrival of millions of European immigrants. Still, this internal movement was huge, and should have stood out even more once European immigration was curtailed by World War I and the restrictive immigration laws passed in the 1920s.

Yet this rural exodus had nothing like the same impact on white writers that the Great Migration had on black writers, except in the subgenre of Appalachian literature, including Harriet Arnow's great novel *The Doll-maker*—and as James Gregory notes, even within that genre, Arnow is relatively singular in her representation of the mass migration from Appalachia in the 1940s and 1950s rather than the more common literary treatment of the individual expatriation of the southern white artist-intellectual (Gregory, 195).[1] Popular culture was another story—with white migration to the city (and from the South and the Southwest to the West Coast and the industrial centers of the North) being an important country music theme in such songs as Tompall Glaser's and Harlan Howard's "The Streets of Baltimore," Mel Tillis's "Detroit City," and Merle Haggard's "Big City." And, it is worth noting that the Great Migration of African Americans was a significant presence in works by white writers in the early twentieth century, such as Fanny Hurst's *Imitation of Life* (1933) and William Faulkner's *Light in August* (1932).

Those novels by white authors that did feature such a move of white Americans from the country to the city or from the provinces to the metropolis, such as Nathanael West's *Day of the Locust* and F. Scott Fitzgerald's *The Great Gatsby*, gave the move a much different cultural framework from that used in works by African American writers—though I argue in the conclusion that the early migration narratives, and the tropes of passing and the mixed-race protagonist that are prominent features of many early migration novels, had a significant influence on *Gatsby*. Even in what is probably the most famous ur-story of rural white migration in U.S. popular culture and literature, the so-called "Okie" exodus of the Great Depression, the symbolic landscapes and the racial dynamics are quite different. While the notion of a yeomanry or peasantry deformed and destroyed by migration might be a common feature of the "Okie" exodus stories, and many African American migration stories, almost always the "Okies" are seen moving from one rural site to another, from farm to agricultural labor camp, as they are in *The Grapes of Wrath*, rather than to, say, the oil fields and refineries of Bakersfield and shipyards of the San Francisco Bay Area, where many of the actual migrants from the Dust Bowl did in fact find work. Much of the power of the typical story of the Dust Bowl exodus from farming to migrant agricultural labor turns on displacement of white native-born, "Anglo-Saxon," Protestant farmers (invoking images that go back in the United States to Thomas Jefferson and his vision of an American republic based on a white yeomanry). These "real Americans" are driven from their homesteads and arrive in the golden land of California, where they are treated the same as the Mexican and Filipina/Filipino workers they to some extent displace, evoking a sort of outrage that both produces a sense of class solidarity, in some cases across racial lines, and reaffirms a sense of whiteness as a default characteristic of the American citizen to whom such things should not happen.[2] In other words, vitally important events do not necessarily achieve the sort of literary centrality that the black movement North in the twentieth century did.

The point here is that migration and urbanization may have been a central fact of African American life (and U.S. life generally) in the twentieth century, but that does not completely explain the degree to which the African American migration North would occupy the minds of black novelists (and poets, playwrights, musicians, and visual artists) as well as a considerable number of white artists. In fact, as seen with respect to white writers and the great white migration and, for that matter, black novelists and their (with the exception of Arna Bontemps) avoidance of slavery in the first half of the twentieth century, there were no compelling reasons why it would have to be such a central subject from the beginning of the twentieth century to the present — at least no compelling reasons that issued directly from historical experience. Or perhaps it is more accurate to say that there were compelling reasons that did not derive simply from migration and the shock of the rural folk confronting urban life and northern-style racism. Rather, the impetus for the centrality of migration in black literature was significantly the result of a reconfiguration of the territory of race in the modern city of the Jim Crow era in the North and in the New South.

Racial Geography, Migration, and Nineteenth-Century African American Literature

Obviously, the centrality of the migration narrative in modern African American writing was in part due to a long literary foreground antedating the final demise of Reconstruction and its institutions and ideals. As Robert Stepto pointed out in *From Behind the Veil*, before the rise and triumph of Jim Crow, "the seminal journey in Afro-American narrative literature is unquestionably the journey north"—a journey introduced into U.S. letters by the genre of the fugitive slave narrative in the nineteenth century (67). One might add that the genre introduced the North-South axis to literature by white Americans, with a significant impact on such crucial mid- and late nineteenth-century U.S. works as Harriet Beecher Stowe's *Uncle Tom's Cabin* and Mark Twain's *The Adventures of Huckleberry Finn* (which becomes an inverted and terrifying, if often humorous, slave narrative after Huck and Jim miss the turn onto the Ohio River at Cairo and find themselves traveling South deeper and deeper into slave territory) and such early twentieth-century modernist literary landmarks as Fitzgerald's *The Great Gatsby* and Faulkner's *Light in August*. Interestingly, these white modernist migration stories are connected not to the great white migration from the South to the North but to the black migration narrative tradition.

The most famous treatments of this journey in the genre of the slave narrative, and certainly among those most available to black writers in the late nineteenth and early twentieth centuries, were the autobiographical works of Frederick Douglass, the 1845 *Narrative of the Life of Frederick Douglass, An American Slave*, the 1855 *My Bondage and My Freedom*, and the 1881 *The Life and Times of Frederick Douglass* (which was republished with considerable revision in 1892). In the course of Douglass's narratives, a boy grows up and is brutalized, literally rendered a brute in Douglass's accounts, by slavery in the South, rebels, and ultimately escapes north to the more or less free state of Massachusetts. As with the later representations of the Great Migration north, Douglass's autobiographies have some considerable basis in actual experience—Douglass indeed grew up in slavery in Maryland and did in fact escape to the North, where he ultimately became a leader in the abolitionist movement and the most prominent postbellum leader of the African American community.

In Douglass's narratives, though, the journey north was as at least as much symbolic as it was an actual trip. Drawing on a range of literary sources, including other slave narratives, autobiography, gothic literature, and Protestant allegory, Douglass's autobiographies consist largely of several inter-related journeys, physical and spiritual, literal and symbolic. These journeys include the movement from the Eastern Shore of Maryland (by way of Balti-more) to New Bedford, Massachusetts, from slavery to freedom, from slave/brute to man, from orality to literacy, from the margins to the mainstream, from common man to representative man, from mass man to individual, from a backward past to gleaming modernity. What is meant here by the opposition of the common man to the representative man is that Douglass claims narrative authority, not on the basis that he somehow embodies the common characteristics and aspirations of enslaved African Americans, but rather because he is an average individual who, after the manner of the pro-tagonists of Christian allegories such as *Pilgrim's Progress*, discovers the path to true selfhood and freedom. At the same time, Douglass goes out of his way to avoid being seen as exceptional, though he clearly could have made such claims based on his actual abilities and achievements. Even in his third autobiography, in which he details many of the honors he received, the great leaders he met, and the important posts he held (ending with his ap-pointment as consul general to Haiti in the 1892 revised edition), he strikes a note of modesty, asserting that "if I have pushed my example too promi-nently for the good taste of my Caucasian readers, I beg them to remember that I have written in part for the encouragement of a class whose aspirations need the stimulus of success" (*Autobiographies*, 913). His success, though noteworthy, is one to which an entire class or people might aspire. His indi-viduality, too, is paradoxically typical—much as individuality is said to be a prominent feature of the collective American (read native-born, white) temperament. In other words, he is representative because he embodies the capacity of the average slave for self-development. He becomes a guide to African Americans and an argument against the ideological underpinning of slavery for white people.

Douglass's journeys take him away from the African American commu-nity and folk culture of the South, a culture described as still much influ-enced by African cultural practices and sensibilities toward the individualis-tic, free-enterprise culture of the industrial North represented by Douglass's idealized vision of New Bedford as a sort of modern Utopia. In *Narrative* and *My Bondage*, we see a methodical distancing of the narrator from African-influenced culture as embodied, for example, in the rootworker Sandy Jenkins. And possibly more importantly, in terms of later literary represen-tations of the folk culture, Douglass implicitly and explicitly distances him-self from the language of the African American folk, as when he recalls his arrival on Lloyd's plantation in *My Bondage and My Freedom* and the "bro-ken," nearly unintelligible (to him) speech of the slaves there:

> There is not, probably, in the whole south, a plantation where the English language is more imperfectly spoken than on Col. Lloyd's. It is a mix-ture of Guinea and everything else you please. At the time of which I am now writing, there were slaves there who had been brought from the coast of Africa. They never used the "s" in indication of the possessive case. "Cap'n Ant'ney Tom," "Lloyd Bill," "Aunt Rose Harry," means "Cap-tain Anthony's Tom," "Lloyd's Bill," &c. "*Oo you dem long to?*" means, "Whom do you belong to?" "*Oo dem got any peachy?*" means, "Have you got any peaches?" I could scarcely understand them when I first went among them, so broken was their speech; and I am persuaded that I could not have been dropped anywhere on the globe, where I could reap less, in the way of knowledge, from my immediate associates, than on this plan-tation. (*Autobiographies*, 168–69)

One can also see this sort of distancing in an 1880 speech commemorating the emancipation of the slaves in the British Caribbean colonies with which Douglass concluded the 1881 edition of *The Life and Times*. In that speech Douglass pointedly separates himself from the sort of black folk Christianity that later writers, such as Du Bois, Fenton Johnson, Jean Toomer, and James Weldon Johnson would extol in the early twentieth century:

> My hope for the future of my race is further supported by the rapid de-cline of an emotional, shouting, and thoughtless religion. Scarcely in any direction can there be found a less favorable field for mind or morals than where such a religion prevails. It abounds in the wildest hopes and fears, and in blind unreasoning faith. Instead of adding to faith virtue, its tendency is to substitute faith for virtue, and is a deadly enemy to our progress. (*Autobiographies*, 937)

Douglass's point here is not necessarily or simply assimilationist — though he clearly champions both the idea and, in 1880, the viability of true black citi-zenship in the United States. But, again, he does set himself as the represen-tative man against the culture of the black rural folk, suggesting that a new sort of modern culture will have to replace — and, indeed, is replacing — the old linguistic, expressive, and spiritual practices. This is quite different from the positing of the folk culture as the bedrock from which a new black high culture will rise, a position that will become quite common among writers later in the Nadir. At the same time, Douglass does promote the notion of a distinct, but fading culture of the rural folk, a notion of potential cultural extinction that will be very powerful in black literature of the early twentieth century — albeit in a more plaintive and elegiac or preservationist register.

Also, Douglass's concern for family ties is of secondary importance in his first two narratives to his individual self-development — though family ties are of far more importance in his second narrative than his first and more significant yet in the third. For example, near the end of the first narrative, Douglass mentions his marriage in passing and then makes virtually no further reference to his wife again — or for that matter to the children, Lewis and Rosetta Douglass, that he had by the time of the antislavery convention in Nantucket with which he concludes. One might guess that the marriage is mentioned in the first place because the ability to marry, like the ability to name one's self, is a sign of the true American individual. However, once that particular mark is noted, it seems unnecessary for Douglass to return to it, even though his family was undoubtedly of great importance in his "real life." In short, we see the development of a radical individualism in which community is of little concern and sometimes an actual impediment to true black self-realization.

Douglass could have told a different story in his first autobiography — and he does in part in his second narrative. As he notes briefly in *Narrative* and at slightly greater length in *My Bondage*, Douglass, a skilled ship caulker, was unable to find work in New Bedford, a major port and center of what was then perhaps the leading industry of the United States, whaling, because of racial discrimination. In *Narrative*, Douglass could well have written a story of betrayal and disappointment and the futility of depending on the goodwill of those white people, North or South, whose conception of their identity as free individuals, not to mention their material well-being, depends on the subordination of African Americans ideologically and practically in a myth of race and the natural hierarchy of races.

Douglass chose not to tell that story in *Narrative* and did so only partially in *My Bondage* under the impact of the Fugitive Slave Act and in order to justify the establishment of a black abolitionist journal in the face of white abolitionist objections. Perhaps because of this sense of betrayal and increased ambivalence about the North, displayed, for example, in a story about an experience with a "Jim Crow car" in Massachusetts in *My Bondage* (closely resembling a similar scene in William Wells Brown's pseudo–slave narrative novel *Clotel*), it has a much closer resemblance to later Jim Crow, and even post–Jim Crow, narratives.

However, even in the second narrative with its greater tone of disillusionment with the North, and its new emphasis on black institution building, one does not find the same sort of secular black public spaces found in the literature of the Jim Crow era by African American writers. When northern black institutions are discussed, particularly the church and the press, what is seen is the black individual (and, to a lesser extent, family) and semiprivate sacred and secular political institutions intervening in the broader society for African American freedom and attempting to "improve and elevate the character of the free colored people of the north" (*Autobiographies*, 398). While in the antebellum narratives by black women, particularly Harriet Jacobs's *Incidents in the Life of a Slave Girl*, black family spaces are of paramount importance, secular public spaces are notably missing. In short, black is not yet imagined as a country or even a city.[3]

The master narrative of this journey north, then, is one of individual self-development and self-realization, with at least the potential of genuine citizenship in an ideal America, or a combination of that individual self-creation with group elevation. This self-development tied to group elevation also entails a flight from the southern black folk and southern black folk culture — and an avoidance of the sort of secular spaces in the North where that culture might be re-created or revised with some eye to the past as well as the present along the lines of Amiri Baraka's notion of the "changing same." At the same time, this story of self-fashioning differs from, say, *Gatsby*, in that the protagonist is not exceptional, not a sort of Romantic superman (or, perhaps in the case of Jay Gatsby a deformed or stunted superman), but instead representative of the broader group, so as to demonstrate a general African American capacity for self-development and citizenship, often, as many have remarked, through a demonstration of literacy.

The Journey Back and Forth: The Rise of the Jim Crow Migration Narrative

As Stepto also notes, the "immersion narrative" of the "journey into the Black Belt" of the South became an established trope in African American literature by the turn of the century — though, as we shall see, the early versions of the "immersion narrative" typically feature a sort of yo-yoing between South and North, between inside and outside the Black Belt that never really comes to rest (66–91). Again, this story has some basis in objective fact insofar as Reconstruction saw many African American students, intellectuals, and professionals (and many white abolitionists), some of whom had been born in slavery or relative freedom in the South and some of whom had never been below the Mason-Dixon line, travel from the North to the South to work in the schools, the government programs, and so on, serving the newly freed African American community. One could think of these people as the Student Non-Violent Coordinating Committee or Congress of Racial Equality of their time — except they got a lot more federal support (at least initially) than SNCC or CORE ever did. But as in Douglass's narratives, the literary representations of this reverse migration were symbolic as well as actual. In Frances E. W. Harper's *Iola Leroy* (1892), the protagonist is the daughter of a very light-skinned former slave and the mother's white former master. The father frees the mother and they are married, producing three children, Iola, Gracie, and Harry. Both Harry and Iola are educated in the North where they are unaware that their mother is a "Negro." However, after the untimely death of Iola's father shortly before the Civil War, a judge, at the behest of the father's nefarious cousin, finds that Iola's parents' marriage and her mother's manumission papers are illegal.

As a result Iola, her mother, her sister, and her brother are judged to be the property of the cousin — though Gracie dies of shock and grief before she can be enslaved. In short order, Iola is returned to the South and faces a momentary identity crisis when she finds out she, like her mother, is a "Negro" and a slave. Harry, warned against returning South by a letter from his sister, more quickly embraces his identity as a "colored" man in the North and eventually joins a black regiment to fight against slavery in the Civil War. One obvious question here, especially given the greatly increased interest in the construction of racial categories over the past decade or so, is what do "Negro" and "white" mean here? After all, Iola and Harry look "white," were raised "white," and are overwhelmingly of European descent, so why are they "Negro?" This is not a question that Harper takes up in any real depth. Instead, she goes out of her way to avoid it in her argument for a united black community that might have the political leverage to head off the final victory of Jim Crow. And, in fact, other authors, notably James Weldon Johnson in *Autobiography of an Ex-Colored Man*, will raise this question in the first two decades of the twentieth century, though they, too, will not pursue it at any great length.

For my purposes here, however, the most important aspect of the novel is the return of Iola, her brother, and various other African Americans with formal educations and professional skills to the South as citizens where they live and work with and among the folk for the elevation of the race and the preservation of black citizenship. In doing this, Iola rejects both the half-freedom of living as a Negro in the North (which is shown to have its own virulent brand of discrimination) and the self-hating and family-denying opportunism of passing for white in either the North or the South. This is a sort of counternarrative to the one told by Douglass. In Douglass's narratives, there is a journey toward individual selfhood and away from the folk. In Harper's novel, there is a journey toward a communal identity in which individual self-interest is sacrificed for a larger good linked with the southern folk. While there is still a sense of the intellectual-professional as the leader who uplifts the folk, and a sense of a certain hierarchy resembling Du Bois's notion of the "talented tenth," the novel also promotes the concept that the southern folk and southern black culture are the locus of African American identity, and that the trip North is ultimately one of self-denial and even self-hatred.

One obvious aspect of *Iola Leroy* is the way in which the rural South is posited as a black space or homeland. Once again, this vision of the former plantation South (or what the journalist and poet Frank Marshall Davis would call the "Cotton South") has a certain demographic reality. However, it is worth noting that the antebellum narratives of Douglass, Brown, Jacobs, Frank J. Webb, Martin Delany (*Blake*'s secret government in the Great Dismal Swamp, notwithstanding), and others did not in general tie African Americans to the South in any essential, organic way. While one might see a political imperative in such an association during Reconstruction, as noted in the previous chapter, even in the earlier poetry by black authors featuring the trope of the Civil War veteran, where there is a physical movement to the South rooted in the historical record, such a link is not proposed, perhaps because, as citizens, African Americans are deemed by the writers to have a claim on every section of the United States. It is really not until considerably after 1877, with the onset of disenfranchisement and Jim Crow segregation, that black authors, such as Harper, Chesnutt, Dunbar, Washington, and Du Bois, elaborate such a connection between African Americans and the southern soil.

Washington's 1901 autobiography, *Up from Slavery*, makes this connection, while sounding a note of movement, migration, and modernity from the very start, declaring in the preface that "much of what I have said has been written on board trains, or at hotels or railroad stations while I have been waiting for trains" (n.p.). In some respects, *Up from Slavery* is anomalous in that its movement is not exactly on the symbolic North-South axis — though the Tuskegee Institute is obviously south of the sites of Washington's youth and early adulthood. In fact, the actions of the narrative take place entirely within the South and "Border" region, from the plantation of Washington's slave childhood in Virginia to his later childhood and early adolescence in industrial or quasi-industrial West Virginia to his days at the Hampton Institute to the establishment of Tuskegee Institute in Alabama to the triumph of his 1896 speech at the Atlanta Cotton Exposition. Even his relatively short sojourn in Washington, D.C., though unquestionably urban, is regionally ambiguous. In this respect, it is an ancestral mirror image of Malcolm X's later autobiography, which is in many respects a neo–slave narrative set entirely within the North.

Despite this anomaly, Washington's autobiography is significant in the way it represents his family's new neighborhood in Malden, West Virginia, as a sort of degraded, checkered industrial center in which there is no true community, resembling, despite the town's small size, similar descriptions of northern urban precincts where migrants arrive in the early migration novels:

> At that time salt-mining was the great industry in that part of West Virginia, and the little town of Malden was right in the midst of the salt-furnaces. My stepfather had already secured a job at a salt-furnace, and he had also secured a little cabin for us to live in. Our new house was no better than the one we had left on the old plantation in Virginia. In fact, in one respect it was worse. Notwithstanding the poor condition of our plantation cabin, we were at all times sure of pure air. Our new home was in the midst of a cluster of cabins crowded closely together, and as there were no sanitary regulations, the filth about the cabins was often intolerable. Some of our neighbours were coloured people, and some were the poorest and most ignorant and degraded white people. It was a motley mixture. Drinking, gambling, quarrels, fights, and shockingly immoral practices were frequent. All who lived in the little town were in one way or another connected with the salt business. (15–16)

Washington's description of Malden recalls antebellum proslavery and postbellum "Lost Cause" representations of the treatment of industrial free labor as more degrading in many respects than slavery. Indeed, Washington depicts industrial free labor as a sort of trap that brutalizes those caught in it in much the same way that Douglass argues slavery does, perhaps setting up the depiction of Malden in opposition to the near-utopian portrait of New Bedford that Douglass compared favorably with the landscape of both the urban and rural slave South: "Many children of the tenderest years were compelled then, as is now true I fear, in most coal-mining districts, to spend a large part of their lives in these coal-mines, with little opportunity to get an education; and, what is worse, I have often noted that, as a rule, young boys who begin life in a coal-mine are often physically and mentally dwarfed. They soon lose ambition to do anything else than to continue as a coal-miner" (23). Washington here is engaging in a typically double game because his formal education truly begins in Malden after a fashion that would not have been possible on the antebellum plantation. It is in Malden that he learns the value of education, of literacy, of thrift, of hard work, and of a job well done (though as a house servant rather than an industrial worker); it is in Malden that he renames himself. (And, as he notes, his brother John helps support him at Hampton Institute from wages earned in a West Virginian coal mine.)

Yet there is a sense that Washington must return to the plantation South to fulfill his destiny, as do Iola Leroy and the other educated black characters of Harper's novel. While he never precisely lives in the North, he does describe a stay in the border city of Washington, D.C., much of which is devoted to what he sees as an unhealthy dependence on government support and the seduction of even working-class African American families, especially young people, by popular culture and incipient consumerism—Washington must be among the earliest critics of American consumer culture—in part inculcated by the lack of a practical education:

> How many times I wished then, and have often wished since, that by some power of magic I might remove the great bulk of these people into the country districts and plant them upon the soil, upon the solid and never deceptive foundation of Mother Nature, where all nations and races that have ever succeeded have gotten their start—a start that at first may be slow and toilsome, but one that nevertheless is real.
>
> In Washington I saw girls whose mothers were earning their living by laundrying. These girls were taught by their mothers, in rather a crude way it is true, the industry of laundrying. Later, these girls entered the public schools and remained there perhaps six or eight years. When the public-school course was finally finished, they wanted more costly dresses, more costly hats and shoes. In a word, while their wants had been increased, their ability to supply their wants had not been increased in the same degree. On the other hand, their six or eight years of book education had weaned them away from the occupation of their mothers. The result of this was in too many cases that the girls went to the bad. I often thought how much wiser it would have been to give these girls the same amount of mental training—and I favour any kind of training, whether in the lan-

guages or mathematics, that gives strength and culture to the mind—but at the same time to give them the most thorough training in the latest and best methods of laundrying and other kindred occupations. (53)

Here again, as in *Iola Leroy*, one sees a linking between the southern soil and a black homeland, one that is explicitly connected to race, nation, community, and culture, a community that is threatened by the practical and ideological alienation and individualism of the urban North—and the popular culture associated with the North. Yet, as he signals almost immediately in the preface, Washington himself does not remain tied to the land, but is in almost perpetual motion, claiming to write much of the autobiography on the road.

Popular Culture, Black Public Spaces, and the New Black Territory

Of course, there was already in existence an enormous body of popular literature, music, and drama that made such a connection between African Americans and the southern land (and between migration and the destruction of organic community), though in a different register perhaps. Many of the most popular minstrel tunes of the antebellum period as well many of the early "coon songs" of the Reconstruction and immediate post-Reconstruction eras, both by black performers, such as Bert Williams and George Walker, black songwriters, such as James Bland, and white tune-smiths, such as Stephen Foster and Daniel Emmett, virtually defined the southern plantation as *the* black territory. Interestingly, these songs often anticipated such early migration novels as Dunbar's *Sport of the Gods* and Toomer's *Cane* in that they were based on the conceit of an alienated migrant speaker sadly roaming (to quote Foster's ubiquitous 1851 "The Old Folks at Home") "up and down de whole creation" and longing for the organic community with its connection to nature that he (it is almost always a he) experienced in his youth or else feels through some ancestral osmosis. For example, Bland's famous 1878 "Carry Me Back to Old Virginny," adopted as the state song of Virginia in 1940, reads (or sounds):

Carry me back to old Virginny,
There's where the cotton and the corn and tatoes grow,
There's where the birds warble sweet in the spring-time,
There's where the old darkey's heart am long'd to go.

There's where I labor'd so hard for old massa,
Day after day, in the field of yellow corn,
No place on earth do I love more sincerely
Than old Virginny the state where I was born.

Bland's song also envisions a reunion of the former slave speaker with his former "massa and missis" on the "bright and golden shore" of heaven.

As was so often the case with minstrelsy, ragtime, the "coon song," and early vaudeville, especially as created and performed by black artists, Bland's song might be said to have a bifurcated character. Some listeners (the Virginia legislature in 1940, perhaps) might imagine it a close cousin to the plantation literature–reconciliationist tradition that pictures a reuniting of North and South, and even black and white, on the basis of a separate, subjugated status for African Americans. However, others might hear something more like the black reconciliationist tradition that proposes regional and racial reunion on the basis of African American equality and the recognition of the wrong of slavery by the former slaveholders. After all, nowhere in the song does it say that the speaker plans to labor "so hard for old massa" "day after day" in heaven as he did when he was a slave on earth. Instead, in this world, as in *Up From Slavery* (anticipating the dilemma of Ralph Kabnis in Jean Toomer's *Cane*), the singer foresees being planted (or replanted) "upon the soil, upon the solid and never deceptive foundation of Mother Nature"—with both former slave owner and slave presumably removed from both antebellum and postbellum alienation and exploitation.

While the Jim Crow–era migration narratives are clearly indebted to earlier narratives of Douglass, Harper, and Washington (and the popular music of Bland and other songwriters, as well as the plantation tradition, for that matter), they differ in that black public spaces deeply tied to popular culture are crucial to the movement of the narratives in new ways, whereas in earlier narratives distinctly African American spaces were largely restricted to home and family. Such family sites are still present in the Jim Crow narrative and often set in opposition to the public, commercial spaces that are seen as inimical to family in many respects. Interestingly, in many of these later stories the very designation of these public spaces as black makes them unusually vulnerable to invasion by white seekers of blackness in ways that are perhaps analogous to the violation of family spaces (and even the idea of black family spaces) in the antebellum South that was a recurrent motif in the slave narrative. At the same time, it is often suggested that this redefining of racial territory provides the basis of what might be a distinct national or quasi-national culture. Such redefinition had much to do with the vast migration of African Americans from the countryside to the city and from the South to the North, greatly swelling the new urban ghettos, but in fact the formation of the modern ghettos, North and South, and the increasing location of interracial vice districts in these ghettos, antedated the Great Migration.

A recurring motif of the migration genre is the individual or family that leaves the folk in the South only to be destroyed in the North. Perhaps the earliest example of this sort of character is the corrupt politician and lawyer John Langley in Pauline Hopkins's 1899 novel *Contending Forces*. In many respects, one might consider this the first of the Jim Crow migration narratives. *Contending Forces* contains some of the earliest depictions of urban black territories and public or semipublic spaces in the North, specifically Boston's "Negro quarter" in the West End (really the adjoining North Slope of Beacon Hill), the site of the church of the Smith family as well as of the home and business of the black fortuneteller Madame Francis. The Smiths' boardinghouse is located in the emerging ghetto of the South End. Much of the action of *Contending Forces* occurs in the semipublic space of the boardinghouse, the scene of a "literary and musical programme" and the sort of setting that, as is discussed in the next chapter, would become a hallmark of artistic representations of the new bohemias in the United States, black and white.

Contending Forces is a hybrid of the gothic romance and the related genre of the melodrama.[4] The novel is filled with familiar gothic topoi of doubling (and redoubling), secrets, incest, stolen birthrights, sexual coercion, prophetic visions, curses visited down through the generations, and so on. As is often the case with the gothic, from *The Castle of Otranto* to *Dracula*, but less common in the Victorian melodrama, the novel's ostensibly happy ending has a strangely melancholic air that refuses any final closure. Will Smith and Sappho Clark have been reunited; they marry and Smith adopts Sappho's son Alphonse. The Smiths have also been restored to their ancestral birthright (stolen by a slave master who is an ancestor of John Langley through a coercive relationship with a slave) and acknowledged by their English relatives. Will's sister Dora, the former fiancée of Langley, has married Doctor Lewis and is contented, if not precisely passionately in love. Yet it is significant that the final scene takes place on a Cunard Line ship bound for Europe, suggesting that such a restoration and acknowledgment, such a happy ending was impossible to imagine occurring in the United States. The penultimate scene is that of the death of the peripatetic John Langley, the man who drove Sappho back to the South, in the ice fields of the Klondike as foretold by the medium Madame Francis.

Though in a sense the villain (or, at least, a villain) of the novel, Langley anticipates the protagonists, whom we might think of as black marginal men (after Robert Park) or even flaneurs (after Walter Benjamin), of the later migration novel, especially those of Paul Laurence Dunbar's *The Sport of the Gods*, James Weldon Johnson's *Autobiography of an Ex-Colored Man*, Jean Toomer's *Cane*, Claude McKay's *Home to Harlem* and *Banjo*, and Nella Larsen's *Quicksand*. He is a mixed-race character, "a mixture of 'cracker' blood of the lowest type on his father's side with whatever God-saving quality that might have been loaned the Negro by pitying nature" (221). While the narrator suggests some biological origin for Langley's behavior, inverting the normative hierarchy of black and white, much of his character derives from his essential rootlessness, migrating as he does from the South to the urban North with no lasting connection to family or soil other than his descent in part from one of the "first families" of the South that is, with heavy irony, described as the original source of his low "cracker" blood. He remains perpetually in rootless motion and permanently "between" (as embodied in his mixed-race origins), not able to come to rest anywhere until forced to do so by death in a cold white place where nothing grows. He is both a libertine and a crass arriviste, thinking constantly and cold-bloodedly about his material and social advancement. He is a version of what Robert Alter calls the "new urban man, grasping shards of sensory data and jagged ends of recollected images, [who] becomes a maelstrom in which the centrifugal elements of experience are whirled together in dizzying combinations" (20–21), a recurring figure of modernist fiction. Yet, despite all this, there is a sense that if he chose differently, if he could root himself, say, in marriage to Dora (which he considers almost entirely in a pecuniary light), then he might be saved. However, he fails in this. This sort of failure, leading to permanent movement, or yo-yoing generally, between North and South, without any genuine resolution except perhaps through death (or something like a social death), becomes the mark of the early migration novel.[5]

A more developed early example of this motif can be found in Paul Laurence Dunbar's 1902 naturalist novel *The Sport of the Gods*. Dunbar's novel starts in the South where a wealthy white landowner, Maurice Oakley, becomes convinced that his loyal, hardworking, self-reliant black servant Berry Hamilton is a thief. In a perfunctory trial, Hamilton is condemned to prison. (Ultimately, Oakley discovers that Hamilton is innocent and that his own bohemian expatriate artist brother, Francis, is in fact the criminal, but decides that it is better for a black man, however upright, to remain in jail than to admit the truth of his brother's guilt and to put the public honor of his family in jeopardy.) Unable to bear the scorn of the small rural town in which it lives, the Hamilton family moves to New York City. There, the Hamiltons lose the values of the rural South and are seduced by the glamorous evils of the metropolis in the first major fictional showcase of the "black bohemia" of clubs, dancehalls, gambling joints, theaters, hotels, and boardinghouses that will become a hallmark of modern African American urban literature.

"Fate Me": The Circumscribed Fin de Siècle Black Flaneur and the Modernist Protagonist

As Dunbar's *The Sport of the Gods* unfolds, Berry's son Joe joins a memorable cast of grifters, barflies, sleazy show business people, and white voyeurs in this demimonde. The most memorable and arresting character of the novel is the black, possibly gay grifter-bohemian-dandy-flaneur "Sadness" Williams, who, too, was a migrant to the city driven by Jim Crow and racial terror not unlike Joe. In Sadness's case, the precipitating event is his father's lynching in Texas. Upon his arrival, Sadness was initiated into the interface of crime and popular culture (and deviant sexuality) that is black bohemia through his victimization by a con artist. In turn, he participates in a similar draining of Joe — though Sadness is distinguished from the other grifters by what appears to be a sincere, if self-consciously ironic and ultimately vain, attempt to warn Joe about the dangers of his new environment. One might consider this a sort of gothic vision of black bohemia in which the hard-core bohemian is an urban vampire, both glamorous and trapped, passing on his or her condition and curse to new arrivals to the city. Sadness, even more than John Langley, is a black flaneur whose territory is circumscribed in a way that is directly opposed to the range of mobility of his white counterparts, particularly Skaggs and Francis Oakley. In this one is reminded of Alter's comparison of the Parisian flaneur to the protagonists of Kafka:

K.'s urban habitat, a labyrinth of office buildings and apartment houses, many of them on the seedy side, in which people are closed off from one another in their private rooms, quickly turns into a breeding ground for paranoia. In this generalized and anonymous European city, projected out of the observed features of Kafka's Prague, we have come round 180 degrees from the flaneur of nineteenth-century Paris: the individual, instead of enjoying the pleasures of roaming spectatorship, has himself become a spectacle, the object of curious and perhaps contemptuous or hostile stares from windows. (149)

It is worth recalling that the African American dandy (as well as the tramp) as a form of entertaining spectacle, or even what might be thought of as an entertaining menace, had a long history in the popular culture of the United States. Sadness plays with this history within the context of the new black zones of the urban United States. Thus, the perambulations of the black flaneur are radically circumscribed. However, in an irony much noted by black writers, he becomes extraordinarily mobile within a limited (and sharply delineated) space. In *Turning South Again*, Houston Baker Jr. describes a Jim Crow system, aided and abetted by Booker T. Washington, which attempted to frustrate "Afro-Modernity" by rendering the black male immobile (*Turning South Again*, 60). The restriction on black freedom of movement that Baker touches on here marks a crucial feature of the new racial regime, particularly as urban space comes to be increasingly segregated in the United States. Yet, strangely, it is the African American male who comes to virtually define the flaneur in the United States with the black loafer, dandy, zoot-suiter, bebopper, hipster, b-boy, thug, and so on, becoming models for waves of white, Latina/Latino, and Asian American counter-cultures. The black street observer who is also observed (digging and being dug in return, to paraphrase Langston Hughes's "Motto"), who is mobile within a limited space, pushing up against immobility, combines Baudelairean peripatetic Paris (or at least Benjamin's vision of Baudelairean Paris) with Kafkaesque claustrophobic Prague—only this combination of perambulation and confinement, of recessive gazing, was rooted in the new realities of the Jim Crow urban landscape of the United States with new black and white urban public spaces (Hughes, *Collected*, 398).

Joe Hamilton does not exactly follow the path marked out by Sadness, perhaps because he lacks (and never develops) Sadness's intelligence and ironic self-hating detachment (an essential characteristic in many representations of the successful bohemian). Instead, he follows a more timeworn and familiar trajectory, becoming infatuated with Hattie, a black vaudeville actress on a downward career slide, which in turn leads to his ruin and to his incarceration for the demented murder of Hattie. The daughter Kitty Hamilton, too, joins this world, changing from a fresh-faced country girl into an increasingly hardened and prematurely aged showgirl in "Martin's

Blackbirds," much like Joe's murdered paramour, on her way, perhaps, to being a broken down call girl—or to meeting a violent death as Hattie did. Berry's wife Fannie, with the support of Kitty, gives up on her jailed husband and marries an abusive drunk. This familiar destruction of country folk in the city is what Berry finds when he is released from prison and journeys north in search of his wife and children. As in *Iola Leroy*, we see a journey north that is very different from that of Douglass, a journey into a kind of new slavery to mass culture and the evils of modernity—like many stories in early and mid-nineteenth-century British literature where good yeoman families are destroyed in the metropolis of London or the new mill towns of the North. In Dunbar's novel, Berry and Fannie return south together to their former hometown after the sudden death of Fannie's second husband. But it is a cheerless return that seems itself a sort of death in life that can be resolved or relieved only by actual death: "It was not a happy life, but it was all that was left to them, and they took it up without complaint, for they knew they were powerless against some Will infinitely stronger than their own" (148).

Much of this same unresolved gloom permeates Du Bois's *The Souls of Black Folk* despite its somewhat upbeat ending. Taken as a whole, it, too, features a constant back-and-forth between South and North in which the South is marked as the black homeland (at least in the New World) that is strangely untenable, especially for the black subject who has become both educated and alienated in the North. The miniature fictional migration narrative, "The Coming of John," embedded within the otherwise "nonfiction" text traces the trajectory of a young black man unable to find a place North or South, especially in his home in the South, and by the end so alienated from himself that he generally thinks of himself in the third person and even, for a moment, as another person: "The night deepened; he thought of the boys at Johnstown. He wondered how Brown had turned out, and Carey? And Jones,—Jones? Why, *he* was Jones, and he wondered what they would all say when they knew, when they knew, in that great long dining-room with its hundreds of merry eyes" (263). As is so often the case, John can find resolution only in death, in his case at the hands of a lynch mob.

The death of John, a mixture of sorrow and outrage connected to travel between North and South, and/or city and country, is only one of many such moments in *The Souls of Black Folk*. One thinks about Du Bois the protagonist (as opposed to the author) thinking about the life and death of Josie at the end of "Of the Meaning of Progress" as he rides the Jim Crow car from rural Tennessee back to Nashville. The saddest and angriest moment of all is found in the chapter on the death of Du Bois's infant son, Burghardt, born in Du Bois's native Massachusetts and dying in Atlanta. Both the sadness and rage are most clearly on view in the strange and bitter elation that Du Bois describes as arising in his heart as he considers his son's escape from the veil (and the South): "Not dead, not dead, but escaped; not bond, but free" (133). However, the baby's movement does not even end with death as Du Bois recounts how he refused to inter the body in Georgia and took it back to the North for burial.

One finds the same note of melancholic and unresolved (except by death) movement at the end of James Weldon Johnson's *Autobiography of an Ex-Colored Man*, first published anonymously in 1912 in New York City. As a novel, it seems a bit disjointed if one has a sense of Chekovian unity of plot (in which the gun on the mantelpiece, once displayed, must be fired), because, in important respects, it is three or four books at once. In part, that is because it is addressed to at least two different audiences, a literate white middle-class audience and a literate black middle-class audience. One important part of the book is reportage, documenting various aspects of African American life generally unknown to white people. One thinks of the long passages describing turn-of-the-century African American middle-class life in Jacksonville, Boston, and elsewhere that seem to have nothing much to do with the plot. Again, while these passages might seem to digress or divert attention from the movement of the plot in the book, they have the purpose of showing the wide range of the African American community and African American tastes to middle-class white Americans. There are also the sporting-life scenes of black bohemia, which may have the purpose of selling books because they resemble descriptions of bohemian French life, such as Giacomo Puccini's opera *La Bohème* (1896) and George du Maurier's novel *Trilby* (1894), that were so popular in the United States and in Europe at the turn of the century with a wide reading public, which presumably included both black and white people. The club passages also seem remarkably like scenes of Harlem nightlife during the Harlem Renaissance a decade or so later (which no doubt led to the reprinting of the book, which did not sell very well when first issued, during the height of the Harlem Renaissance in the 1920s).

There are also passages that read as if they are from tracts or political pamphlets. These passages variously exhort white people to recognize the full humanity, the achievements, and the civil rights of black people and encourage African Americans not to lose all hope but to recognize the distance they have come and to keep on going. Then there are passages that sound like the editorials that Johnson wrote in the *New York Age*; generally aimed at a black audience, they instruct it in conduct and in the interpretation of events, culture, and so on. The passages on African American folk and popular culture are particularly significant as early literary arguments for the existence of a distinctly African American folk culture (and a high culture rooted in that folk culture) that has the potential to, perhaps ironically, bring about an integration of African Americans into "America" on the basis of equality through separate cultural solidarity and development:

> There are a great many colored people who are ashamed of the cake-walk, but I think they ought to be proud of it. It is my opinion that the colored people of this country have done four things which refute the oft advanced theory that they are an absolutely inferior race, which demonstrate that they have originality and artistic conception; and, what is more, the power of creating that which can influence and appeal universally. The first two of these are the Uncle Remus stories, collected by Joel Chandler Harris, and the Jubilee songs, to which the Fisk singers made the public and the skilled musicians of both America and Europe listen. The other two are ragtime music and the cake-walk. No one who has traveled can question the world-conquering influence of ragtime; and I do not think it would be an exaggeration to say that in Europe the United States is popularly known better by ragtime than by anything else it has produced in a generation. In Paris they call it American music. (*Writings*, 54.)

Here we see an association of and transition between the landscape of the rural South and the cultural forms, the spirituals and the Uncle Remus stories, linked to that landscape and the new black territory of the urban United States that Johnson ties to popular culture forms, particularly the popular musical theater and ragtime, in both *Autobiography* and the portion of his 1930 social history *Black Manhattan* dealing with turn-of-the-century black bohemia.

One of the notable aspects of Johnson's novel is that it contains both sorts of Robert Stepto's archetypal African American stories, the ascent north to freedom and individualism and the descent south to the folk and cultural rootedness, but, as in *Sport of the Gods* (and, to a large extent, *Contending Forces*), without any satisfactory resolution. The un-named protagonist of the novel is a light-skinned, mixed-race character. Earlier uses of this mixed-race figure by black authors were often designed to show the irrationality of race and U.S. definitions of race in a way that white Americans would find shocking, titillating, and moving—the idea, for example, in William Wells

Brown's 1853 novel *Clotel* that a president, Thomas Jefferson, would, could, and (as we know now) did own his own children. Johnson, however, uses the figure somewhat differently. For Johnson, the mixed-race individual who can "pass" back and forth across the race line (without ever feeling comfortable on either side) is a sort of embodiment of the cultural and social twoness that people such as Dunbar with his famous metaphor of the mask and Du Bois with his metaphor of the veil claim is a mark of the contemporary African American psyche—Du Bois's notion of "double consciousness" (785) and the "remarkable book" *The Souls of Black Folk* are actually referenced in the novel.[6]

The plot of the novel mirrors the narrator's divided state as he yo-yos between North and South. The opening invokes and draws on the early turns of Harper's *Iola Leroy*. The reader discovers that the narrator was born in the South, which he vaguely, though fondly, recalls as a land of nature and music. However, his first clear memories are of a small northern city where he has moved with his mother and where he becomes a sort of musical prodigy. Like the experiences of Iola and her brother Harry, the narrator's first existential crisis takes place when he discovers at school that his mother is a light-skinned former slave and that his father is in fact her former owner—and both his parents have decided that it would be better for him if he were brought up in the North. In short, he is, despite all appearances, a Negro (as such things were adjudicated in the United States).

Interestingly, in a major departure from the trajectory of Harper's novel, other than some brief initial comments by both black and white students, he is not treated much differently by his classmates at school. Perhaps the most telling thing in this respect is the narrator's potentially explosive relationship to his partner in musical performances, a beautiful, young white woman several years older than he is who inspires a puppy love that finds its expression in secretly written, overwrought poetry. There is no moment of recognition of the shadow of racism through some rejection by the young woman along the lines of the white girls' refusal of the young Du Bois's valentines in *The Souls of Black Folk*. In fact, the musical partnership is begun after the moment of racial revelation in the school. While the age difference, the shyness, and perhaps the "race" of the narrator prevent the young woman from treating him seriously in an emotional way, these things do not stop her from embracing and kissing him after a successful performance—anticipating his successful wooing of a young white woman near the end of the novel even after he has revealed to her that he is a "Negro." The ex-colored man's youthful crisis is largely internal: his own sense of self has been turned upside down. He is a Negro—but what is a Negro? What does it mean to him to be a Negro?

The ex-colored man attempts to solve his crisis by going south to attend the historically black Atlanta University instead of Harvard. In part, he justifies his choice as financial prudence, but he admits that it is largely driven by his fascination with the South, seeking, by implication, to really learn what it is to be black among the best of "his" race. However, en route he is robbed by a black railroad porter. Without the money to pay for his tuition, the narrator drifts farther south and finds himself in Jacksonville—James Weldon Johnson's hometown. He soon finds work in a cigar factory. What follows is largely reportage about middle-class black life and the rise of Jim Crow segregation in the South in the late nineteenth century. While the ex-colored man mixes with the best of black society in Jacksonville and takes up music again as a performer and music teacher, he feels increasingly hemmed in by Jim Crow. So when he is laid off at the cigar factory, he is drawn to the metropolis of New York City.

In New York, he stumbles into a club in the center of black bohemia on the Middle West Side. In short order, in a way that recalls Sadness in *Sport of the Gods*, he is drawn into the sporting life of sex, drinking, gambling, and ragtime; of black rounders, gamblers, and performers; and of white interlopers in black bohemia. These interlopers include both occasional slummers and regulars, often white women seeking (and finding) sexual relationships with black men. In some ways, he is even more clearly a member of black bohemia with its familiar connection between art and crime, than Sadness, becoming both a skilled gambler and ragtime pianist.

For a while it appears that the main question of the novel is whether the narrator will drink himself to death or be killed by a jealous black lover of "the widow," a white regular at "The Club," who is in fact murdered by her lover. The narrator is rescued by a rich European man, a slummer, who hires him to play ragtime at his social gatherings, first in New York, then in Europe. While the ex-colored man is at first overwhelmed by the art, architecture, and relative racial tolerance of Europe, he comes to long for the United States. He desires to return to the South and study the music and culture of the black folk with the idea of using the skills that he has developed in both the classical European and ragtime musical traditions to create a "high" African American art that would truly express the African American spirit much as European nationalist artists, such as Synge, Bartok, Sibelius, and Janacek, attempted to do with Irish, Hungarian, Finnish, and Czech folk cultures.

So the narrator returns to the South, where he is at least as overwhelmed by the spirituals and sermons of the black folk as he had been by Notre Dame. However, after that promising start, he witnesses a lynching in which a man is burned alive. He is revolted by the experience and traumatized to know that he, as a Negro, is held in such contempt that he could be treated more cruelly than one would treat any animal. He flees the South and returns to New York, where he works as a clerk and through some shrewd moves becomes a prosperous businessman. During this period, he does not exactly claim to be white; rather, he avoids any mention of his racial identity, letting (as did Iola Leroy during much of her northern adult sojourn) others make their own assumptions. Eventually, he meets a woman (white as far as the narrator and the reader know) and falls in love. There is a crisis when he reveals that he is a "Negro," but she eventually accepts him. They marry—though again, the fact that he is "colored" is unspoken even to his children. As he prospers in business, he abandons his musical ambitions— which is only natural, seeing how important his identification as part of a Negro people was to those ambitions.

When we leave the narrator, he is full of regret. His wife, the only person in his current life to know that he is a Negro, has died. His life after his abandonment of his project of creating a new type of high African American music has been basically good, but as he sees black artists and activists attempting to achieve the sorts of things he intended to do when he left Europe, he feels that he sold his birthright for a mess of potage. It is worth noting that if we take the conclusion of the narration to be close to the date of the book's publication, then the work of these artists and activists is contemporary with the formation of the new black ghettos, even if the traditional date for the start of the Great Migration is still a couple of years off.

One might say that his melancholy lot is pretty typical of the narratives, generally by white writers, of what was called the "tragic mulatto," except that the narrator's problem is not that he is constitutionally crippled by his mixed-race status. His real problem is that he does not take his identity crisis to resolution, that he does not create the music that is the transmutation of the folk culture and popular heritage into a new high form, making an irresistible claim on America. This is due not just to the protagonist's weakness, or even to the weaknesses of the African American community generally, but more importantly to the legal and extralegal duality imposed by Jim Crow in both its northern and southern, urban and rural variations. After all, the thing that sends the narrator back north after his descent into the southern black folk is his confrontation with the depth of white racist violence and oppression culminating in a lynching, that is, the sort of extralegal violence that was a crucial tool in the establishment and maintenance of Jim Crow in the South.

In other words, it is hard to maintain hope that the sort of cultural work (and, by extension, political work) that the protagonist sets out to do will have a real impact on the situation of black people in America, even if Johnson the author suggests through the novel that such hopes are necessary. So that at the end of the novel we are left with the ex-colored man wracked with regret because he never attempted to bridge the gap between the two parts of his consciousness, which are not really black and white so much as different modalities of being black, and instead tried to solve the problem by rejecting the folk and "passing." This solution ultimately leaves him isolated and lost, especially once he begins to "pass" in earnest after the death of his wife — as long as she knows he is a "Negro," he cannot be said to be completely passing. (And, it might be noted, one hallowed feature of the African American passing story is that secretly passing from one "life" to another is inherently unstable and anxious because one is never certain when someone from one life might pop up in another.) Of course, as long he thinks he is in some sense a "Negro," he, after *The Souls of Black Folk*, forever feels his twoness in a melancholic ending that seems hardly more cheerful than that of *Sport of the Gods* — or, in fact, than the tone of the final third or so of Du Bois's book.

As discussed in the conclusion, this sense of melancholy pervades many of the migration narratives of the Harlem Renaissance and, in fact, takes on a new intensity.[7] The black subject is caught in an impossible existential bind in the United States. As in *Sport of the Gods*, *Autobiography*, and, in many respects, *Contending Forces*, the old home of the South, with its connection to nature and the line of cultural transmission seen reaching more directly to Africa, is either practically or spiritually untenable. In Rudolph Fisher's influential Harlem Renaissance short story, "City of Refuge," which draws much on *Sport of the Gods*, the protagonist King Solomon Gillis flees the South just ahead of the lynch mob; Uggam, Gillis's North Carolina homeboy transformed into Harlem grifter, is a World War I veteran who cannot bring himself to go back south after he has seen Paris. Both are ruined by the city, Uggam morally and Gillis physically in all likelihood. This sense of the urban ghetto as simultaneously new home, refuge, trap, and exile, of black metropolis and destroyer of black culture and racial values pioneered by Dunbar and Johnson (and Hopkins), and further developed by such authors of the Harlem Renaissance as Fisher, Jean Toomer, Nella Larsen, and Claude

McKay obviously was immensely strengthened by the continued growth and hypersegregation of African American populations in the urban centers of the United States.

The initial black migration narratives, like the later poetry of Dunbar, are forerunners of a certain modernist sensibility in U.S. and European fiction. The protagonists of the early migration narratives in their yo-yoing between North and South, black and white, citizen and some other less classifiable status, private space and public space, are radically divided intellectually. The sort of radical alienation and fragmentation that will come to be associated with artistic modernism is here writ large and early. If one compares the novels of Hopkins, Dunbar, and Johnson to perhaps the most similar contemporary novel of migration from the provinces to the city by a white U.S. author, Dreiser's *Sister Carrie*, for many critics another landmark of a truly modern American literature, one notices that Carrie, last seen unconsciously floating like a bubble to the top of a corrupt and vacuous New York fashionable world, lacks the sort of agonized, if sometimes delusional and unreliable, self-consciousness characteristic of the early migration protagonist as well as of the later modernist protagonist, sometimes one and the same, from Prufrock to Gregor Samsa to Stephen Daedalus to Gustav Aschenbach to Nick Carraway to Ralph Kabnis to Helga Crane to Joe Christmas. Finally, along with the slave narrative (and such permutations of the slave narrative as *Uncle Tom's Cabin*, *The Adventures of Huckleberry Finn*, and *Iola Leroy*) and the poetry invoking the black Civil War veterans, the early migration novels inscribed the North-South axis in the literatures of the United States, often combining with and reshaping the symbolic valence of the East-West axis in the high age of U.S. colonialism. So, although the overt narrative directly engaging the movement of millions from the country to the city is relatively rarely written by white authors, a sort of sublimated migration narrative linking the North-South axis to anxieties about race and culture became a hallmark of U.S. modernism.

chapter four

Somebody Else's Civilization

African American Writers, Bohemia, and the New Poetry

In the United States, as elsewhere, the rise of artistic modernism and the emergence of indigenous bohemias in the late nineteenth and early twentieth centuries were closely linked, though not twinned phenomena. I use the plural rather than speak of bohemia in the singular because, nearly from the beginning, bohemia in the United States was characterized by racially and ethnically distinct, though significantly overlapping, communities, whether one is speaking of "black bohemia," the largely white bohemia in such communities as New York's Greenwich Village and Chicago's Towertown, or the avant garde artistic subcultures of immigrant communities, such as the circles of Yiddish- and Russian-speaking Jewish artists and intellectuals who frequented the cafés of New York's Lower East Side. Given the increasingly rigid segregation of urban space and the debates about race and citizenship that roiled the United States, such distinctions are not surprising. However, somewhat paradoxically perhaps, it was the intersection between these bohemias, particularly between "black" and "white" (especially as the importance of the older "white ethnic" artistic circles faded as the twentieth century wore on), even as distinct predominantly black and white bohemian spaces were maintained, that came to define the ideas of bohemia and the artistic avant garde in the United States.

Early bohemia in the United States grew out of a complicated triangulation between primarily literary and musical representations of European bohemias (generally French and, to a lesser extent, English), actual bohemian communities abroad (themselves much shaped by a dialectic of imitation and rejection of popular representation), and local conditions and imperatives. As Christine Stansell points out, for example, women and organized feminism played a far more prominent role in the New York and Chicago bohemian communities of the early twentieth century than was true of London or Paris, even if their counterparts in bohemian Paris and London were unquestionably influential in shaping these new U.S. countercultures (231–34).

In fact, one of the things that makes early literary modernism and what

Harriet Monroe and others termed somewhat vaguely the "new poetry" complicated is that they were significantly a product of circles and institutions rooted in the new bohemias of the United States in dialogue with American writers and intellectuals based in or on the fringes of the bohemias of London and Paris that had much different gender and ideological dynamics. Thus, the political radicalism, especially the socialism and anarchism (in the days when anarchism and anarcho-syndicalism were a significant, if seemingly counterintuitively, organized section of the Left) of such journals as *The Little Review*, *The Masses*, *Others*, and even *Poetry*, not to mention the key roles that women had in these journals, distinguished these journals from their pre-Dada counterparts in London and Paris. These distinctions made for some contradictions in the journals' relationships with expatriate artists, such as Ezra Pound and T. S. Eliot, based in the far more masculinist and often relatively apolitical bohemias of London and Paris, relationships that were crucial to the development of modernism in the United States. Pound, in particular, had difficulty adjusting to the leading roles that such women writers and editors as Amy Lowell and Monroe played in the early modernist literary circles of the United States—though, ironically, he would support Monroe in her conflict with the black poet, critic, and editor, William Stanley Braithwaite.[1]

As such critics as Lorenzo Thomas and Kenny Williams (and James Weldon Johnson, for that matter) have pointed out, black writers and intellectuals, especially Braithwaite and Fenton Johnson, were significant players in the rise of U.S. poetic modernism and the idea of a "new poetry." Braithwaite in particular joined his sometime antagonist Harriet Monroe as a crucial critic and editor in promoting the new poetry—or the "poetry renaissance" as Braithwaite preferred.[2] To this one might add that black writers, including Dunbar, James Weldon Johnson, and Fenton Johnson, were important early commentators on indigenous U.S. artistic bohemias—black, white, and black and white. At the same time, Braithwaite, Fenton Johnson, and James Weldon Johnson championed new African American writing, seeing what they posited as an upsurge in black poetry as simultaneously a part of the larger U.S. poetry revival and of a Negro "renaissance." They certainly did not invent the idea of a "New Negro." Still, they did much to take what had been primarily a political term and concept and use it to imagine a black artistic counterculture that paralleled, touched on, and influenced (and was influenced by) largely white circles while retaining a separate existence and character.[3]

The notion of social bohemianism appears to have entered the English-speaking world in the mid-nineteenth century with the commercial success and international fame of Henri Murger's sketches of Parisian bohemian life on page and stage—though perhaps Murger's work did not reach its apogee of influence until 1896 with its adaptation by Puccini in the opera *La Bohème* (in turn adapted and transposed to the Lower East Side by Jonathan Larson in *Rent* a century later).[4]

It is worth thinking about what made this bohemia a new phenomenon. After all, unconventional artists à la François Villon, William Blake, or Christopher Smart antedated the Victorian age. And circles of artists, writers, intellectuals, and students meeting in sometimes seedy taverns, coffeehouses, salons, and so on to talk about art, letters, and politics certainly did not begin in nineteenth-century Paris. Even the detachment of artists from aristocratic patronage and the rise of market relations between the artist, the work of art, and the bourgeois art patron or consumer in which novelty and rebellion become valuable attributes of the art commodity (which includes the artist who increasingly must sell himself or herself), as well as the enmeshment of writers and artists in emerging popular culture industries, had a considerable history before the nineteenth century, perhaps most famously (among English speakers) in the floating hack literary world of London's Grub Street in the eighteenth century.

Perhaps the thing that really first distinguishes the idea of bohemia in the nineteenth and twentieth centuries from these protobohemian figures and sites is geography, that is, the notion of a space or community that is larger than a bar, coffee shop, or restaurant—Grub Street notwithstanding—and the importance of bohemian geography in the rise of artistic modernism. The name bohemia, denoting a region and former principality in the Hapsburg Empire (and later Czechoslovakia and the Czech Republic) and connoting the notoriously and romantically transnational Roma, suggests the peculiar ways in which bohemia is a place or quarter, but one of shifting, mobile, and unusually permeable boundaries.[5] In that sense, while one might consider the scene at Walt Whitman's favored watering hole in the mid-nineteenth century, Pfaff's Cellar, to be an early bohemian outpost in New York, something changed by the end of the century when bohemia began to be associated with particular neighborhoods, often overlapping with immigrant or African American communities.

From its beginning as a recognized social formation, one of the most notable and most noted features of this bohemian space, especially in its artistic representations in the English-speaking world, is as a location where boundaries of class, gender, race, ethnicity, and nationality grow thin and become more permeable in stark contrast to the rigid limits of the "mainstream" society that surrounds it. In the circle of bohemia, middle-class, working-class, and peasant participants in this counterculture might adopt the persona of some fantastic aristocratic dandy, while, perhaps even more frequently, aristocrats and burgers might take on some stylized appearance of a farmer or working man or woman. People of different national citizenships, ethnic or national groups (which were not necessarily the same as national citizenships, especially in a Europe dominated by huge multiethnic empires that coexisted with a plethora of German and Italian states when Henri Murger began to chronicle French bohemia), regions, religions, and races (as race was understood then) intimately mingled in such countercultural zones as Paris's Latin Quarter and Montmartre, London's Soho, Chicago's Towertown, the North Slope of Boston's Beacon Hill, New Orleans's French Quarter, and New York's Greenwich Village in the nineteenth and early twentieth centuries. Again, these zones usually overlapped with or were proximate to immigrant communities, concentrations of so-called transients, and centers of illegal or semilegal vice industries.

In the case of the United States, sometime bohemian areas bordered on or overlapped with neighborhoods with significant numbers of African Americans. If, as Christine Stansell argues, it is not clear whether African Americans would have been served in Greenwich Village restaurants frequented by the bohemians of the early twentieth century, white and black bohemians certainly would have been able to (and did) have a drink together at the "black and tan" bars of Greenwich Village's "Little Africa" that Jacob Riis wrote about so scathingly in *How the Other Half Lives* (Stansell, 67). Perhaps not surprisingly, then, some of the most prominent early representations of a U.S. bohemia took place in poetry and prose by African American authors. And representations of both black bohemia and its intersection with a multiracial and multiethnic, if largely white, bohemia became important topoi of modern black literature through the New Negro Renaissance.

As noted in the previous chapter, one aspect of the new urban Jim Crow regime was the creation of more or less new black territories and secular public spaces in modern industrial and commercial cities of the United States at the turn of the twentieth century, what Paul Laurence Dunbar described as a "tendency to colonise, a tendency encouraged, and in fact compelled, by circumstances" (*Heart of Happy Hollow*, 5). Not coincidentally, this expansion of new types of Jim Crow (or intensification of older practices of segregation) outside the South took place at almost exactly the same time as the emergence of both bohemia, and bohemian neighborhoods, in the United

States and something that might be called modernism in the arts. The 1913 Armory Show, for example, occurred in the same year that Woodrow Wilson greatly increased the segregation of federal employment. Because the black intelligentsia had often directly or indirectly benefited from government patronage during Republican administrations, Wilson's move had considerable impact, leading James Weldon Johnson, for instance, to leave the consular service. Bohemia did not escape the intensification of residential segregation and the growth of the new type of African American ghetto (a term that at the time was still almost entirely associated with Jews as seen in U.S. bohemian Hutchins Hapgood's classic 1902 account of the Lower East Side, *The Spirit of the Ghetto*). Indeed, bohemia was increasingly shaped by this segregation as the century wore on and it came to be more and more defined as a space of racial liminality in the segregation regime. Of course, this liminality was only relative, as a picture of a "black bohemia" appeared in literature by African American authors almost as soon as the idea of an "American" bohemia became plausible. However, one of the things that marked both bohemias, *especially* as seen in works by black writers, is how the attenuation or crossing of public boundaries defined the bohemian space (and the bohemian in the racialized space).

"Why Not Don My Spangled Jacket?": Paul Laurence Dunbar Looks at Bohemia

One of the earliest writers in the United States to represent the encounter of Americans with the older bohemia of Paris and London and among the very first to envision an indigenous bohemia in New York was Paul Laurence Dunbar. Echoing, perhaps, Henri Murger's claim that bohemia was possible only in Paris, those American-born writers before Dunbar who described the bohemian type (or types) in their fiction, such as Henry James in his 1878 novel *The Europeans*, generally portrayed it as either coming to the United States from Europe or being encountered by Americans abroad. Though Dunbar's take on bohemia was, as William Maxwell points out, a mixture of fascination and scorn, that stance has long been typical of representations of bohemia, not only by outsiders but also by countercultural insiders (Maxwell, 342–43).[6] That Dunbar's representations of an "American" bohemia essentially describe what James Weldon Johnson and others retrospectively entitled "Black Bohemia" suggests the centrality of African Americans to the development of what Dunbar, Johnson, and other black Nadir writers saw as a truly modern "American" art.

One of the peculiarities of bohemia, or at least artistic representations of bohemia, is the jaundiced eye that artists, even those associated with the scene they describe, frequently cast on the various bohemian countercultures. As Christine Stansell points out about recollections of early twentieth-century bohemian New York, many retrospective accounts of, say, Greenwich Village in the 1910s and the 1950s, fin de siècle Paris, North Beach and Venice Beach in the 1950s, Haight-Ashbury in the 1960s, and so on, are largely positive in a nostalgic sort of way. Or, if these recollections are not entirely upbeat, they often follow a trajectory that posits an authentic revolt against society resulting in a pure bohemian moment, which is subsequently subverted by external and internal pressures, most often deriving from official repression, materialism, careerism, consumerism, and tourism, but sometimes, too, from what are seen as false or sterile ideological and aesthetic temptations, say Stalinism or black nationalism.

However, it is remarkable how often more or less contemporary participants in various artistic countercultures represent bohemia as a sort of trap and, somewhat contradictorily, as a transitory phase, and how frequently the bohemian subject considers himself or herself and his or her peers with a sort of self-disgust, largely because of, as Michael Soto remarks, the parasitical relationship of bohemia to bourgeois society (96). The notion of bohemia as a stage in the life of the artist that will end in a pitiful decline and death (following the maxim that people who live on the edge sometimes fall off), undistinguished conformity, or counterbohemian stardom goes back to its earliest appearance on the stage and in literature in Henri Murger's *La Vie de la Bohème*. In perhaps the quintessential document of mid-twentieth-century bohemia in the United States, Jack Kerouac's *On the Road*, the literary counterculture holds a fascination for the narrator Sal Paradise that is tempered by a sort of repugnance not simply for the poseurs but also for the authentic hard-core bohemians. Part of the attraction of Dean Moriarty for Paradise is Moriarty's position both inside and outside the counterculture, a son of the West (Colorado, not California) whose yea-saying physicality is contrasted to the gloomy nay-saying intellectuals of Paradise's circles in Boulder and, especially, on the East and West Coasts (even if Moriarty soon becomes ensconced in the counterculture milieus of New York and San Francisco). One also frequently finds insider accounts of bohemia, say Jean Rhys's 1928 novel *Quartet*, that present the allegedly unconventional life of the artistic counterculture as allowing people, frequently white men, to behave badly, often brutally replicating hierarchies of race, class, and gender without the restraint of bourgeois niceties.

It is in this spirit that Dunbar's work skewers the poseurs, prisoners, and professionals of bohemia, both at home and abroad. As William Maxwell notes, Dunbar's first direct commentary on bohemia comes in a pair of poems in the 1899 *Lyrics of the Hearthside*, "The Bohemian" and "The Garret" — though, as Maxwell also suggests, they can be retrospectively connected to Dunbar's earlier poem, "The Dilettante: A Modern Type" in *Lyrics of Lowly Life* (where a rich family underwrites a would-be artist's vanities) (Maxwell, 342). In "The Bohemian," Dunbar comments scathingly on the quintessential bohemian move of making one's life a sort of artwork, in fact, substituting the bohemian persona or mask for actual work on page, stage, or easel:

> Bring me the livery of no other man.
> I am my own to robe me at my pleasure.
> Accepted rules to me disclose no treasure:
> What is the chief who shall my garments plan?
> No garb conventional but I'll attack it.
> (Come, why not don my spangled jacket?) (*Collected*, 92–93)

This aspect of self-fashioning, despite the speaker's protests otherwise, is manifestly not outside of fashion or social narrative but absolutely dependent on it. Dunbar develops this critique with a more extended treatment of bohemian types in his 1902 novel *The Sport of the Gods*. The first bohemian that the reader encounters in Dunbar's novel is the expatriate artist Francis Oakley. Oakley, a figure with the "face and brow of a poet, a pallid face framed in a mass of dark hair" (325), is not unlike the bohemian described in "The Dilettante." He is a painter from a southern planter family who devotes far more effort to his self-presentation in the Parisian counterculture than to actual painting:

> Francis's promise had never come to entire fulfillment. He was always trembling on the verge of a great success without quite plunging into it. Despite the joy which his presence gave his brother and sister-in-law, most of his time was spent abroad, where he could find just the atmosphere that suited his delicate, artistic nature. After a visit of two months he was about returning to Paris for a stay of five years. At last he was going to apply himself steadily and try to be less the dilettante. (325)

Francis Oakley is strangely mirrored by Skaggs, a white habitué of the Banner Club, a bastion of black bohemia in New York. As James Weldon Johnson would do later in *Autobiography of an Ex-Colored Man*, Dunbar makes the black bohemia of the Banner Club and the demimonde of black musicians, actors, vaudeville producers, artists, would-be intellectuals, journalists, pimps, drunks, grifters, voyeurs, and the wayward young more "bohemian" in the sense of *La Vie de la Bohème* than was the case of such actual landmarks of black bohemia as Marshall's Hotel, Ike Hines's 53rd Street bar, and John Nail's saloon, where the scene was considerably more refined in fashion and manner than Dunbar's description of the Banner Club:

> The Banner Club was an institution for the lower education of negro youth. It drew its pupils from every class of people and from every part of the country. It was composed of all sorts and conditions of men, educated and uneducated, dishonest and less so, of the good, the bad, and the— unexposed. Parasites came there to find victims, politicians for votes, reporters for news, and artists of all kinds for colour and inspiration. It was the place of assembly for a number of really bright men, who after days of hard and often unrewarded work came there and drank themselves drunk in each other's company, and when they were drunk talked of the eternal verities. (*Sport*, 372)

Skaggs might seem to be, and is in some senses, the opposite of Francis Oakley. He is a product of a poverty-stricken farm in Vermont and one of the professionals of bohemia, enmeshed in the marketplace of the new mass journalism epitomized by William Randolph Hearst's *New York Morning Journal*, one of the early bastions of "yellow journalism." Yet Skaggs passes himself off as the son of a southern planter family, "who played with little darkies ever since I could remember" (374). This disturbing statement from an adult white man in its claim of racial familiarity and transgression, like the stereotypical European bohemian pose of the actual plantation scion Francis Oakley, is seen in the novel as all too familiar, as "the same old story" (374).[7]

One might imagine Dunbar titling these two portraits of white bohemians "They Wear the Mask." In the case of Francis Oakley, his bohemian sojourn in Europe is dependent on the knowing and unknowing support of his planter family, the origin of whose money and position lies in the slave era and continues to rest in the postbellum, post-Reconstruction era on the subordinate labor of African Americans. As noted in the last chapter, it is Francis's theft of his brother's money, and Maurice's eventual coverup of the theft, that sends his own butler Berry Hamilton to prison and the rest of the Hamilton family to New York. Thus, one is reminded of the doubly parasitical nature of Oakley's bohemianism, in both cases ultimately relying on black labor (or hard labor, in the case of Hamilton's incarceration). One might add there is also a double masking in which Berry Hamilton is convicted because a "coon" persona that is completely at odds with his actual upwardly mobile, American individualist beliefs is superimposed on him. Hamilton remains in jail because Maurice, hiding the guilt of his brother (despite Francis's willingness to be revealed once he learns of Berry's incarceration), prefers to keep the mask lowered on Hamilton rather than expose his family as in some stereotyped manner "blacker" than Berry.

Skaggs's mask, too, relies on African Americans, both in the sense that his planter fantasy imagines a past life dependent on black labor, making an apparently easy and democratic association with African Americans in New York a sort of bohemian transgression, and in the sense that he actually makes a living writing "racy" stories about black bohemia and the black underworld of New York for the commercial press. Skaggs, the habitual liar who believes his own lies as he tells them, is a figure not unlike Henri Murger, who himself lived off of his accounts of bohemia for decades. So one of the things that Skaggs attempts to mask in his tales of a pseudoaristocratic southern upbringing is the familiar conjunction of bohemia and the bourgeois economic order, particularly the emerging popular culture industries of mass journalism, popular music, vaudeville, and the like in the urban centers of Europe and North America.

This conjunction can be seen as the universal condition of bohemia, both black and white. As Walter Benjamin famously said about the bohemian artist in Charles Baudelaire's early poetry, "Baudelaire knew what the true situation of the man of letters was: he goes to the marketplace as a flaneur, supposedly to take a look at it, but in reality to find a buyer" (*Charles Baudelaire*, 34). It is this aspect of the bohemian as a hack with visions of liberty and iconoclasm who nonetheless has an ironic sense of his poverty and dependence on the marketplace that Dunbar also addresses in his poem, "The Garret" from *Lyrics of the Hearthside*:

> Within a London garret high,
> Above the roofs and near the sky,
> My ill-rewarding pen I ply
>   To win me bread.
> This little chamber, six by four,
> Is castle, study, den, and more,—
> Altho' no carpet decks the floor,
>   Nor down, the bed. (*Collected*, 96)

Again, this ironic self-consciousness that is simultaneously a boast and indictment of a literally studied rebellion enmeshed in the bourgeois marketplace against which it ostensibly rebels is characteristic of the earliest representations of the bohemian type (or types) by American authors. To return once again to James's *The Europeans*, the sympathetically rendered young bohemian Felix Young makes a living producing poor but flattering portraits for the well-to-do and knocking off sketches for the mass-circulation press. When the reader first encounters Young, the artist rapidly produces two such sketches for a European illustrated newspaper, which is paying him fifty francs a piece, as he sits talking to his sister.

Such an enmeshment with the marketplace might be seen as particularly true of the early bohemians of the United States. As Gerald McFarland observes, an inordinately high percentage of the emerging bohemian community centered on the south side of Washington Square Park in Greenwich Village at the turn of the twentieth century labored in the popular culture industries, particularly journalism (169–72). The young Stephen Crane (not that he lived to be very old) wrote crime stories and sketches for the commercial press, including the *New York Morning Journal*, the *New York Herald* and the *New York Tribune*. Most notably for the purposes of this study, one such sketch, "Stephen Crane in Minetta," describing the largely African American demimonde of the interracial "black and tan" bars of the old black community of Minetta Lane and Minetta Place in the "Little Africa" of fin de siècle Greenwich Village, seems as if it could have issued from the pen of Dunbar's Skaggs. In fact, one is tempted to view the name of Dunbar's Sadness in *Sport of the Gods* as perhaps a pointed riff on the more sensationally named "Bloodthirsty" in Crane's piece (McFarland, 11–13).

It is worth recalling that, as scathing as Dunbar can be about bohemia in prose and fiction, his work, as William Maxwell says, frequently engages the "mythology of the modern artist calculated to manage jump-cuts between bourgeois exactness, doomed romantic love, picturesque artistic destitution, and the compulsive desublimation of the senses" (343). As Maxwell recalls, Dunbar had a firsthand encounter with London bohemia while on an extended 1897 visit (during which Dunbar did apparently live for a time in a garret). While in London, he made pilgrimages to such literary landmarks as the Cheshire Cheese and the Savage Club (the self-proclaimed, if somewhat well-heeled, "bohemian" gentlemen's club and site of one of Dunbar's most successful poetry readings during his often financially and emotionally chaotic trip) (Maxwell, 343–44; Cunningham, 161). Dunbar's picture of the bohemian "within a London garret high" resembles not only, as Maxwell suggests, the mirrored poet and caged bird of "Sympathy" but, in fact, Dunbar's composite semi-self-portrait of the poet drawn over and over in his poetry, especially the "literary English" poems (Maxwell, 344). Throughout this body of work one finds a picture of the poet-dreamer caught in the marketplace and filled with the alternately (or sometimes simultaneously) angered, ironic, satiric, and despairing sense that he has sold himself and will do so again. In short, Dunbar represents himself as a "true" bohemian along the lines of the visionary-hack (who contradictorily believes in "Art" as a sort of sacred vocation and as a commodity produced for the free market of the fallen world in which he lives) as opposed to the other bohemian type of the well-heeled dilettante.

And, in fact, episodes of Dunbar's life in various accounts sound like scenes from some popular travelogue of bohemia (albeit in New York and Washington rather than in Paris or London), such as the story of how Dunbar and Will Marion Cook worked on the musical *Clorindy; or, The Origin of the Cakewalk* in a basement apartment without a stove, consuming in one evening two dozen bottles of beer, a quart of whiskey, and steak eaten raw (Sotiropoulos, 86). Nonetheless, despite a shared entanglement with the market, this Dunbar as a black bohemian, or as someone who at least participated in black bohemia, stands in contrast to Skaggs. The hallmark, then, of the black bohemian, of whom the memorable character Sadness in *The Sport of the Gods* is perhaps the most extreme case (other than that of the poet himself) is a condition of restriction, of enclosure and entrapment, that differs from Francis Berry's (and even Skaggs's) freedom of movement outside the bohemian space. Skaggs may be using black bohemia to escape the poverty of his youth in Vermont, but he is not tied to it in the way that Sadness and the other denizens of the Banner Club are chained. As noted in the previous chapter, the grifter-dandy Sadness, like the poet (and perhaps the actual) persona of Dunbar, maintains a kind of ironic awareness about his status in bohemia as a masked flaneur restricted to a few square blocks of cityscape (or to the New New Grub Street of dialect poetry, which Dunbar claims in "The Poet" as the primary source of his professional success) as opposed to Skaggs, who moves in and out of black bohemia as pleasure and commerce demand, or to Francis Oakley, who roams the world on his family's money.

The Europeans and subsequent, if lesser known, novels by American writers that sought to capitalize on the huge popular success of British novelist George Du Maurier's 1894 gothic rendering of British artists in mid-nineteenth-century Paris, *Trilby*, depicted the encounter of Americans with European bohemia and European bohemians with the United States (Stansell, 11–12; Soto, 102–3). However, few, if any, attempted to set out a developed indigenous "American" bohemia before Dunbar's novel (which, too, may have been attempting to capitalize on the increased fascination with bohemia in the United States caused by the success of *Trilby* and Puccini's *La Bohème*). While the notion of a "black bohemia" as the first true "American" bohemia anchored (restricted even) to a particular quarter might seem surprising, the development of the black flaneur (zoot-suiter, hipster, b-boy, and so on according to the historical period) as the quintessential bohemian role model in the United States during the course of twentieth century makes Dunbar's novel seem prophetic.

Blacks in Bohemia, Black Bohemia, and the Rise of the New Poetry and the New Negro Renaissance: Fenton Johnson

When Harriet Monroe attempted to define the "new poetry" in *The New Poetry: An Anthology* (1917), she described a body of work that

> strives for a concrete and immediate realization of life; it would discard the theory, the abstraction, the remoteness, found in all classics not of the first order. It is less vague, less verbose, less eloquent, than most poetry of the Victorian period and much work of earlier periods. It has set before itself an ideal of absolute simplicity and sincerity — an ideal which implies an individual, unstereotyped diction; and an individual, unstereotyped rhythm. (vi)

She goes on to add that "great poetry has always been written in the language of contemporary speech, and its theme, even when legendary, has always borne a direct relation with contemporary thought, contemporary imaginative and spiritual life" (vi). African American culture and the work of black writers served as both a resource and a marker for the sort of "immediate realization of life" and "ideal of absolute simplicity and sincerity" to which Monroe refers, ironically in part because of the very stylized nature of the representation of black culture, speech, and bodies. It is also at this moment, particularly as African Americans began to interact with the largely "white" bohemian scenes of Chicago, New York, and Boston, that many of the key journals and institutions promoting the "new poetry" in the United States arose.

Chicago in particular was the site of many of the new literary institutions that would undergird modernist poetry in the United States. Again, these institutions were largely rooted in the bohemian communities and neighborhoods on the North Side, South Side, and in the Loop, particularly the Near North Side neighborhood known as Towertown and the South Side neighborhood of Jackson Park, at the turn of the century. As the twentieth century wore on, Towertown increasingly became the center of Chicago's bohemia. Chicago was where Harriet Monroe's *Poetry* magazine, Margaret Anderson's *The Little Review* (founded 1914), and an office of Alfred Kreymborg's *Others* (founded 1915) were based.

While organized political radicalism (e.g., radical feminism, anarchism, socialism, syndicalism, communism, and so on) was a defining characteristic of bohemianism in the United States (as opposed to Europe) in the early decades of the twentieth century, bohemianism in Chicago was particularly inflected by such organizations as the anarcho-syndicalist Industrial Workers of the World (IWW) or Wobblies, the Socialist Party (SP), and, eventually the Communist Party of the United States of America (CPUSA). The labor movement in Chicago had a long history of militant anarchist and socialist leadership reaching back into the nineteenth century. Both the IWW and CPUSA were largely founded in Chicago, and both, for a time, had their national headquarters there. The IWW was a particular presence in Chicago's North Side bohemia in the 1910s and 1920s. Chicago was the epicenter of huge union-organizing drives in the meatpacking and steel industries. Led by William Z. Foster, the former Wobbly who went on to become the long-time chair of the CPUSA, and other trade union radicals, these organizing campaigns recruited an unprecedented number of African American and immigrant workers into the labor movement, culminating in the Great Steel Strike of 1919 in which several hundred thousand striking workers paralyzed the steel industry. Though the strike was eventually crushed, the Chicago affiliate of the generally conservative American Federation of Labor (AFL), the Chicago Federation of Labor, remained a bastion of left-wing unionism until the middle 1920s.

These radical organizations varied in their approaches to African Americans and what became known as the "Negro Question." None of them at first really saw African Americans as a distinct group with its own history and culture in the way that the CPUSA would in the late 1920s with the rise of its "Black Belt Thesis" that posited African Americans in the rural South as a "nation" and in the urban centers as a "national minority." However, generally, if unevenly, all saw African Americans, particularly in the urban centers, as members of the working class — though the Socialists were often condescending, and even contemptuous, toward rural African Americans.

Race and racism were seen basically as divisive forms of false consciousness that needed to be and would be transcended with the advent of the new socialist or syndicalist workers' society. The IWW (and later the Communists) were notably opposed to any sort of Jim Crow labor arrangements, organizing black and white workers in the South as well as the North. In fact, the most stable East Coast IWW organization was that of the Philadelphia longshoreman led by the African American Ben Fletcher.

Given the presence of the Left, especially the IWW, in bohemian Chicago, it is not surprising that African Americans found bohemia a comparatively welcoming interracial space in a city increasingly segregated not only by restrictive housing covenants, redlining, and so on but also by acts of violence and intimidation ranging from the individual beating, burning, or bombing to mass assault (a phenomenon that stretched, at least, from the Chicago Riot of 1919 through the Cicero Riot of 1951 to the mobs threatening Martin Luther King Jr.'s Open Housing marches of 1966).

In the 1910s and 1920s, the epicenter of Chicago's bohemia shifted from the South Side to the Towertown neighborhood of the Near North Side, an area largely inhabited by migrant workers, transients, grifters, immigrants, artists, and political activists — with some residents combining several or all of the above categories. The center of this political and artistic floating world was Washington Square, a small park better known then as "Bughouse Square." Bughouse Square was the North Side's equivalent of New York's Union Square or the Speaker's Corner of London's Hyde Park, an open-air center of soap box orators speaking on a huge range of topics. While virtually every variety of cultural and political radicalism could be encountered in Bughouse Square, the Wobblies, whose national headquarters was not far away on West Madison Street, were the dominant group through the 1910s and much of the 1920s. Other Wobbly-inflected bohemian centers in Towertown included the Hobo College, run by the anarchist-impresario Ben Reitman (who was also the longtime manager and lover of anarchist and radical feminist icon Emma Goldman) and the Dil Pickle Club, a combination coffeehouse, nightclub, performance center, and lecture hall in which one might encounter a lecture on any subject or a performance of any style, media, or genre in which the generally raucous audience would play a considerable part.[8]

Again, one of the notable features of this politicized bohemia was its relatively integrated character. The radical racial egalitarianism of the IWW no doubt played a considerable role in this openness. Bughouse Square was not the center of African American street speaking in Chicago — that was, and would long be, Washington Park on the South Side. However, it was a place where black artists and political radicals interacted with their white counterparts, participating as both speakers and auditors. The longtime Communist activist (and one of the architects of the CPUSA and Comintern's "Black Belt Thesis") Harry Haywood recalled how he and other members of a loose group of black radicals would listen to black and white speakers in Bughouse Square and at the Dil Pickle Club. Hubert Harrison, a radical nationalist who had been a member of the IWW, the Socialist Party, and the Garveyite Universal Negro Improvement Association (UNIA) also spoke at Bughouse Square when he was in Chicago. Some of these speakers (and listeners), including Haywood and his brother Otto Hall, became involved with the socialist–black nationalist African Blood Brotherhood and, eventually, the CPUSA (Haywood, 130; Rosemont, introduction, 19).

The little magazines of Chicago promoting the "new poetry" interacted with this radical bohemia to varying degrees. Harriet Monroe and *Poetry* remained generally aloof from the more political side of bohemia—the journal would not embrace the literary Left in any consistent manner until the death of Monroe in 1936 and George Dillon's assumption of editorship in 1937. *The Little Review* and its editor Margaret Anderson were far more open to the prolabor, anarchist, and antiwar sentiments of the Wobbly-dominated North Side bohemia—though not, apparently, to the publication of black authors. Alfred Kreymborg's *Others* embraced the radical bohemias of the North Side and of Greenwich Village the most deeply. While Kreymborg remained based primarily on the East Coast, he frequently shuttled to Chicago and the Midwest for extended periods of time. His journal, too, shifted its editorial offices, but was based for a time on North Clark Street in Chicago (Churchill, *The Little Magazine Others*, 52–58).

While a distinct black bohemia appears not to have developed on the South Side to the degree that one would grow in Harlem (and, indeed, already had emerged on the Middle West Side of Manhattan), an interlocking network of African American artists, political activists, and journalists began to take shape, anticipating the far larger circles of black cultural and political radicals—and a much greater interaction between black and white artists and intellectuals—in Chicago during the 1930s. Organizations such as the Free Thought Society, the UNIA, and the African Blood Brotherhood, journals such as *Champion Magazine* and *Favorite Magazine*, and newspapers such as the *Chicago Defender*, which had perhaps the largest national audience of any black paper of the era, and the *Chicago Whip* provided spaces for this network. While the *Defender*'s ideological stance at that time could be described as liberal and race conscious, the *Whip* declared itself as resolutely radical, prolabor, "new Negro," and sympathetic to the Bolshevik Revolution (though strangely ambivalent about the Palmer Raids and the deportation of "anarchists").

The most noteworthy figure of these networks, at least as far as literature is concerned, is the poet and editor Fenton Johnson. Johnson operated in an extraordinarily complicated set of spheres. He was for a time the leading literary figure of the black South Side of Chicago, lionized by leading mainstream African American social and cultural institutions. As Lorenzo Thomas notes, Johnson also found his way into black nationalist and radical circles that grew out of the upsurge of Left and Pan-African activity during and immediately after World War I and the Bolshevik Revolution.[9] Johnson, too, was the first black writer of Chicago to attract significant attention in the new bohemian literary circles there and in New York. Johnson's generation of black writers and intellectuals and those from the subsequent age cohort, such as James Weldon Johnson and Sterling Brown, saw Johnson as both a herald of a black experimental or modernist poetry and a founder of the "new poetry" of the United States generally: "It is also a fact that Johnson belongs in that group of American poets who in the middle of the second decade of the century threw over the traditions of American poetry and became the makers of the 'new' poetry. He was among those writers whose work appeared in *Others* and in *Poetry: A Magazine of Verse*" (James Weldon Johnson, *Book of American Negro Poetry*, 1931, 141). While Johnson's white contemporaries generally did not assign to him the same importance as a progenitor of the "new poetry," some, such as Kenneth Rexroth and Alfred Kreymborg, did see Johnson as a visible part of Chicago's bohemia, giving to the bohemian spaces of the North Side a sense of racial liminality or permeability in defiance of the increasingly rigid northern-style Jim Crow regime in the city.

Johnson came from a family extraordinarily well connected in local business and politics on the South Side. His background is sometimes described as "middle-class," but such a characterization makes Johnson's family sound far more genteel (and less influential) than it actually was in many respects — though family members, especially his aunt Eudora, were certainly active in middle-class social and cultural networks and institutions of the black South Side. His uncle John "Mushmouth" Johnson made a fortune through his saloon and gambling house, his control of the numbers game on the black South Side, and his collection of protection money from black and Chinese gambling houses for the largely Irish-dominated crime syndicate that operated through the local Democratic Party organization. John Johnson was a key figure in the emerging network of often race-conscious black gamblers, entrepreneurs, and Democratic Party operatives in the Second and Third Wards of the South Side in which the new ghetto took shape during the 1910s. He also worked closely with the black city Republican councilman, and later congressman, Oscar De Priest. De Priest used his power to shield the black gamblers who were among the few sources of black-controlled capital on the South Side. Fenton Johnson's father, Elijah, was a partner in his brother John's gambling operation and became an important nightclub operator after John's death in 1907 (Haller, 723.).

Fenton Johnson's aunt (and the sister of John and Elijah) Eudora married the realtor and banker Jesse Binga. Binga, in part funded by the portion of John Johnson's estate that his wife inherited, was the leading black banker and entrepreneur of Chicago until the onset of the Great Depression and the failure of the Binga State Bank. When the Bingas moved into a previously all-white section of the South Side in 1919, their house was bombed several times, anticipating similar moments (as with the family of Lorraine Hansberry) where race-conscious black businessmen and professionals put themselves on the frontlines of what literally seemed a war to extend the boundaries of Bronzeville. One of Jesse Binga's partners in the Binga State Bank was Robert Abbott, who founded the *Chicago Defender* in 1905 (Thomas, 15–16; Haller, 723–24; Spear, 74–79). While Fenton Johnson lived much of his adult life in poverty, his family and business associates of his family helped fund the publication of his books and his various literary and journalistic projects until the onset of the Great Depression.

During the 1910s Fenton Johnson cut a large figure in black Chicago's arts and journalistic institutions. He contributed to the *Chicago Defender*, the first African American daily paper and eventually the preeminent African American newspaper of the twentieth century, circulating throughout black America. It frequently covered Johnson's activities in both its news pages and its gossip column, lauding Johnson as "a remarkable literary find" and "the noted poet" and declaring "his works entitle him to high rank among our great poets" ("Pleasant Sunday," 12; Cleveland G. Allen, "Fenton Johnson," 4).[10]

Some of Johnson's high profile was due to his family connection to Binga, Abbott, and the new interlocking network of black politicians, gamblers, and entrepreneurs on the South Side. He also took part in a network of middle-class black cultural, social, fraternal, and religious institutions as journalist, literary author, performer, and lecturer. His work was read and discussed at meetings of the Phyllis [*sic*] Wheatley Club, a prominent black women's club active in the social, intellectual, philanthropic, and political life of the South Side. Johnson himself performed (and his drama was staged) at the club's fundraising events. He presented his poetry at black churches on the South Side and in Harlem. His lyrics for "The Lost Summer" (dedicated by Johnson to Ernestine Schumann-Heink, the contralto and longtime star at the Metropolitan Opera in New York) were set to music by B. Consuelo Cook, a local art song composer, and sung at South Side community centers (Knupfer, 224, 228; "Fenton Johnson Triumphs," 5; "Fenton Johnson Makes Hit East," 4; "Phyllis Wheatley Club," 1; "Pleasant Sunday," 12).

Johnson also attempted to make a more direct mark on the cultural and intellectual infrastructure of the black South Side and beyond through the founding of a journal, *The Champion Magazine*, in September 1916. Perhaps because much of the funding of the magazine came from Jesse Binga (who took over the running of the journal from Johnson in the spring of 1917), *Champion Magazine* was not precisely radical, in either politics or aesthetics. Instead, it presented a race-conscious mixture of news, political commentary, reportage, arts and literary criticism, sports coverage, graphic art, poetry, and short stories—something like a cross between the *Chicago Defender* and *The Crisis* in New York. While most of its readers and contributors were in Chicago, Johnson sought with partial success to gain a national audience. For example, the black Boston critic, editor, and poet William Stanley Braithwaite wrote the journal a congratulatory letter that was published in its second issue. Johnson was also able to attract poems, stories, and articles from outside the region, by such writers as Alice Dunbar-Nelson, Benjamin Brawley, Georgia Douglas Johnson, Arthur Schomburg, Marcus Garvey, and Joseph Seamon Cotter.

Despite the early article by Garvey in the January 1917 issue, *Champion Magazine* was not militantly nationalist as such but promoted "the reconciliation of the races" as its "great mission" ("The Champion Magazine," 1). The journal also took a decidedly evenhanded stance in the ongoing debate about black education between Du Bois and the partisans of the recently deceased Booker T. Washington. Of course, in many respects Washington was a major influence on the development of twentieth-century African American nationalism and was much admired by Garvey himself. Even Johnson's notion of "reconciliation," a cause he would promote for the rest of the decade, did not involve the disappearance of race and African American cultural identity or the creation of an "American race" along the lines of Jean

Toomer, but instead advocated black pride, declaring that "THE CHAMPION MAGAZINE will do all in its power to impress upon the world that it is not a disgrace to be a Negro, but a privilege" ("The Champion Magazine," 1). As Lorenzo Thomas observes, perhaps through the influence of the journal's associate editor William Ferris (who would leave the magazine to become an editor of the UNIA's *Negro World*), *Champion Magazine* under Johnson's editorship not only published Garvey and other nationalist-influenced writers but also featured the Egyptian and Ethiopian visual iconography that was such a central feature of the more nationalist, Afrocentric side of the New Negro Renaissance (Thomas, 17–20).

For the most part, however, the literature published in *Champion Magazine*, including Johnson's stories and poetry, remained relatively conservative formally. The first issue, for example, featured a neo-Romantic poem of Johnson's in which the speaker pines for "Beatrice" in an iambic pentameter quatrain, declaring that despite the fact that a "vampire woman lived within her soul," "he longs to be with her adown the knoll" ("Beatrice," 37). Ironically in view of Johnson's later poetry (and William Stanley Braithwaite's central place in the promotion of Amy Lowell and the Imagists), the journal also hailed the establishment of Braithwaite's *The Poetry Review* by asserting:

> A certain group of American poets have great hope that this venture will be successful. This group feels that Mr. Braithwaite is not entirely in sympathy with the so-called "new poetry." Vers libre is at its best a poor substitute for emotion; its present vogue is similar to that of the pseudo historical novel at the opening of the twentieth century. A reaction will set in that will free poetry from everything that was extreme even before the imagists came into power. ("Braithwaite's 'Poetry Review,'" 12)

It is only midway through Johnson's short tenure as editor in December 1916 with the publication of one of his free verse "spirituals," "Swing Ajar the Gates of Heaven," that something like modernism or the "new poetry" enters the journal.

Johnson seems to have gone through a further aesthetic and political radicalization after his departure as editor of *Champion Magazine*. The precise motivation for this radicalization is not clear, though one of the causes might be the international and domestic growth of nationalist, anticolonialist, and Left activism as a result of World War I and the Bolshevik Revolution in 1917. The fact that Chicago was at the heart of militant, Left-led labor struggles in the meatpacking and steel industries involving (especially in the case of the meatpacking industry) tens of thousands of African Americans, might, too, have contributed to this sense of new possibilities.

Chicago was also the site of greatly intensifying segregation and racial violence (as attested by the multiple bombings of Jesse and Eudora Binga's house when they violated the housing color line), culminating in the massive race riot of 1919 — only one, albeit perhaps the most prominent, of many eruptions of antiblack mob violence during the "Red Summer" of 1919. Certainly, this sort of violence fostered the radicalization of many African American artists, intellectuals, and political activists. Whatever the precise cause or set of causes, while Johnson appears not to have had much to do with the *Whip*, perhaps out of loyalty to his family (which was more closely allied to Abbott and his competing *Defender*), there is considerable evidence that he was active in growing Left African American circles. Johnson was a speaker at the People's Education Forum of the Twenty-first Assembly District branch of the Socialist Party in Harlem, led by such black Harlem radicals as Hubert Harrison, Otto Huiswoud, W. A. Domingo, Grace Campbell, and Richard Moore — some of whom would be among the founders of the African Blood Brotherhood and the earliest black members of the CPUSA (Turner, 53–54).

As mentioned previously, Chicago, birthplace of *Poetry* and *The Little Review* and home of *Others* in 1917 and 1918, played an enormously important role in the gestation and circulation of the "new poetry" in the United States and was the site of a related bohemia rivaled only by New York's Greenwich Village in the early twentieth century. While quite a few black activists, musicians, actors, writers, and artists took part in Chicago's new bohemia, none had a higher profile than Johnson — and certainly none had the same visibility among the writers, editors, and journals of the "new poetry." It was this visibility that made Johnson's work the leading exemplar of black modernist verse among African American artists and intellectuals before the publication of Jean Toomer's *Cane* in 1923. Johnson, who, again, had made a considerable reputation in black cultural and political circles through his at times uneasy connections to a matrix of black entrepreneurs, numbers racket bankers, newspaper publishers, machine politicians (both Democratic and Republican), and radical black political and arts activists, began to successfully gain the attention of the predominantly white U.S. bohemia in the second half of the 1910s. In part, he was able to break through because of the interest shown him by William Stanley Braithwaite, who did so much to advance the "new poetry." Braithwaite was an early and appreciative reader of Johnson's *Champion Magazine* and, later, *Favorite Magazine*, promoting Johnson's poetry in both his criticism and anthologies.[11] However, equally important was Johnson's relationship to the journals *Poetry* and *Others* and their respective editors, Harriet Monroe and Alfred Kreymborg.

It was Fenton Johnson's poems modeled on spirituals that first made a mark beyond the black community, appearing in both *Poetry* and Braithwaite's influential annual *Anthology of American Verse*. Like James Weldon Johnson's poems that drew on the black sermon genre, Fenton Johnson's neospirituals, which were first collected in the 1915 *Visions of the Dusk*, can be seen as growing out of his earlier Dunbarian work, attempting to find a form and diction for a modern and distinctly African American poetry while negotiating the problems presented by popular culture representations of the black folk and their culture. While minstrel performances sometimes invoked or parodied the black performance of the spirituals, nonetheless versions of black sacred music had a life in U.S. high and popular culture outside minstrelsy and the popular stage. Versions of the spirituals or the "sorrow songs" had been widely circulated in North America and Europe since the success of the Fisk Jubilee Singers and their arrangements of the spirituals for the concert stage in the 1870s. Some black authors, such as James Weldon Johnson in *Autobiography of an Ex-Colored Man*, suggested that these songs, created by "black and unknown bards," were performed most authentically and most powerfully by black congregations in the rural South. Thus, Fenton Johnson's spirituals-based poetry can be seen as anticipating efforts by Langston Hughes, Waring Cuney, and Sterling Brown to use secular black music, particularly the blues, as the basis for a body of distinctly African American lyric poetry.

These poems can also be viewed as part of the modernist effort to create a closer relationship between poetry and song as a means of reinvigorating lyric poetry. As Lorenzo Thomas points out, the spare and precise rhythm, various types of sonic bonding (assonance, near-rhyme, anaphora [or blues-like repetition of lines with a certain amount of variation or "worrying"], but often not end-rhyme), diction, and imagery of Fenton Johnson's spirituals suggest or invoke vernacular language, rhythms, apostrophe, and rhyme without replicating them. Johnson's spirituals, such as "Song of the Whirlwind," might also be seen as close kin of (and perhaps an influence on) the intertwining of music and text in modernist poetry by Ezra Pound and Jean Toomer (Thomas, 33):

Oh, my soul is in the whirlwind,
I am dying in the valley,
Oh, my soul is in the whirlwind
And my bones are in the valley;
At her spinning wheel is Mary
Spinning raiment of the lilies,
On her knees is Martha honey
Shining bright the golden pavement,
All the ninety nine is waiting
For my coming, for my coming. (Fenton Johnson, *Visions of the Dusk*, 32)

Here Johnson seeks to create a distinctly "American" diction that is rooted in African American expressive culture but avoids the dualist Dunbarian split between "high" and "popular."

Though embracing much of the same approach to diction and syntax as in his "spirituals," Johnson's later and most self-consciously "modern" poetry incorporated and thematized this split within the body of single poems. Eugene Redmond has called Johnson a groundbreaking "poet of the blues," a perceptive sobriquet that allows the reader to see a line between Johnson's "The Scarlet Woman" and the blues poems from a woman's perspective, such as "Young Gal's Blues," in Langston Hughes's *Fine Clothes to the Jew* (1927). However, Johnson also plays with the images of minstrelsy and vaudeville, both black and white, unpacking the ambivalence of those images, most overtly in "Tired," first published in the January 1919 issue of *Others*.

The diction of the speaker of "Tired" is a colloquial American speech that is largely unmarked as to his race or regional origin. In those moments where the language is self-consciously "poetic" ("Pluck the stars out of the heavens. The stars mark our destiny. The stars marked my destiny. / I am tired of civilization" [James Weldon Johnson, *Book of American Negro Poetry* (1931), 145]), the speaker is also clearly mocking. This is not a stock "Zip Coon" figure humorously pretending to an intellectual, aesthetic, and linguistic prowess ridiculously beyond his "natural" place, but a bitter denial by the speaker that a broad white group capable of seeing him as more than a minstrel or vaudeville type, or a composite of such types, could exist. In fact, the poem primarily consists of a series of these types melded into a pair of composites: a drunken, happy-go-lucky, lazy, crapshooting man and an equally indigent gin-drinking, promiscuous woman, neither of whom cares to any great degree about their many children.

The unfolding of these stereotypes is set against the contrary images that they replace of a striving, hardworking, church-going nuclear family. The linked statement "I am tired of work; I am tired of building up somebody else's civilization" and the images that follow remind the reader that the speaker and his wife do two sorts of work. They (as their ancestors have done for generations) literally build up "someone else's civilization," providing much of the basic economic underpinning as well as much of what might be considered the familial infrastructure (e.g., the performing of basic domestic functions so that others are freed of those functions) through their labor without the sort of compensation or advancement (or even strengthening of the family and increase of opportunity for future generations) that is supposed to come from hard work in the United States. However, they also do symbolic work as their images build up the cultural and ideological infrastructure of the United States. The irony, one might say, is that, by not laboring, they do critical cultural work. And, like Bert Williams in his tramp role, Johnson as Johnson is not the speaker and is in fact working hard, recalling in a racialized modality Benjamin's comment about the flaneur and the marketplace.

Most accounts of Johnson's career suggest that he was crushed by poverty and the failure of his political and cultural efforts to create and sustain black journals that would simultaneously promote his notion of radical reconciliation between the races and black artistic and intellectual life. Lorenzo Thomas suggested that the virulently racist and antiradical spirit of the immediate post–World War I era intimidated, frustrated, and exhausted Johnson (Thomas, 40–44). This may well be true. But even in the 1920s, Johnson was apparently a significant participant in a comparatively integrated bohemian circle on the North Side. The poet Kenneth Rexroth recalled Johnson as a close friend and mentor who frequently read his poetry in the bohemian dive bar hotspot, the Green Mask, and served as a conduit through which such New Negro Renaissance figures as Langston Hughes, Claude McKay, and Countee Cullen found their way to the artistic circles of the North Side (Rexroth, 165–67).[12]

Before the 1920s, Johnson became something of an icon to the more politically radical bohemians of New York and Chicago. "Tired" and "The Scarlet Woman" are among several of Johnson's poems printed in *Others*, appearing to be a part of a group portrait of the new Chicago ghetto somewhat in the spirit of Masters's *A Spoon River Anthology* or a verse version of Anderson's *Winesburg, Ohio* (though formally more like the work of Carl Sandburg), anticipating later modernist or neomodernist collective portraits of black neighborhoods, such as Gwendolyn Brooks's 1945 *A Street in Bronzeville*,

Langston Hughes's 1951 *Montage of a Dream Deferred*, and Melvin Tolson's 1965 *Harlem Gallery*. In a 1918 poem published in *The Crisis*, "Red Chant," *Others* editor Alfred Kreymborg names Johnson and urges:

Let us go arm in arm down State Street
Let them cry, the easily horrified:
Gods of my fathers,
Look at the white man chumming with the black man! (31)

If this urging is, as Lorenzo Thomas argues, a not entirely effective response to "Tired," it still makes Johnson (and African Americans) a necessary constituency of radical bohemia. In fact, to a considerable extent it is the physical presence of Johnson on Kreymborg's arm, and presence of Johnson's poetry in Kreymborg's journal, that makes Kreymborg (and *Others*) truly radical (Thomas, 35). Kreymborg's poem also remarkably foreshadows, in perhaps a less homoerotic manner, a similar scene in Countee Cullen's "Tableau" several years later, where the "fair folk" are "Indignant that these two should dare / In unison to walk" (Cullen, *My Soul's High Song*, 86).

Johnson through his later work, then, became a figure of significance to both black and white avant gardists. To African American writers and critics of the New Negro Renaissance, he served not only as an early exemplar of black literary experimentalism (and, perhaps paradoxically to some, social realism) but also as a visible sign of African American participation in the making of early U.S. modernism, countering the persistent notion that the modernist avant garde was something that black writers joined after it was fully formed. For radical white bohemians such as Kreymborg and, later, Rexroth, the presence of Johnson himself in bohemian places and his work in bohemian literary spaces signified, in the increasingly rigid segregation of the urban North (especially Chicago), a racial liminality and even a permeability of racial divisions that became a hallmark of bohemia and the avant garde in the United States, though such liminality and permeability depended on the continued significance of race in defining self and community in the United States.

A Black Bohemian Critic in the Mainstream: William Stanley Braithwaite, the New Poetry, and the Negro Renaissance

The Boston in which William Stanley Braithwaite came of age at the end of the nineteenth century was in many respects a city in dramatic social and political transition. The last couple of decades of the century saw the increasing displacement from political dominance of the old-line Yankee "Brahmins" by the Irish. While this struggle was protracted, the election of the city's first Irish American mayor, Hugh O'Brien, in 1884 signaled the beginning of the end of Brahmin electoral power. Though the Brahmins were able to regain city hall after O'Brien's third term because of Irish factional disputes, by the turn of the century, the Irish were clearly in the ascendant. The 1914 election of James Curley (who would go on to dominate state politics) in a contest with another Irish American candidate marked the complete triumph of the Irish over their former adversaries — at least in the political arena of Boston. Irish Americans would continue to dominate the office of mayor until the election of Thomas Menino in 1993.[13]

The Brahmins retained strong connections to the abolitionist movement. Indeed, some of the older Brahmin leaders of the late nineteenth century, such as Thomas Wentworth Higginson, had been abolitionist leaders and proabolitionist officers in the Union Army, even, like Higginson, officers in black regiments. As has been seen, Robert Gould Shaw was a virtual Brahmin saint. As elsewhere in the United States, the Boston Irish were in general considerably less sympathetic to abolition, having long seen African Americans both as competition for jobs and as the embodiment of a social inferiority from which the Irish were trying to distinguish themselves. In some cases, Irish Americans in Boston not only opposed abolition but actively backed enforcement of the Fugitive Slave Act. Still, Irish mob violence toward African Americans in Boston was far less common in the nineteenth and early twentieth centuries than in New York City. There was also a significant, if minority, current of support for abolition and black civil rights among Boston's Irish, led most prominently by the Fenian editor of the *Boston Pilot*, John Boyle O'Reilly.

The postbellum Massachusetts Brahmins preferred not to use nativism and anti-Catholicism directly to attack their Irish opponents. Rather, they used "Good Government" and "Reform" as rallying cries against what they portrayed as the corruption and cronyism of Irish-dominated ward politics. Also, visions of abolition and the Union cause became Brahmin tools used to consolidate their political base — much as the antebellum Know-Nothing movement in Boston had used Irish support of the Fugitive Slave Act. Thus, the commemoration of the Saint-Gaudens memorial to Shaw and the Fifty-fourth Massachusetts Regiment can be seen as a sort of Brahmin political rally. Similarly, Yankee-dominated Boston districts elected a number of black candidates to office in the 1880s, not only reflecting sympathy for African Americans in the South as Reconstruction faded but invoking the abolitionist and Unionist spirit in the struggle for the maintenance of Brahmin political power. In return, Boston Irish political antagonism to the legacy of abolition was less rooted in visceral antiblack sentiments (unlike the case in Boston later in the twentieth century) than that legacy's association with the Brahmins.

Though by the turn of the century Brahmin political power was in decline, the Brahmin elite maintained (and even now still maintains) much influence over the most important cultural, educational, and journalistic institutions of Boston, including what William Stanley Braithwaite called the leading "literary" paper, the *Evening Transcript* (Braithwaite Oral History, 15).[14] While it would certainly be an exaggeration to say that the Brahmins and the institutions they dominated took an egalitarian stance toward the average African American, especially those actually living in Boston and Cambridge, there was an openness to individual African Americans that allowed them opportunities seldom found in other northern cities, even New York — and not only for those from the small black elite but also for ambitious intellectuals such as Du Bois or Braithwaite who came from modest means, if not outright poverty. This is not to say that they did not encounter much racism, as when Harvard refused to allow Du Bois to stay in a dormitory during his graduate education or when the treasurer of the Boston Authors Club attempted to discourage membership for Braithwaite, who was nominated by Thomas Wentworth Higginson.[15] And Boston, along with the rest of the urban North, became increasingly segregated racially as the center of the African American community moved from the relatively multiracial and polyglot West End and the North Slope of Beacon Hill (then more or less one neighborhood) to the South End and Lower Roxbury, beginning at about the turn of the century — with the city becoming known as one of the most rigidly segregated Eastern cities by the later twentieth century.

Though other cities, especially New York and, later, Chicago, increasingly challenged Boston's status as the literary capital of the United States, Boston publishing houses, journals, newspapers (especially the *Transcript*), colleges and universities, editors, and critics still exerted an inordinate influence over U.S. letters in the fin de siècle. As in Chicago and New York, if not to the same extent, the end of the nineteenth and the beginning of the twentieth century saw the growth of a bohemian artistic community, often with significant, if uneasy, connections to the Brahmin cultural establishment. As in New York's Greenwich Village, the largest bohemian cluster gathered in a neighborhood that had long been a center of black life in Boston, the North Slope of Beacon Hill around Pinckney and Joy Streets (Shand-Tucci,

24–33). Though black families were relocating to the South End and Lower Roxbury, a considerable African American population and such important institutions as the Charles Street AME Church remained well into the twentieth century. To a large extent, it is the combination of Boston's surviving turn-of-the-century abolition legacy, its status as an (if not the) intellectual "hub" of the United States, and a still considerable cultural infrastructure with a national reach that allowed Braithwaite to become one of the chief arbiters of U.S. poetry and the "poetry renaissance" by the second decade of the twentieth century.

Braithwaite was born in 1878 and raised in what is now the Bay Village/ South Bay section of Boston, an area that was constructed on similar lines to the more elite sections of Beacon Hill but chiefly inhabited by people of much more modest means, many of them artisans. The neighborhood, now greatly changed by construction of the Massachusetts Turnpike and various urban renewal projects, lay between downtown Boston and the South End, increasingly the center of the black community in Boston as well as an early bohemian hub. In those days before the construction of the turnpike, the neighborhood was far less separate from the South End than it is today — though apparently the overwhelming majority of Braithwaite's neighbors during his childhood were white.

Braithwaite's father, an immigrant from British Guiana (and the scion of influential "colored" families scattered across the British Caribbean), was a man of strange contrasts. He had received medical training as a doctor in Britain, but left before he finished his course of studies and gained certification, working as a nurse in Boston. He remained a British subject and in many respects a complete Anglophile and yet spoke on programs with John Boyle O'Reilly, the Irish nationalist and prominent supporter of African American civil rights. Despite wide social contacts in Boston, he was paranoid about the association of his children with others in the neighborhood, home schooling them until his early death when William Stanley Braithwaite was seven (Braithwaite, "House under Arcturus," 121–36). William Stanley Braithwaite's mother, a severe woman born in Boston of parents from North Carolina, also maintained a genteel demeanor despite the family's often-dire financial straits. (Interestingly, a couple of his mother's sisters became well-known performers, the DeWolfe Sisters, in the popular black musical theater of the 1890s.)

In childhood, Braithwaite gravitated toward "Newspaper Row" on nearby Washington Street, where nearly all of the then numerous newspapers of Boston were located (and the home of yet another bohemian nexus), and worked as a paperboy. Because of his family's financial problems, Braithwaite left school at twelve and a half, working in a series of menial jobs, chiefly as a stock boy or errand boy (Braithwaite, "House under Arcturus, Second Installment," 128–36; Braithwaite Oral History, 1). After a sojourn with his family in Newport, Rhode Island, where he worked as a "brush boy" in a barbershop catering to some of the richest men in the United States, Braithwaite returned to Boston.

A friendly superintendent at Ginn and Company, a children's and textbook publisher where he found a job in the typesetting composition room, encouraged Braithwaite to read during slack periods, developing his interest in literature, particularly works by Keats and other Romantic poets. Coming across Keats's "Ode on a Grecian Urn" in a volume he was typesetting gave Braithwaite an epiphany of the sacred vocation of the poet (Braithwaite, "House under Arcturus, Part III," 257–59; Szefel, "Beauty and William Braithwaite," 562). From this point on, not unlike Paul Laurence Dunbar's, Braithwaite's development as an intellectual and writer was essentially the autodidact's.

Braithwaite's early career as a neo-Romantic poet was filled with rejections from many magazines. He found more success when he proposed an article surveying magazine verse to the editors of the *Boston Evening Transcript* in 1905. Though the editors were dubious about the value of such poetry, they agreed, launching Braithwaite's career as a freelance critic for the *Transcript* that would last for many years (Braithwaite Oral History, 7–17). As Lorenzo Thomas, Lisa Szefel, Kenny Williams, and others have recalled, it was this position as critic at the *Transcript* and, later, editor of many anthologies, especially the annual *Anthology of Magazine Verse* beginning in 1914, that allowed Braithwaite to champion the "poetry renaissance" and promote the careers of such early modernists as E. A. Robinson, Vachel Lindsay, Edna St. Vincent Millay, Robert Frost, and Amy Lowell and the Imagists. He was especially close to Robinson. In this capacity, Braithwaite was quite possibly the most influential newspaper critic of poetry in the United States, maybe the most powerful critic of poetry in a U.S. newspaper ever. Many poets, black and white, felt that a favorable column in the *Transcript* or an appearance in one of the annual anthologies was an enormous aid in making a literary career.[16] Certainly Frost's career received a tremendous boost from Braithwaite, though Frost would not hesitate to use racial slurs in describing Braithwaite when he (and Ezra Pound) sided with Harriet Monroe and *Poetry* in a dispute over who would be the chief doyen(ne) of the "new poetry" upsurge.[17] Beyond the influence Braithwaite exercised through his position as critic and editor, he also worked closely with poets on their manuscripts, making practical suggestions to such writers as Robinson, Sara Teasdale, and James Weldon Johnson.

Again, what made it possible for Braithwaite to gain this sort of authority, in addition to his drive and critical intelligence, were the peculiarities of Boston, in which the Brahmin leaders of the literary, cultural, journalistic, financial, and (to some diminishing degree) political institutions of the city maintained a strong connection to the abolitionist and Reconstruction legacy. Friendships (or at least friendly acquaintanceships) with Thomas Wentworth Higginson, Julia Ward Howe, and other Brahmin cultural leaders gave Braithwaite access to the *Transcript*, the Boston Authors Club (whose members included much of the Brahmin intellectual elite, such as its founder Higginson, Howe, Thomas Aldrich, and Bliss Perry), and other important literary and cultural institutions—which, in turn, provided him entrée to similar organizations and circles outside of Boston. Despite the fact that Fenton Johnson had far more formal education than did Braithwaite (including a year at Columbia University's School of Journalism), it is hard to imagine him being hired for a post at a non-African American paper in Chicago equivalent to Braithwaite's at the *Transcript*. While the members of the Authors Club were largely conservative aesthetically, if often comparatively liberal in matters of race, there was a considerable radical Brahmin streak in the Beacon Hill bohemia to which Braithwaite also attached himself.[18] Though Braithwaite has rarely, if ever, been described as a bohemian, it is telling that one of the chief pillars of New England bohemia, Bliss Carman (the "vagabond poet" who is now better known as a poet of his birth country, Canada) was the godfather of Braithwaite's daughter (Shand-Tucci, 39). Certainly, Braithwaite published many of the leading East Coast bohemians, such as Carman, Millay, Lowell, Kreymborg, and Maxwell Bodenheim (who began his career in Chicago but was a very visible bohemian fixture in New York for many years).

However, despite the relatively integrated (though largely white) circles through which Braithwaite's professional life moved for the most part until he joined the faculty of Atlanta University in 1935, he also did much to promote the writing that would underpin the other U.S. literary "renaissance" of the early twentieth century, the New Negro Renaissance. He was one of the original staff members of *The Crisis* in 1910, assisting W. E. B. Du Bois in the founding of the journal that would be a major vehicle of the later renaissance. As Michael Soto points out, he was among the first (in fact, perhaps the first) to promote the idea of a "Negro Renaissance" in the pages of a

1901 issue of *The Colored American* (79–80). Braithwaite expressed ambivalence, however, about the actual New Negro Renaissance in the later 1920s. Much as Wallace Thurman argued in *Infants of the Spring*, he saw anything smacking of the relegation of literature by African Americans to the status of "social experiment" as a form of racist dismissal and second-class citizenship (Braithwaite Oral History, 82–85).[19]

Nonetheless, Braithwaite significantly advanced the careers of key players whose writing and editorial work announced the existence of a new sort of black literary movement. He was a close friend and mentor of James Weldon Johnson, reading and commenting on Johnson's manuscripts, praising his poetry in his *Transcript* column, and including Johnson's work in the *Anthology of Magazine Verse*, beginning in 1915. Despite Jean Wagner's unsupported claim that he was trying to hide his identity as an African American, Braithwaite attempted to put together an anthology of African American writing from at least as early as the first years of the twentieth century (128). As late as 1919 Braithwaite was still discussing the possibility of publishing such an anthology — though he was never able to secure the financial backing for it.[20] His friend Johnson was inspired to bring out such a volume a few years later, *The Book of American Negro Poetry* (1922), in which Johnson paid deep tribute to Braithwaite, saying that "no future study of American poetry of this age can be made without reference to Braithwaite" and his efforts as a "friend of poetry and poets" (James Weldon Johnson, *Book of American Negro Poetry*, 43). The 1922 edition of Johnson's anthology, more than any other single volume, announced a new moment in modern black literature; and the 1931 edition did much to codify that moment.

There have been claims that Braithwaite was skeptical about poetry too overtly "racial" in form and theme during the Harlem Renaissance, but evidence suggests that in Johnson's case at least Braithwaite was an enthusiastic reader of the early versions of Johnson's poetry based on the black sermon tradition later collected as *God's Trombones* (Letter from James Weldon Johnson to William Stanley Braithwaite, January 15, 1919, William Stanley Braithwaite Papers).[21] So if, as Jervis Anderson suggested some time ago, Johnson was a "midwife" of the Harlem Renaissance, then Braithwaite was a midwife of the midwife who helped transform the former diplomat, journalist, and song lyricist into a major literary figure. As noted earlier, Braithwaite also strongly supported the poetry and journal projects of Fenton Johnson, praising Johnson's work in his newspaper columns and in journal essays, and including Johnson's poetry in the *Anthology of Magazine Verse*.

He also published the work of Georgia Douglas Johnson in his 1917 anthology and promoted her poetry in his column, again serving as a midwife of a New Negro Renaissance literary midwife. He wrote the introduction to her 1918 *The Heart of a Woman* (and included it in the listing of the most important volumes of poetry of the year in the annual anthology). In the years immediately after World War I, Johnson was at the center of a salon of black writers, including Jean Toomer and on occasion Alain Locke, that was the anchor of the New Negro Renaissance in Washington through the 1920s and an important incubator of Toomer's writing.[22] Braithwaite also was among the earliest editors to print the work of Jessie Fauset, soon to become the literary editor of *The Crisis* (and yet another midwife of the New Negro Renaissance), in the 1918 anthology — the same volume in which he printed Fenton Johnson's "The Lost Love" and criticized Vachel Lindsay's "The Congo" for completely misunderstanding "Negro" culture and sensibilities). Finally, Braithwaite was an early supporter of the work of Claude McKay and Countee Cullen, whose early poetry (especially that of McKay) came to be seen by a broad reading public as announcing a black poetry revival or renaissance.[23] It is also worth noting that Braithwaite's prominence as critic and his role in promoting the U.S. "poetry revival" was a matter for great pride among many in the black intelligentsia and in the African American press.[24]

Black writers of the Nadir, then, were far more important to the shaping and reception of an "American" bohemia and artistic avant garde than has been generally acknowledged. African American writers, particularly Dunbar and James Weldon Johnson, were among the very first to represent such a bohemia in their poetry and fiction. At the same time these writers, along with Fenton Johnson, also depicted a "black bohemia" that intersected with the predominantly white bohemian communities, but that, nonetheless, remained a distinct formation. In the work of these writers, these bohemias were linked to particular geographic spaces and in various ways were related to the hyperracialized urban geography of the United States in the early twentieth century.

Also, the participation of African Americans in the institutions of the new literary avant garde, whether, like James Weldon Johnson and Fenton Johnson, as poets and fiction writers or, like William Stanley Braithwaite, as editors and critics, not only helped build the infrastructure of the new avant garde and the emerging bohemias but also began to establish bohemia in the United States as a place where the relatively porous nature of racial boundaries became a defining feature — a feature of bohemia and the artistic avant garde that remains largely intact a century later. At the same time, the invention and persistence of both the idea and actual existence of a black bohemia, standing in uneasy and sometimes hostile relationship with the African American community, "mainstream" U.S. society, and even the predominantly white bohemia, created a new cycle of migration and circulation in African American literature, as members of bohemia are represented as yo-yoing between these various locations within a particular city or region as well as between the stops on the North-South axis established by the migration narrative.

chapter five

A Familiar and Warm Relationship

Race, Sexual Freedom, and U.S. Literary Modernism

One of the problems in discussing an "American" modernism or avant-garde before the 1920s is the confusion about whether one is talking about art and artistic circles within the United States or whether one includes such expatriates as Henry James, T. S. Eliot, Gertrude Stein, and Ezra Pound. While it certainly makes sense to include the expatriates, doing so without some attention to their geographic location has given rise to distorted notions about modernism and U.S. bohemia, creating a vision of modernism centered in the United States that is far more apolitical (or even politically conservative), racist, anti-Semitic, masculinist (and actually misogynist) than was actually the case. This distortion has been only partly corrected by more recent scholarship on feminist modernism (and modernist feminism) and the "Lyrical Left" of Greenwich Village and Towertown during the first two decades of the twentieth century by such scholars as Christine Stansell, Suzanne Churchill, and Franklin Rosemont—but only Rosemont really recognizes the contributions of African Americans to that Left milieu.

Again, one thing that distinguished early bohemia in the United States from its western European counterparts by and large was the degree to which it was connected to organized political radicalism (e.g., the Socialist Party, the IWW, the early Communist parties [the Communist Labor Party and the Communist Party of America], and smaller Marxist and anarchist groups). Radical political figures, such as Big Bill Haywood, Emma Goldman, Carlo Tresca, Lucy Parsons, and Elizabeth Gurley Flynn, were familiar participants in the bohemian communities of Chicago's Towertown and New York's Greenwich Village. The bohemias of London and Paris before the rise of Dada and ensuing engagement of surrealism and expressionism with Communism and/or Trotskyism were far less engaged with organized radical politics.

U.S. bohemia was also marked by the way feminism and various struggles for sexual freedom were woven into its fabric. Obviously, U.S. feminism in the late nineteenth and early twentieth centuries reached far beyond the emerging boundaries of bohemia. The ratification of the Nineteenth Amend-

ment in 1920 demonstrates that in many respects it was a mainstream movement. The notion of a "New Woman" who redefined the economic, political, intellectual, psychological, physical, and sexual horizons of women (and
men) was not restricted to bohemia and other sorts of radical enclaves but
circulated widely through U.S. society. And, as Judith Schwarz notes about
Hutchins Hapgood and other heterosexual male bohemians, sometimes men
in Greenwich Village, Towertown, and other countercultural centers valued
the erotic access that "free love" allowed them while rejecting the notion of
equal rights for women (Judith Schwarz, 81–82). Still, bohemia with its overlapping worlds of political and cultural radicalism in the United States was
to a large extent the home soil of radical feminist activists and organizations
promoting sexual freedom, often under the cry of "free love," and the idea of
women as sexual agents and sexual citizens, both heterosexual and lesbian,
as important political issues. This agency was seen as issuing primarily from
the desires and actions of women under the mentorship or in the company
of other women rather than the tutelage of a virile and erotic man along the
lines of D. H. Lawrence's *Lady Chatterley's Lover* (1928).

A significant aspect of both the bohemian conception of free love, to the
extent that one can speak of it as a unified idea, and the promotion of contra-
ception was the decoupling of women's sexuality from procreation and the
legally sanctioned nuclear family. Once women were acknowledged as sexual
agents not necessarily bound to family and procreation, then lesbianism
(and, by extension, male homosexuality) could be seen as a legitimate subset
of sexual freedom — though even in such relatively radical feminist groups
as the Greenwich Village–based Heterodoxy, the identification of members
as lesbians remained publicly submerged, if common on a more internal or
informal level, particularly after the 1910s (Judith Schwarz, 85–93).

These struggles had a particular significance and inflection for African
Americans. After all, much of the power of the argument for Jim Crow segregation, particularly in popular culture, turned on the question of sexuality,
both male and female. The archetypal justification for the wave of lynching and mob violence that accompanied and helped enforce the rise of Jim
Crow was the alleged violation of "white womanhood" by black men. The
second wave of Jim Crow that saw the beginnings of the urban ghetto in the
United States during the first two decades of the twentieth century prominently featured the enactment of "antimiscegenation" laws prohibiting consensual sexual or marital relationships across the color line. These laws owed
much of their motivation to the popular culture image of the 1912 marriage
of the boxer Jack Johnson to Lucille Cameron, a young white woman from

Minnesota whom he had previously been accused of abducting (Gilmore, 30–34). The passage of such legislation was seen as a major civil rights issue by black activists as the laws marked black men as sexual aggressors and black women as sexually depraved.[1]

An increasing number of scholars, including George Chauncey, Kevin Mumford, and Siobhan Somerville, have made the Foucaultian observation that this hardening and policing of racial boundaries took place at the same time that the boundaries of heterosexual and homosexual were being drawn and aggressively defended, producing homosexuality as a coherent identity (or set of identities) and forging the beginnings of modern gay and lesbian communities. As these scholars in particular have also claimed, this syn-chronicity was not random but was closely intermeshed. During the first three decades of the twentieth century, it was precisely around these issues of sexual coercion and sexual freedom and of the making of gay and lesbian, and queer if you will, Americans that most closely connected bohemia black and white and the new African American ghettos, ultimately providing much of the seedbed for the New Negro Renaissance, especially in Harlem.

Much as the peculiar location of African Americans in law and culture during the Nadir led black writers to be among the first in the United States to take up what would be the modernist (and postmodernist) staple of the divided or fragmented subject, so, too, did that location and its linkage to sexuality push African American authors to take up the issues and tropes of sexual coercion and sexual freedom. Of course, the racist identification of African American women (in both antebellum and postbellum eras) and men (especially in the postbellum period) with sexual abandon and vari-ous forms of sexual deviance (including cross-racial desire) placed tremen-dous pressure on black authors to at least acknowledge the desirability of normative heterosexual monogamous intraracial relationships resulting in stable marriage. Still, one characteristic of African American literature, par-ticularly the novel, in the late nineteenth and early twentieth centuries is the frequency with which consensual interracial romantic or sexual rela-tionships occur. It is true that racial solidarity is often ultimately upheld over racial "crossing," even willing "crossing," in this literature. And some could be considered only semiconsensual in that only one partner, gener-ally the "black" partner, is aware of the "cross"—though there is usually some moment of racial revelation in these texts. Still, this sort of transgres-sive heterosexual pairing anticipates the remarkable number of times openly homosexual figures, not to mention homoerotic and homosocial (and, again, often interracial) pairings, appear in Harlem Renaissance literature.

The Birth of Tragedy: The Mixed-Race Figure
and Sexual Freedom and Sexual Coercion

It has been more than two decades since Hazel Carby in her landmark book on early African American women novelists, *Reconstructing Womanhood* (1987), made a case for a more complicated view of the mixed-race figure in African American fiction than the then (and, even to some extent, now) dominant one that saw the so-called mulatto as a trope aimed at a white audience and, even, an embodiment of surrender to white notions of beauty and femininity:

> I would argue that historically the mulatto, as narrative figure, has two primary functions: as a vehicle for an exploration of the relationship between the races and, at the same time, an expression of the relationship between the races. The figure of the mulatto should be understood and analyzed as a narrative device of mediation. After the failure of Reconstruction, social conventions dictated an increasing and more absolute distance between black and white as institutionalized in the Jim Crow laws. In response, the mulatto figure in literature became a more frequently used literary convention for an exploration and expression of what was socially proscribed. (89)

Racially mixed figures had been a feature of black and white U.S. literature for some considerable time, from the African-European "cross" of Cora Munro, perhaps the original "tragic mulatto," in James Fenimore Cooper's *Last of the Mohicans* (1826) and the crossings of "Negro" and "white" in the nineteenth-century narratives of such black authors as William Wells Brown, Frederick Douglass, Harriet Jacobs, and Harriet Wilson on. The mixed-race figure in antebellum black literature served multiple ideological and aesthetic purposes, pointing up, among other things the ways in which southern slavery (and, to paraphrase Harriet Wilson, its shadow in the North) destroyed "natural" family bonds and family feeling among slaves and slaveholders alike—though, as in Harriet Jacobs's autobiography *Incidents in the Life of a Slave Girl* (written under the pseudonym of Linda Brent), the mixed-race figure often is deployed to argue that African Americans are in fact the true conservators of family and family values under the slave regime. After all, in Jacobs's narrative, slavery has so depraved Mr. Flint and deprived him of natural family sentiments that he proposes to move Linda/Harriet into the nursery of his infant child so as to make her more accessible to his sexual predations. Ironically, then, Linda/Harriet's efforts to evade Mr. Flint's attempt preserve not only her agency and at least her impulse toward womanly virtue (even if that virtue as represented in sentimental literature was not possible under Jacobs's portrait of the slave system) but also some measure of propriety within the Flint family.

Black writers also took up the mixed-race figure to illustrate the arbitrariness of racial distinctions in the United States that undergirded the caste nature of the slave system. African American authors often contested white writers' deployment of the trope to embody either tragic or villainous results of cultural mixing across various racial divides, again starting with Cooper's Leatherstocking novels. For black authors, the tragedy arose outside of, not within, the mixed-race body and psyche, and villainy is practiced on, not practiced by, mixed-race characters.

As Carby observes, there was an increased use of the mixed-race figure by African American writers as Reconstruction failed and Jim Crow arose at the end of the nineteenth century and the beginning of the twentieth. As she says, the mixed-race figure was a vehicle for expressing and exploring what was socially proscribed. One might also see the trope as challenging what was proscribed sexually in terms of the limitations of the choices of the black subject and of the notion of women, black and white, as sexual beings. These characters are very often the offspring of consensual relationships, even marriage, between black and white parents. Or perhaps it is more accurate to say that a range of interracial relationships, consensual, semicoercive, and coercive, are represented in many of these narratives—with women's sexual desire and sexual agency as prominent features.

As quite a few scholars have discussed, stereotypes of black women as antifeminine, lacking in beauty, "natural" maternal instincts, and sexual restraint, permeated both "high" and popular culture in the United States during the nineteenth and twentieth centuries (Carby, 20–39; Tate, 23–26). Again, the problem for African American writers was not that black women needed somehow to be written into the republic of letters (and U.S. culture generally) because representations of them were practically everywhere in "high" and popular culture. Instead, the difficulty was to challenge, or at least evade, these representations.

The mixed-race character provided African American writers an opportunity to engage the contradictions of these stereotypes. In antebellum black literature, the origins of the tragedy of the figure of the mixed-race woman lay not, as was often the case in the use of the mixed-race figure by white authors, in her "cross" as such but in the fact that she was perceived by white (and, often, black) men and women as beautiful and sexually abandoned while being absolutely beholden to those who owned her. At the same time, she called into question and destabilized the boundaries between the paired categories of black and white, beautiful and ugly, sexual virtue and sexual abandonment, and so on. For example, in Harriet Wilson's *Our Nig*, Mrs. Bellmont literally attempts to blacken her mixed-race servant (and virtual slave) Frado through exposure to the sun so as to avoid any comparison of complexion between Frado and Mrs. Bellmont's daughter Mary — just as Mrs. Bellmont and Mary "blacken" Frado's name by calling her "Nig."

Some of these representations, in which slavery makes the pursuit of a "virtuous" life impossible for black women, graphically demonstrate the fundamental immorality of the slave system and its special horrors for slave women. But they also provide a space in which sexual agency and sexual desire might be expressed in contravention of the reigning models of domesticity and female propriety. As such astute commentators as Carby and William Andrews have long argued, Jacobs's *Incidents in the Life of a Slave Girl* is among the most remarkable nineteenth-century U.S. texts in that respect (Andrews, *To Tell a Free Story*, 251–52; Carby, 58–59). Much of Jacobs's narrative describes the efforts of Linda/Harriet to avoid the sexual aggression of her master, Mr. Flint. In the narrative, Linda/Harriet is able to ward off Mr. Flint's advances. In this, as has often been remarked by scholars, Jacobs hews closely to the line of sentimental literature. However, as Carby, Andrews, and others have also pointed out, there is an obvious departure from the sentimental genre in the description of Linda/Harriet's relationship with Mr. Sands, a nearby "white unmarried gentleman," which results in the birth of two children:

> Of course I saw whither all this was tending. I knew the impassable gulf between us; but to be an object of interest to a man who is not married, and who is not her master, is agreeable to the pride and feelings of a slave, if her miserable situation has left her any pride or sentiment. It seems less degrading to give one's self, than to submit to compulsion. There is something akin to freedom in having a lover who has no control over you, except that which he gains by kindness and attachment. A master may treat you as rudely as he pleases, and you dare not speak; moreover, the wrong does not seem so great with an unmarried man, as with one who has a wife to be made unhappy. There may be sophistry in all this; but the condition of a slave confuses all principles of morality, and, in fact, renders the practice of them impossible. (Jacobs, 84–85)

Undoubtedly, as William Andrews argues (and Jacobs herself asserts, speaking of "revenge and calculations of interest"), elements of extrasexual self-interest and of sociopolitical struggle against the slave system are significant parts of Linda/Harriet's affair with Mr. Sands (*To Tell a Free Story*, 252). One noteworthy aspect of the slave narrative (and, indeed, much abolitionist literature) is the way it necessarily anticipated the second-wave feminist slogan that the "personal is political," given that the most intimate details of African American personal life were regulated by the laws supporting chattel slavery. Still, it is worth remarking that, according to Jacobs, such feelings of revenge and calculation enter into the equation only after the beginnings of the affair with Mr. Sands when Linda/Harriet discovers that Mr. Flint is building a secluded cottage for her outside of town so as to further his sexual campaign against her. Her initial sentiments have more to do with being desired without compulsion and with her own desire (choosing "to give one's self"). While these initial sentiments, as well as later considerations of self-interest and revenge on Mr. Flint, are framed and hedged with apologies for her "immoral" behavior and indictments of the immorality of slavery that urges both black and white to such behavior, there is no sense that Linda/Harriet is a "ruined" woman after the manner of sentimental literature, despite Jacobs's use and, indeed, acknowledgment of the conventions of that literary genre. It is hard to take her comment about "sophistry" seriously, but to the degree one does, her initial self-justification still precedes the comment. The reader is left with at least the possibility that virtue resides in sexual choice rather than chastity until marriage, and that various sorts of psychosexual pleasures were possible and even desirable, so to speak, outside of marriage. Where vice resides is in sexual coercion that is inextricably tied to slavery and its racialized caste system.

Coercion, choice, and the color line are also notes that are struck repeatedly in Frances E. W. Harper's 1892 *Iola Leroy*, even if sexual desire, particularly on the part of black women, is definitely a muffled chord in the novel. The dialectic of choice and coercion in the novel is set in motion by the marriage of Iola and Harry Leroy's parents, Eugene and Marie, across the color line (and the line of master and slave) — though the reader does not discover their story until well into the novel. Harper reconciles these transgressions of race and gender boundaries with a feminist version of sexual propriety. They take place after Eugene has returned to the South following a season of debauchery in Europe (perhaps in bohemian Paris) that has wrecked his health. Marie, a mixed-race slave on his plantation, nurses him back to health. She strikes him as a paragon of womanhood. He declares his love for her, and they marry following her manumission and formal education at a school in the North. Marie subsequently educates her husband in the evils of slavery, particularly with respect to the unequal, and generally coercive, sexual relations of master and slave. As noted in chapter 3, the machinations of their unscrupulous white cousin, Alfred Lorraine, result in the enslavement of Marie and her daughters Iola and Gracie and their public reclassification as Negroes following Eugene's early death. Iola's and Gracie's brother Harry does not return South and so escapes a firsthand experience of slavery.

After this original example of consensual interracial union, mixed-race characters in the novel are repeatedly offered the choice to be "white," choices that would entail considerable material advantages. Both Harry Leroy and Harry's and Iola's light-skinned uncle, Robert Johnson, are encouraged by white recruiting officers to enlist in white Civil War regiments and further their chances of promotion. Iola's eventual husband, Dr. Lattimer, has the opportunity to become the heir of his wealthy white grandmother if he is willing to "pass." And the white Dr. Gresham proposes to Iola with the assumption that she would also "pass" if she were to accept him. In each instance, the mixed-race character elects to be "Negro." Even Harry's decision to marry a woman much darker than he is one that effectively forecloses any possibly of opting to be "white." Interestingly, not only do the mixed-race characters of the novel choose to be (or remain) "Negro," but, other than Marie Leroy, they almost always marry within the same class. Still, the original choice of Iola's and Harry's parents to marry across lines of race and class remains.

Similarly, Pauline Hopkins's *Contending Forces* is filled with acts of sexual coercion, employing and revising gothic tropes of doubling, repetition, curses handed down through generations, the usurpation of birthrights, hauntings, and prophecies. Rape and attempted rape are recurrent and even cyclical events. One also finds in the novel examples of both the "tragic mulatto" in the figure of Sappho Clark and the villainous "cross" in John Langley.

However, as is generally the case in the work of black writers in the nineteenth and early twentieth centuries, the origin of tragedy and villainy lies in slavery and the "new slavery," that is, the *modern* slavery, of Jim Crow, and the strictures of those racial regimes, not in the crossing of races as such. As noted earlier, in describing Langley, Hopkins invokes the familiar racist language of blood and of the tragedy and dangers of racial crosses that took on such power in the post-Reconstruction United States, whether in the figure of the "tragic mulatto" or in the rapacious "mulatto":

> Langley's nature was the natural product of such an institution as slavery. Natural instinct for good had been perverted by a mixture of "cracker" blood of the lowest type on his father's side with whatever God-saving quality that might have been loaned the Negro by pitying nature. This blood, while it gave him the pleasant features of the Caucasian race, vitiated his moral nature and left it stranded high and dry on the shore of blind ignorance, and there he seemed content to dwell, supinely self-satisfied with the narrow boundary of the horizon of his mental vision. (221)

Langley's "cracker" blood, however, turns out to derive from one of the "best" families of North Carolina, which is to say a prominent slave-owning family, inverting the normative class associations of "low" and "best" — and, indeed, "cracker." The pattern of sexual coercion and the literal theft of person in the novel originate with Langley's ancestor, the planter Anson Pollock, who stole the birthright of a pair of the Smith family's progenitors, Charles and Grace Montfort. In true gothic complexity, the Montforts were themselves planters who migrated with their children, Charles Jr. and Jesse, and their slaves to North Carolina from Bermuda in order to avoid the manumission of their human property with the end of slavery in the British Empire. Their envious neighbor Pollock murders Charles and charges that Grace was partially of "African" blood, seizing Grace, Charles Jr., and Jesse as slaves. Pollock's motivation is not so much the desire for property but the desire for the body of Grace — which only truly becomes property after her enslavement. When Grace commits suicide rather than submit, Pollock instead forces himself upon another slave, Lucy. The younger Charles is hired out and eventually purchased by a sympathetic Englishman, who takes Charles Jr. back to Europe. Charles Jr. and his progeny vanish from the plot until the end of the novel. Jesse Montfort escapes from bondage and marries a black New England woman, joining the African American community. He and his descendants are described as being "absorbed into that unfortunate race" (79) — with even the name "Montfort" being absorbed by "Smith."

In cyclical gothic fashion, the tragic pattern of racially inflected choice and coercion is reenacted through the generations, much as the original sin of property theft and a subsequent curse ties together the Pyncheon and Maule families in Hawthorne's *The House of the Seven Gables*. John Langley, for example, is the product of a coercive and probably incestuous relationship, perhaps involving rape, between Anson Pollock's grandnephew, also named Anson Pollock, and Lucy's (and presumably the senior Anson's) granddaughter. Langley in turn attempts to blackmail Sappho Clark (already the victim of incestuous rape) into a sexual relationship, causing her to flee. In this, Langley betrays his fiancée Dora Smith and her brother and his supposed friend Will Smith, who loves Sappho. Again, both of the Smiths are descended from Jesse Montfort.

As in *Iola Leroy*, the origin of tragedy, and villainy, is not in the cross but in the twinned curses of slavery and racism. In part, it is a tragedy in which Charles and Grace Montfort share the blame because they came to North Carolina in order to avoid the manumission of their slaves. As the narrator remarks, however, it is quite possible that Grace and even the senior Charles *do* have some degree of African ancestry, a possibility that does not disturb them in the least. Even if the couple is wholly "white," any tragedy adhering to the marriage of Jesse to the African American Elizabeth is shown to be a product of slavery (and, later, Jim Crow) rather than the cross itself. The curse, at least so far as the Smiths are concerned, is at least partially lifted only after Mr. Withington, the "white" English descendant of the younger Charles Montfort (who was able to successfully sue for reparations of his family's loss of freedom and property in England), chooses to acknowledge his relative and returns to the Smith family the patrimony (and family) stolen by the elder Anson Pollock and the institution of slavery.

Siobhan Somerville uses an exchange between Hopkins and one of Hopkins's readers to show that Hopkins "located a powerful project within her fiction — the right of African Americans to claim and represent their own desires" ("Passing through the Closet," 140). Perhaps more precisely, Hopkins argues for the right of African Africans to claim, represent, and act on their own desires within a context of mutual consent, a revolutionary and potentially hazardous act in both the slave and Jim Crow eras — though one in keeping, at least in part, with Reconstruction and its notion of true African American citizenship and democratic rights.

As Somerville also notes, both of the chief female characters of the novel, Sappho Clark and Dora Smith, strain at the constraints of the expectations of heterosexual marriage — even if both are depicted as happily married by the end of the novel (151). Their mutual physical attraction is certainly described far more vividly than their physical desire for the men they ultimately marry. Sappho (née Mabelle Beaubean) is a mixed-race woman from Louisiana, who was raped by her white uncle, a coercive union that produces her son Alphonse. She renames herself, taking (as, again, Somerville and other commentators remark) a name variously linked with lesbianism (itself a term that becomes commonly used in English to denote erotic relations between women in the late nineteenth century) roughly at the time Hopkins was writing *Contending Forces*. Dora's brother Will ultimately marries Sappho and adopts Alphonse. Manipulated and jilted by John Langley, Dora ultimately marries a steady, decent man, Dr. Lewis, whom she comes to love in a quiet, passive way without any of the passion that marked her relationship with Langley (or, indeed, Sappho Clark).

In short, the novel is marked by repeated and even cyclical inter- and intraracial attempts of men to coerce women into sexual relationships and by the resistance of many of these women through a wide range of methods, including suicide. Again, the origin of the tragedy of these women is not in their mixed-race status. The possibility that even the "white" Grace Montfort (and Charles Sr. for that matter) might in fact have some African ancestry is raised to remind the reader of the instability of U.S. racial definitions. After all, once that possibility is admitted, the category of "white" (and, by extension, its opposite "Negro") can never be definitively assured. Instead, tragedy issues from slavery and its legacy for *both* black and white.

Not only do the women, with the possible exception of Lucy, resist compulsion and attempt to assert their own choices and terms in their romantic relationships by whatever means available, but at least the existence (and even potential primacy) of same-sex female desire is raised in the novel. And, as in *Iola Leroy*, though the Smiths (and their ancestors from Jesse Montfort on, so far as the reader knows) and Sappho Clark of the novel opt to remain "black" even when the possibility of other choices exists, their choice is framed by the consensual, possibly mixed-race union of Charles and Grace Montfort (and the consensual, definitely mixed-race marital choice of Jesse Montfort and Elizabeth).

Consensual interracial relationships are even a larger part of James Weldon Johnson's *Autobiography of an Ex-Colored Man*. In fact, it is striking how overtly coercive sexual unions are missing from the novel, given how frequently such coercion was featured in earlier African American narratives. Again, it is a consensual union of a white man and mixed-race (hence "Negro") mother in Georgia that is the starting point of the narrative:

> I have a dim recollection of several people who moved in and about this little house, but I have a distinct mental image of only two: one, my mother, and the other, a tall man with a small, dark mustache. I remember that his shoes or boots were always shiny, and that he wore a gold

chain and a great gold watch with which he was always willing to let me play. My admiration was almost equally divided between the watch and chain and the shoes. He used to come to the house evenings, perhaps two or three times a week; and it became my appointed duty whenever he came to bring him a pair of slippers, and to put the shiny shoes in a particular corner; he often gave me in return for this service a bright coin which my mother taught me to promptly drop in a little tin bank. I remember distinctly the last time this tall man came to the little house in Georgia; that evening before I went to bed he took me up in his arms, and squeezed me very tightly; my mother stood behind his chair wiping tears from her eyes. (*Writings*, 6)

Unlike Eugene Leroy in his bond with Marie Leroy in *Iola Leroy*, the narrator's father is not prepared to publicly acknowledge his relationship with his mother though marriage — a legal and social impossibility in Georgia. In any event, the father is unwilling to abandon his identity as "one of the greatest men in the country — the best blood of the South" (*Writings*, 14) in order to follow the narrator's mother to the North except for a single visit. (In fact, as the narrator discovers, the father has another family, a "legitimate" white one, including a sister whom he sees from a distance but never meets.) However, the novel makes clear that is not simply lust and the desire to possess that motivates the father. Rather, the father genuinely loves the mother (and she him) and the son, even if that love is debased and perverted by the legacy of slavery and the rise of Jim Crow — as suggested by the gold coin the father ties around his son's neck in an act of love and commodification. This pattern of both consent (and one might even say obsessive fascination) across the color line and the distortion of love and familial ties by racism is repeated several times through the novel.

One peculiar aspect of this pattern is that, after the initial relationship of a white man and an African American woman (albeit a light-skinned African American woman), black women basically fall out of the story as romantic objects (or subjects) or even as figures attractive in any sort of sexual manner. All the women whom the narrator describes in detail as sexually attractive (his youthful musical partner, "the rich widow" at the black bohemian "Club," and his wife) are white so far as we (and the narrator) are able to tell. The one exception is found in a couple of sentences about a "young school teacher" in Jacksonville of whom he "began to have dreams of matrimonial bliss" (*Writings*, 52). However, there is no description of the schoolteacher's appearance or character. In fact, one can only assume that she is black (and a woman, for that matter) because the narrator is thinking about legally marrying her and "raising a family" (*Writings*, 54) in Jacksonville, Florida, as the tide of Jim Crow flows in and after he has decided to go South for the first time as an adult and embrace an identity as a "Negro." Certainly, the reader is unable to determine the depth of his physical attraction to the young woman other than to conclude that it could not be that great because he leaves for New York without her after being laid off from his job in a cigar factory—which can be contrasted with his feelings for the (as far as is revealed) "white" woman who becomes his wife, feelings that ultimately cause him to conceal his "race" from his children.

This dynamic is more complicated than it might first seem. The narrator, as his millionaire patron points out, is by appearance and education "white." He spent his early years under the impression that he was "white" (and will adopt a more or less "white" identity again by the end of the novel). His attraction to and for "white" women, such as "the rich widow" (who, he notes, is not distinguishable in appearance from some light-skinned "colored" women at the "Club"), then, is not easily relegated to any simple notion of "forbidden fruit" or, on the part of the widow, bohemian slumming. Of course, one of Johnson's points here is how little the fears and fantasies of "race" in the United States are rooted in any biogenetic or even visual difference—and how often these fears and fantasies can color one's self in his or her own eyes as well as the eyes of others.

"The rich widow" is quite explicitly identified with bohemianism, reminding the narrator of an older version of George Du Maurier's famous bohemian heroine, Trilby O'Ferrall. Even if the aristocratic widow's search for Negro sexual partners, such as the "very black young fellow" (*Writings*, 67) (a sort of "bad Negro") who is her regular companion, in black bohemia indicates a sort of "Crow Jim" sexual color complex fetishizing African American men, her attraction to the very light-skinned narrator suggests that her tastes are complicated—as, indeed, is the sexual scene at the "Club," where dark-skinned and light-skinned "colored" men and women mix with white men and women ranging from aristocrats and millionaires to vaudeville performers.

Still, the reader is struck by the sheer number of consensual and even loving relationships across the color line *without* a balancing number of coercive relationships. Perhaps one could deduce a history of coercion in the mixed-race ancestry of the narrator's mother, who was born in the slave era on a Georgia plantation. Quite possibly the relationship of the narrator's parents began as one between master and slave because the narrator was born "a few years after the close of the Civil War" (*Writings*, 5). Under those conditions, the line between consent and coercion is nebulous, if not non-existent. However, again, the narrator goes to some length to show that the attachments between his parents and between himself and his father were genuine (and continued even after the son and mother moved to Connecticut), if twisted by racism, the legacy of slavery, and Jim Crow. And, while race and racism distort all of the narrator's romantic or quasi-romantic attachments (and, indeed, all the romantic relationships encountered in the novel), none involve force or even overt deceit—and virtually all except the briefly described love for the young schoolteacher are interracial as people in the United States understand race. In other words, all these pairings are entered into willingly, and all entail the awareness on the part of both participants that it crosses the color line.

"About All a Man Could Wish to Be": Homosexuality and Black and White Bohemia

The love that only partially speaks its name and is shown as only partially consensual is homosexuality. While *Autobiography of an Ex-Colored Man* may well be the first African American novel to clearly foreground homosexuality and describe an interracial gay and lesbian bohemian scene, Sadness Williams in Dunbar's *The Sport of the Gods* can be seen as the first gay black bohemian dandy:

> There was not a lie in all that Sadness had said either as to their crime or their condition. He belonged to a peculiar class,—one that grows larger and larger each year in New York and which has imitators in every large city in this country. It is a set which lives, like the leech, upon the blood of others,—that draws its life from the veins of foolish men and immoral women, that prides itself upon its well-dressed idleness and has no shame in its voluntary pauperism. Each member of the class knows every other, his methods and his limitations, and their loyalty one to another makes of them a great hulking, fashionably uniformed fraternity of indolence. Some play the races a few months of the year; others, quite as intermittently, gamble at "shoestring" politics, and waver from party to party as time or their interests seem to dictate. But mostly they are like the lilies of the field. (386)

Sadness's sexuality is never directly indicated in *The Sport of the Gods*. That in and of itself is telling in a novel in which the heterosexuality of virtually all the other significant characters seems firmly established—or at least virtually all the other characters are shown in some sort of heterosexual pairing. More importantly, Sadness is what was by the turn of the century a recognizable gay type, a decadent Wildean dandy marked as much by his fantastic, yet polished linguistic exuberance as his dress. Sadness's predilection for double entendre, circumlocution, and witty capping corresponds to long-standing African American rhetorical traditions, but the manner of his speech, unlike that of the other denizens of the black bohemian Banner Club, is more clearly Wildean than traditionally "black":

> Sadness put his arm about his shoulder and told him, with tears in his eyes, that he looked like a cousin of his that had died.
> "Aw, shut up, Sadness!" said someone else. "Be respectable."
> Sadness turned his mournful eyes upon the speaker. "I won't," he replied. "Being respectable is very nice as a diversion, but it's tedious if done steadily." (371)

As Monica Miller and Elisa Glick have noted, the postminstrel black dandy, or flaneur if you will, has a significant connection to the figure of the "Zip Coon" type in minstrelsy and black and white vaudeville. However, an important aspect of Zip Coon is the way in which he is sartorially and linguistically out of control, unable to truly master the visual and verbal style to which he aspires (Glick, 415–16; Miller). Though he resembles the type of this minstrel dandy in his avoidance of gainful employment, a quality shared with the Anglo-European dandy, Sadness differs from Zip Coon in that he is always linguistically in control—however rococo and bravura his performance and how little political agency he might have in the Jim Crow United States. In this, Sadness is perhaps at least partly modeled after the on- and offstage persona of the most famous black vaudeville dandy of the era, George Walker, who made mastery of fashion, deportment, and language his hallmarks (Webb, 15–19). Sadness in black Wildean fashion, though, is shown in repartee with a white character who, with the audience (as was often the case in black vaudeville), understands he has been capped or "topped":

> "I tell you, Sadness," he said impulsively, "dancing is the poetry of motion."
> "Yes," replied Sadness, "and dancing in rag-time is the dialect poetry."
> The reporter did not like this. It savoured of flippancy, and he was about entering upon a discussion to prove that Sadness had no soul, when

Joe, with bloodshot eyes and dishevelled clothes, staggered in and reeled towards them. (409)

As in the work of Wilde, homosexuality is never mentioned openly. However, where in Wilde's plays gay identity figured indirectly through the trope of the Dandy, the very invocation of a Wildean dandy in the era after Wilde's sensational trial and conviction for "gross indecency" in 1895 made Sadness a recognizably gay type. Importantly, as discussed previously, Sadness as the prototype of the black flaneur-dandy is distinguished from the dandies of Wilde in the socially and geographically circumscribed nature of his perambulations and in the sense that all his choices are virtually unbearable and to some degree tragic—a hallmark of the black dandy-aesthete through at least the Harlem Renaissance (Glick, 414; Sinfield, 74–75).

Real Black, Real White, and Half-White: Gertrude Stein's "Melanctha" and the Mixed Origins of Modernist Dualism

Sonia Saldivar-Hull, Aldon Nielsen, and Michael North, among others, have observed that the "Melanctha: Each One as She May" section of Gertrude Stein's 1909 *Three Lives*, seen by many modernist writers in the United States (e.g., Sherwood Anderson, F. Scott Fitzgerald, Ernest Hemingway, Nella Larsen, and Carl Van Vechten) as a, if not *the*, seminal document of U.S. modernist fiction, is marked by openly racist statements of biological essentialism. Certainly, the story is a very complicated and contradictory treatment of racial/ethnic identity as transmitted through "nature" or "blood" and "habits" (which is to say culture) in ways that were seen as "dubious generalizations" (to use Sterling Brown's characterization) earlier in the twentieth century as well as in our own time (Brown, 112).

Yet it might be worth noting that Stein clearly did not perceive "Melanctha" as racist in the sense of consciously being antagonistic or patronizing to African Americans. After all, she sent a copy of *Three Lives* to Booker T. Washington and to her fellow former student of William James, W. E. B. Du Bois. While there is no record that Du Bois responded directly to Stein, *Three Lives* was included on the "What to Read" list published in the first issue of *The Crisis* (Wineapple, 299). Of course, modern U.S. literature is filled with liberal "friends of the Negro," from Fannie Hurst to William Styron, who were surprised and even outraged when the befriended responded negatively to what they saw as recycling of racist types and stereotypes. And that, say, Hemingway or Sherwood Anderson found "Melanctha" a realistic, if not realist, portrait is not necessarily convincing. However, Du Bois's indirect response to Stein's gift points to another puzzling issue raised by commentators on racism in the long story: the praise of "Melanctha" by several generations of black writers and intellectuals. Even Sterling Brown, who demolished Fannie Hurst's *Imitation of Life* for its patronizing racism in a famous review, "Once a Pancake," in the Urban League's *Opportunity*, praised Stein's "Melanctha" as "a convincing portrait of a mysterious, uncertain girl . . . a Negro Madame Bovary or Esther Waters" despite his aforementioned reservations about the "dubious generalizations" of the story (Brown, 112). James Weldon Johnson was so impressed with Stein's work that he sent her a copy of *God's Trombones*—which Stein said she enjoyed "enormously" (Letter from Gertrude Stein to James Weldon Johnson, no date, box 20, folder 459, James Weldon Johnson Papers [Correspondence], Beinecke Library, Yale University). Nella Larsen and Richard Wright were even more effusive in their admiration (Sollors, 30–31; Weiss, 116). Some of this praise no doubt owed to the low bar for realist representations of African American characters, speech, expressive culture, and even bodies by white writers.

Still, as Laura Doyle remarks, it is possible to think about the complex and often contradictory ways that race works in the story without ignoring the racist aspects of the work (Doyle, "The Flat, the Round, and Gertrude Stein," 255–56). And while some critics, notably Carla Peterson, Lynn Weiss, and Geoffrey Jacques, have considered the impact of black music and popular theater on Stein's early writing, it also is worth questioning how African American literature influenced, to use Jacques's formulation, the "racial imaginary" of "Melanctha."

Generally, most critics concerned with the racist elements of "Melanctha" focus on the formulaic descriptions that are repeated more or less verbatim through the story, such as "the subtle intelligent attractive half white girl Melanctha Herbert" and the "warm broad glow of negro sunshine."[2] It might, however, be worth worrying those tags a bit more than is often done. After all, in what sense is Melanctha Herbert "half white"? She is not a "mulatta/o" in the sense of the original Spanish meaning of the term of having a "purely" African-descended parent and a "purely" European-descended parent—or in the sense of Harper's Iola Leroy or Larsen's Helga Crane in the novel *Quicksand*. Both of her parents are "Negro" as such things were adjudicated at the time (and even now, to a large extent). Her mother was a "pale yellow" woman and her father was a "black" man. Unlike Iola Leroy or Helga Crane, or even the "real black" Rose Johnson of "Melanctha," Herbert had always lived among African Americans in a black community.

Her appearance, in a book, as Margo Crawford notes, obsessively and minutely concerned with skin color (among "white" as well as "black" characters), is closely connected to that of her mother. Both are described as "pale yellow" (Crawford, 36).

One might ask further, if Herbert's father is "black" and her mother "pale yellow," and if Melanctha resembles her mother in appearance, in what sense can one say, as the narrator does, that she "had been half made with real white blood" (169–70)? Though Melanctha interacts with and no doubt has sexual relations with white men, and though the major white characters of *Three Lives* are described as "yellow" (Anna in the first story) and even "brown" (Lena in the final story), there is no indication that anyone ever sees her as "white," and one might assume the same of her mother. What does "blood" mean here, then? If the mother (and Melanctha) are visibly "Negro," which is to say that there is some visible mark of Africa, and the father is "black," how then is Melanctha "half white" even in terms of "blood"—unless the father is the possessor of some hidden "whiteness," of some unrevealed European "blood"?

Perhaps one way of approaching an answer is to ask another question. What does Stein mean by "real" in "real white" and "real black"? It seems to have something to do with skin color—at least so far as "black" is concerned. Rose Johnson is "real black" to a large extent because her skin is "real black"—with "real" here serving as an intensifier. Various qualities stereotypically associated with racial blackness (e.g., laziness, stupidity, lack of maternal instinct, and promiscuity) are linked to Rose's skin color by the narrator.

Interestingly, none of the African American characters besides Rose Johnson in the story are "real black" in the sense of skin color. One of the notable characteristics of the narrator is that she or he (let's say she) is far more color struck (and more anguished about color) than any character in the story with the possible exception of the very light-skinned "negress" Jane Harden. The narrator obsessively notes the skin tone of major and minor African American characters in the story: Rose Johnson is "real black"; Melanctha Herbert and her mother are "pale yellow"; James Herbert is "black" (though not described as "real black"); Jefferson Campbell is "dark" or "black-brown" (and his father "light brown" and mother "pale brown"); Jane Harden is "so white that hardly any one could guess" she was "a negress"; "John, the Bishops' coachman" is "light brown"; and the "big, serious, melancholy" porter who tells Melanctha stories is also "light brown." Even though the complexions of the gambler Jem Richards and Rose's husband Sam Johnson are not precisely described, the repeated tags of "mulatto" and "colored" respectively seem, as with the description of Melanctha as "half-white," addressed more to skin than actual parentage. Of course, again, if the stories of *Three Lives* are considered as a sort of triptych with the same narrator, it is worth noting that a great deal of attention is also paid to the skin shades of the "white" characters of "The Good Anna" and "The Gentle Lena." Even so, that attention is not quite so maniacally detailed, for the most part, as it is with even the most minor "Negro" characters in "Melanctha."

One aspect of the narrator's attention to skin color is the collision between literary or popular culture racial types and medical-scientific types as delineated by what Daylanne English calls "medical literary authority" (193). As Eric Schocket observes, as a student of psychology in its early days, both at Radcliffe and at the Johns Hopkins Medical School, Stein became fascinated with psychological types and the relation of those types to physical characteristics (172–75). Not surprisingly, given the powerful nativist and racist and even eugenicist currents in the science and medicine of the day (not to mention white bourgeois opinion and the widely read sort of anthropological criminology promoted by Cesare Lombroso), Schocket and English continue, race figured powerfully in Stein's concern with psychological types. She unquestionably drew on those types as she constructed the characters in *Three Lives*. For one thing, her sense of types and their "bottom nature" influenced her impressions of the black families in Baltimore that she encountered while assisting the delivery of babies during her tenure as a medical student at Johns Hopkins—experiences that she acknowledged as a source for her representations of African Americans in "Melanctha" (Stein, *Autobiography of Alice B. Toklas*, 81–82).

As scholars such as Peterson, Weiss, and Jacques have discussed, Stein also drew on the types and tropes of minstrelsy, the "coon song," ragtime (which was closely allied with, if not indistinguishable from, the "coon song"), and black vaudeville in "Melanctha" (Peterson, "The Remaking of Americans"; Weiss, 117–19; Jacques, 41–51). Peterson convincingly argues that the portrait of the surly, violent, razor-wielding, dark-skinned James Herbert is clearly indebted to the "coon song." Peterson, too, also makes the plausible claim that the name and characterization of Rose Johnson derives in part from an early blackface minstrel song, "My Black Rose" (made famous by George Washington Dixon and long popular in later minstrel sketches of various names built around the song), that features a romantic triangle (Peterson, "The Remaking of Americans," 146–47). (One might also mention the 1904 "My Black Rose" by Joseph Barrett, which is more a straightforward song of romantic longing than the earlier comic song.) And, as Jacques reminds us, there were several "coon songs" that took up the variations of skin color among African Americans.

In addition, Peterson and Weiss make a claim for the influence of "early blues" heard by Stein in Baltimore, a center of black music, particularly ragtime, at the turn of the century. On one level, this influence seems improbable. After all, Stein left Baltimore for London and then Paris in early 1902. The singer Ma Rainey and the composer W. C. Handy, both famously connected with the blues, reported that they heard the blues for the first time down South in 1902 and 1903 respectively. Each described their initial impression of the blues as "weird," though gripping (Handy, 78; Work, 330–31). It is hard to believe that Stein encountered the blues as a coherent form or genre in Baltimore before Rainey and Handy and was somehow able to apprehend this music that sounded weird to these black southern veterans of the African American minstrel tent show circuit well enough to draw on the genre's formal properties to create a blues literature decades before Langston Hughes, Sterling Brown, and Waring Cuney would first write their blues poetry during the New Negro Renaissance. Perhaps in this regard it might be worth recalling Stein's own claim that she was not much interested in music and cared for it only during her adolescence—when it appears that opera was her particular passion (Stein, *Autobiography of Alice B. Toklas*, 75).

Still, Peterson's and Weiss's claims that black music influenced Stein's conception of "Negro" types are certainly plausible. Ragtime and the "coon" song (many of which were written by black composers and lyricists) were at the heart of popular music and popular musical theater and provided the base for the rise of Tin Pan Alley in Stein's young adulthood, and street music of various types was much in evidence in Baltimore then (and, to some degree, now). We do not have much indication, however, that Stein listened to "coon" songs with any particular attention. Again, one might consider her claim that she does not much care for music (or the theater) and that her radical style owes more to literature and visual art than music. To the degree that her consumption of popular music and theater influenced her representation of African Americans, her life in the San Francisco Bay Area, where Stein and her brother Leo *did* spend much time watching popular drama (including a no doubt minstrel-inflected version of *Uncle Tom's Cabin*), might have been more directly influential than her later periods in Baltimore. Even in the case of her viewing *Uncle Tom's Cabin* at the age of twelve, Stein would later claim that she did not retain much of the play beyond a memory of mechanical ice flows (Brinnin, 21–22). In short, while Stein (like William Carlos Williams) displayed much interest in the rhythms and repetitive patterns of varieties of American speech (including African American vernacular speech), it is not clear that she had a deep engagement with the "coon" song, ragtime, minstrelsy, and African American popular music in a deep way — though, clearly, popular culture types circulating generally through U.S. culture do have an impact on "Melanctha."

Stein herself did reference the sung calls of the "arabs" (pronounced "ay-rabs"), "the voices of the negroes singing as their carts go lazily by" (Rosalind Miller, 139) in a reminiscence of her life in Baltimore, written as an undergraduate at Radcliffe College. The arabs were (and still are) African American peddlers who traveled (and, to a reduced degree, still travel) nearly all the neighborhoods of the city in horse and wagon. It is worth recalling that the arabs were (and remain) an urban, commercial phenomenon and their sung calls (e.g., "red hot watermelons!") were and are advertisements of their goods rather than, as some critics have alleged with respect to Stein's comment, a sort of rural-like flourish connecting Baltimore to the land. As Peterson points out, it is probable that Stein also witnessed black marching bands accompanying funeral processions ("The Remaking of Americans," 146). In fact, what Stein calls "Negro sunshine" might well be minstrelsy, "coon songs," *and* the black street culture observable and audible to Stein:

> And they loved it always, more and more, together, with this new feeling they had now, in these long summer days so warm; they, always together now, just these two so dear, more and more to each other always, and the summer evenings when they wandered, and the noises in the full streets, and the music of the organs, and the dancing, and the warm smell of the people, and of dogs and of the horses, and all the joy of the strong, sweet pungent, dirty, moist, warm negro southern summer. (*Three Lives*, 130)

As with black popular music, Stein never gets very deeply into the details of this black street culture. We get no real sense of how this music sounded or how the dances looked. However, we are informed that such a culture exists — though not all the black characters participate in it equally.

Stein, then, is one of the first white writers to represent a black urban space (and to represent blackness as in part a place) at length (as opposed, say, to the brief vignette of a black New Bedford church in *Moby Dick*). Again, this is a space or place that white people can and do visit in the story — even if they remain such minor characters that they are never given names, only such descriptors as "white men," and "white man." Tellingly, "white folks" (as opposed to "white men") do not visit this space. "White folks," instead represent a space from which Rose Johnson, who was "raised by white folks" can return to "colored people." Stein herself emphasized the importance of her exposure to "Negro" space far more than a particular musical genre as a source for "Melanctha": "It was then that she had to take her turn in the delivering of babies and it was at that time that she noticed the negroes and the places that she afterwards used in the second of the *Three Lives* stories, Melanctha Herbert, the story that was the beginning of her revolutionary work" (*Autobiography of Alice B. Toklas*, 82).

As many of the scholars who have dealt with "Melanctha" (as well as most of Stein's biographers) point out, the story is to some degree a rewriting of Stein's early, posthumously published novel *Q.E.D. Q.E.D.* in turn is a fictionalized version of a lesbian love triangle in which Stein was a part while a member of a feminist intellectual and largely (if not wholly) lesbian or polysexual circle in Baltimore made up primarily of graduates of women's colleges, especially Smith College and Bryn Mawr College (Wineapple, 146–47). Apparently, much of the dialogue in "Melanctha" between Jeff Campbell (in part a rewriting of the *Q.E.D.* character based on Stein herself) and Melanctha Herbert (also in part a version of the *Q.E.D.* character drawn from Stein's former lover, May Bookstaver) was at times virtually a transcription of conversations between Stein and Bookstaver (Wineapple, 234–35).

Despite this importation of actual dialogue between Stein and Bookstaver, it is worth remarking, as John Carlos Rowe does, that there is no simple correspondence between the particulars of Stein's romance (so far as we know them — Alice Toklas burned much of the documentary record) and the characters of either *Q.E.D.* or "Melanctha." Stein divides her consciousness and transmuted biography among the various characters (Rowe, 230). For example, while Melanctha Herbert may be significantly based on Bookstaver, her penchant for wandering through a wide variety of places resembles that of the young Stein, and the personality of Melanctha's father echoes that of Stein's own father. Perhaps another way of thinking of *Q.E.D.* and "Melanctha" is as, in part, objective correlatives of an ultimately unhappy lesbian romance. This may explain in part the extended apostrophes ("Why did the subtle, intelligent, attractive, half white girl Melanctha Herbert love and do for and demean herself in service to this coarse, decent, sullen, ordinary, black childish Rose" [70]) that occasionally erupt from the narrator, betraying what seems to be a genuine anguish.

Jaime Hovey makes the valuable observation that *Q.E.D.* is marked by a primitivist transposition of sexual desire onto race (and racial types). Such desire is tied to a "tropical" (read "black") disposition that is often at odds with prim (read "white") appearance (Hovey, 559). In this "Sapphic primitivism," to use Hovey's term, white lesbian bodies (and even white lesbian minds) remain "white," while their desires and passions are (or become) "black." One might expect, then, that this "Sapphic primitivism" would be heightened in "Melanctha."

However, in many ways the text resists such a reading.[5] Some critics, starting with Sterling Brown, have commented on the fact that even the "blackest" characters of the story, James Herbert and Rose Johnson (adopted and raised by "white folks"), are described as not truly being a part of the "Negro sunshine." In fact, none of the major characters really conform to minstrel, coon, plantation, medical-scientific, or even colorist stereotypes. James Herbert, for example, may resemble the belligerent, brutal, razor-wielding "coon," but he is also interior ("fierce and serious") in a way that seems at odds with the "coon" role. It might be added that he is not all that good with a razor and loses a fight to the coachman John, "a decent, pleasant, good natured, light brown negro" (77). Rose Johnson might in some ways exemplify the promiscuity and lack of maternal instincts that have long been traits associated with racist visions of black women, but she also lacks the sensuality or the enthusiastic, if limited emotions and desires that are also hallmarks of those visions—she does not even have "enough emotion to be really roused by a revival." Jem Harris, the gambler, is also "a straight decent man, whom other men always looked up to and trusted"—again, at odds with the image of the black gambler in "coon" songs and sketches.

Jeff Campbell has a capacity for humor and the expression of it that seems, perhaps, most in tune with "the wide, abandoned laughter that makes the warm broad glow of negro sunshine." But he is also wildly pensive and divided mentally and emotionally with a manner of speaking that not only repeats itself but also loops back in tighter and more obsessive coils. If Campbell is Stein's "Sapphic primitivist" attempt to get in touch with her "tropical" sexual and sensual dark side, he seems oddly constructed.

Despite the description of Melanctha as a "subtle intelligent attractive half white girl," linked in appearance to her "pale yellow" mother, it is her "black" father that Jane Harden and the narrator say she resembles most in sensibility:

Melanctha was always abusing her father and yet she was just like him, and really she admired him so much and he never had any sense of what he owed to anybody, and Melanctha was just like him and she was proud of it too, and it made Jane so tired to hear Melanctha talk all the time as if she wasn't. Jane Harden hated people who had good minds and didn't use them, and Melanctha always had that weakness, and wanting to keep in with people, and never really saying that she wanted to be like her father, and it was so silly of Melanctha to abuse her father, when she was so much like him and she really liked it. (93)

The frequently "blue" Melanctha seems unable "to have a good warm nigger time with colored men" (178) for any sustained period of time—as is also true of her father in a homosocial way. It is unclear whether the clearly racist (and minstrel-"coon"-inflected) "good warm nigger time" is the narrator's formulation or that of Rose Johnson, who as an emotional and sexual voyeur likes to see Melanctha play a sort of role that she, despite her blackness, is constitutionally unable to assume herself. Again, this is a role that Melanctha, like her father, is able to play only episodically and for relatively brief periods.

Another striking thing about the story is how the black characters, which is to say all the named and most of the unnamed characters, range in social class. Job titles include longshoreman, workman, porter, college teacher, doctor, gambler, housewife, domestic worker, merchant seaman, coachman, butler, and railroad worker. A couple of the characters, the former teacher at a historically black college, Jane Harden (who "always had a little money" [87]), and Rose Johnson (whose "white folks left a little money" [71]) essentially live off some sort of trust fund. All are urban types (as opposed to the generally rural framing of minstrelsy), and even those characters who owe the most to minstrel/"coon" images are generally portrayed with respect to their jobs in ways that seem at odds with those types. The descriptor "decent" is frequently applied. Even James Herbert is described as "a common, decent enough, colored workman" (74).

The mixing of social classes, not to mention shades of skin color (which are not always tied to social class in the story), becomes even more noticeable as the main characters of the story connect through an interlocking series of romantic or semiromantic triangles that all have Melanctha Herbert in common: Melanctha–James Herbert–the coachman John; Melanctha–Jane Harden–Jeff Campbell; Melanctha–Jeff Campbell–Jem Harris; Melanctha–Rose Johnson–Jem Harris; and Melanctha–Rose Johnson–Sam Johnson. The repetition of Melanctha and two "Js" in each of these triangles reinforces their connection. If, then, "Melanctha" is a racial transposition of *Q.E.D.* and a middle-class (or even upper-class) white lesbian quasi bohemia, it also involves dramatic changes in class and even sexuality from the earlier novel. It sets up a black bohemia in which Melanctha "wanders" sexually, geographically, and emotionally from black and white working men to the very light-skinned "Negro," middle-class, hard-drinking, lesbian bohemian Jane Harden to the brown-skinned doctor Jeff Campbell to the "mulatto" gambler Jem Harris to the "black" Rose Johnson (raised by "white folks" and married to an African American merchant seaman). She is, as she says to Jeff Campbell, a "queer" person and, along with Jane Harden, part of a coterie of "queer folks"—a coterie with which Campbell has a fascination. In fact, Melanctha Herbert is described as a sort of black (or "half-white") lesbian (or polysexual) flaneur in a queer black bohemia.

If vaudeville, minstrelsy, the "coon" song, ragtime, plantation literature, scientific-medical discourse, early modernist primitivism, and Stein's observation of black families and black street life in Baltimore, though influential to varying degrees, inadequately suggest the complexity of "Melanctha," what other sources for her representations of black people might exist and to what end are these sources deployed? One place to look is African American literature at the turn of the century, particularly by W. E. B. Du Bois and Paul Laurence Dunbar. Again, Stein would have been familiar with the work of Du Bois through their common connection with William James, who was particularly enthusiastic about *The Souls of Black Folk*—a connection underlined by Stein's sending of *Three Lives* to Du Bois and the promotion of Stein's book in *The Crisis*. Dunbar, as one of the most successful U.S. writers of the era, would have been familiar to the omnivorous reader Stein, too, especially as she thought about the representation of black subjects.

Quite a few scholars, especially in the past few decades, have disparagingly or approvingly suggested that these representations are closely connected to Stein's own position as "other" and to her feelings of "otherness" as a Jewish American lesbian. This was a time when debates raged about whether members of the "Jewish race" could actually be "Americans" (debates that the advocates of cosmopolitanism ultimately lost with passage of new immigration laws in 1921 and 1924 that virtually shut off legal immigration from southern and eastern Europe) and when the sexuality of African American women was psychologically and physiologically linked to lesbianism through a medical-scientific discourse that dominated the study and treatment of "aberrant" sexualities. The problematic aspect of this identification with a "black" other, as Corrine Blackmer, Sonia Saldivar-Hull, and Jaime Hovey remark, is that it relies on black stereotypes and a primitivism that reinforces racial hierarchy (and Stein's position in that hierarchy).

The point about Stein's primitivism is well taken, though, ironically, perhaps more so with respect to *Q.E.D.* than "Melanctha." Certainly, to use a favorite Stein locution, she engages the primitivist rhetoric of black naturalness in "Melanctha" with phrases such as "a nigger good time" and "the earth-born, boundless joy of negroes." And certainly many of the contemporary white readers of the story, and maybe Stein herself, would be entirely comfortable with these sorts of primitivist stereotypes. However, one still confronts the fact that none of the phenotypically and socially varied Negroes in the story, from the "almost white" to the "real black," from the teacher and the doctor to the domestic worker and porter, actually participate in "the earth-born, boundless joy of negroes" — at least not for any length of time. Instead, almost all the black characters, both major and minor, are divided, unhappy, dissatisfied, "melancholy," "blue," and so on.

If Stein is using African Americans to figure a sense of Jewish lesbian "otherness," perhaps she does so not because of a primitivist notion of a natural Negro groundedness, but because of the visions of black dualism, of the radically divided black subject, that were particularly pronounced in black literature at the turn of the century. In other words, rather than being timeless, premodern noble savages, African Americans (at least in the city) were the modern subjects par excellence. Once more, this division is not simply or even primarily rooted in the psychological (though often rendered through psychological discourse and metaphors such as "double consciousness"), but also in the political, cultural, social, economic, and, increasingly, spatial in the early Jim Crow era. "Melanctha" does, in fact, include a story that testifies to the violence that was essential to the establishment of Jim Crow:

> There was one, big, serious, melancholy, light brown porter who often told Melanctha stories, for he liked the way she had of listening with intelligence and sympathetic feeling, when he told how the white men in the far South tried to kill him because he made one of them who was drunk and called him a damned nigger, and who refused to pay money for his chair to a nigger, get off the train between stations. And then this porter had to give up going to that part of the Southern country, for all the white men swore that if he ever came there again they would surely kill him. (81–82)

In a less direct way, one might also see Rose Johnson's quasi adoption by "her white folks" and her subsequent "drift" "from her white folks to the colored people" as embodying the beginnings of urban residential segregation in the United States.

As discussed earlier in the chapter, the opposition of sexual compulsion and sexual freedom had long been a feature of African American literature, an opposition that gained even more prominence in fin de siècle black writing. In these later texts, one often finds intraracial heterosexual unions within the institution of marriage and interracial and intraracial heterosexual predations by white males (or mixed-race males replicating the behavior of white male ancestors) toward Negro women (often mixed-race women whose experience mirrored that of their black female ancestors). In other words, within the intensification of the Jim Crow regime, the longstanding issue of a black woman's ability to say "no" was joined by that of agency to openly say "yes" and even "I do" across the color line (and by the black male's capability of making a marriage proposal across that line).

If, as Margo Crawford argues, Melanctha Herbert is characterized by insatiable desire, why does she remain unsatisfied (Crawford, 25)? Is it because of the unbridled and monstrous libido often attributed to black women (and to lesbians of all races) in the popular culture, high culture, medicine, and early psychology of the era of "Melanctha"? Or is it because society is structured so that satisfaction is impossible? On a very basic level, her attachment to women is more profound than to men. Melanctha, after all, "wanted Rose more than she had ever wanted all the others." Melanctha's breakup with Rose affects her more deeply than the other splits described in the story. It is Rose's marriage to Sam Johnson that is a large part of the split with Melanctha. At the same time, Melanctha is caught up with "her desire for a right position"—that is to be married—and seems genuinely thrilled that Jem Richards wants to marry her. Next to her split with Rose, the collapse of her engagement to Jem is the most consequential of her many breakups. Melanctha contains, after Du Bois's *The Souls of Black Folk*, "two unreconciled strivings; two warring ideals" (11), the reconciliation of which is prohibited by law and custom. Blackness and lesbianism in "Melanctha" are linked by an externally and internally constrained libido that exists in dialectical opposition to the popularly circulated myths of the unrestrained black and lesbian libidos, myths that, again, as many commentators have noted, are prominently raised by the narrator and many of the characters of "Melanctha."

Black Nationalist Bohemia: Queer Bohemia and the
Emergence of Black Nationalist Modernism

Oddly enough, if Stein creates a vision of a black queer bohemia in order to figure a modernist dualism, black writers in the early twentieth century frequently project an interracial and often significantly queer bohemia as a space through which the black artist and intellectual passes (and ultimately divorces himself or herself from) on the way to a more nationalist stance.

With the rise of an interracial bohemia, the figure of the black dandy-aesthete-intellectual-artist becomes one that strains at the walls of the ghetto as the spatialization of the new Jim Crow regime, attempting to find a place figuratively or actually outside the ghetto. In this respect, emerging African American ghettos, such as Harlem and Chicago's South Side, become paired with the neighborhoods associated with white bohemians, such as New York's Greenwich Village and Chicago's Towertown—with the ghettos representing an authentic blackness that can be visited or returned to and the predominantly white neighborhoods a dream or nightmare of racial egalitarianism that is alternately a refuge or trap for the black artist. To a very considerable extent, these linked spaces are queer, if not openly gay or lesbian, spaces.

Even more overtly than the Banner Club of *The Sport of the Gods*, the "Club" in *Autobiography of an Ex-Colored Man* is a black bohemian space that is the site for the establishment of homoerotic liaisons across the color line. One such pairing is between the narrator and a white bohemian millionaire, who, as Siobhan Somerville observes, gradually seduces (or perhaps purchases the attentions of) the narrator (who has become an accomplished ragtime-stride pianist at the "Club") intellectually and emotionally (*Queering the Color Line*, 117):

Among the other white "slummers" there came into the "Club" one night a clean cut, slender, but athletic looking man, who would have been taken for a youth had it not been for the tinge of gray about his temples. He was clean shaven, had regular features, and all of his movements bore the indefinable but unmistakable stamp of culture. He spoke to no one, but sat languidly puffing cigarettes and sipping a glass of beer. He was the center of a great deal of attention, all of the old timers were wondering who he was. When I had finished playing he called a waiter and by him sent me a five dollar bill. For about a month after that he was at the "Club" one or two nights each week, and each time after I had played he gave me five dollars. One night he sent for me to come to his table; he asked me several questions about myself; then told me that he had an engagement which he wanted me to fill. He gave me a card containing his address and asked me to be there on a certain night. (*Writings*, 71)

Johnson's novel veers here from the interracial and intraracial homosocial and the interracial heterosexual into the openly homoerotic. Johnson sets up a pattern that will become familiar in the New Negro Renaissance in which a homoerotic (and perhaps realized gay) relationship is marked and in a sense vouched for by the presence of openly gay figures in a bohemian environment in which both men and women strain variously against conventions of race and gender — and, to a lesser extent, class:

The men ranged in appearance from a girlish looking youth to a big grizzled man whom everybody addressed as "Judge." None of the women appeared to be under thirty, but each of them struck me as being handsome. I was not long in finding out that they were all decidedly blasé. Several of the women smoked cigarettes, and with a careless grace which showed they were used to the habit. Occasionally a "damn it!" escaped from the lips of some one of them, but in such a charming way as to rob it of all vulgarity. (*Writings*, 72–73)

Here the "girlish looking youth" as a distinctly gay type embodies a sort of love that once its name is spoken cannot be dismissed from the reader's understanding of the relationship between the narrator and "his" millionaire. In other words, the existence of overtly gay characters and/or types presents homosexuality as a viable explanation of the basis of what might otherwise be a homosocial relationship, anticipating similar moves in such Harlem Renaissance novels as Claude McKay's *Home to Harlem* and *Banjo* and Wallace Thurman's *Infants of the Spring*. Unlike intraracial homoerotic relationships in McKay's work, though, the narrator's same-sex attraction, like his heterosexual encounters, seems only to be interracial — again, if one considers him to be a "Negro" (and he never really considers himself anything else after his revelation about his parents). Though, for example, he admires his black classmate "Shiny," no hint of erotic desire seems to enter into that admiration.

At this point, the narrator leaves black bohemia behind for what seem to be entirely queer, if not gay and lesbian, spaces in Europe. He becomes a sort of courtesan whose relationship to the millionaire, as Siobhan Somerville has observed, echoes that of his mother to his father (Somerville, *Queering the Color Line*, 118). However, one significant difference between the two relationships is that the narrator's role in part is to publicly mirror rather than serve as a gender, class, and/or race opposite of the millionaire. The narrator's mother, after all, was a seamstress who presented herself in a normatively feminine way, who was known at least to the school officials as a Negro, and who, in fact, appeared visibly "Negro" to her son once he considered the possibility she might not be "white." His father was a rich, white planter who struck the narrator as "a tall, handsome, well dressed gentleman" (*Writings*, 22).

Conversely, the millionaire takes pains to erase any public signs of racial, class, or gender difference between himself and the narrator:

> He bought me the same kind of clothes which he himself wore, and that was the best; and he treated me in every way as he dressed me, as an equal, not as a servant. In fact, I don't think anyone could have guessed that such a relation existed. My duties were light and few, and he was a man full of life and vigor, who rather enjoyed doing things for himself. He kept me supplied with money far beyond what ordinary wages would have amounted to. For the first two weeks we were together almost constantly, seeing the sights, sights old to him, but from which he seemed to get new pleasure in showing them to me. During the day we took in the places of interest, and at night the theaters and cafés. This sort of life appealed to me as ideal, and I asked him one day how long he intended to stay in Paris. He answered, "Oh, until I get tired of it." (*Writings*, 79)

If the millionaire has any romantic sexual fantasies about the black primitive, at least as far as appearance and demeanor go, he does not seem to project them onto the narrator. In fact, the millionaire goes so far as to try to talk the narrator out of his decision to return to the United States as a "Negro," suggesting that "by blood, by appearance, by education and by tastes" the narrator is far more nearly "white" than "Negro." It is only when the millionaire listens to the narrator play ragtime that he seems to feel any desire for the "Negro" qualities (including the role of servant) of the narrator—and even then it is never really clear to what the millionaire responds in the music:

> He entertained a great deal, some of the parties being a good deal more blasé than the New York ones. I played for the guests at all of them with an effect which to relate would be but a tiresome repetition to the reader. I played not only for the guests, but continued, as I used to do in New York,

to play often for the host when he was alone. This man of the world, who grew weary of everything, and was always searching for something new, appeared never to grow tired of my music; he seemed to take it as a drug. He fell into a habit which caused me no little annoyance; sometimes he would come in during the early hours of the morning, and finding me in bed asleep, would wake me up and ask me to play something. This, so far as I can remember, was my only hardship during my whole stay with him in Europe. (*Writings*, 79–80)

In part, then, this predominantly white queer bohemia is defined by a dialectic of racelessness (or at least a transgression of U.S. racial boundaries and definitions) and racially identified cultural expression.

Strangely enough, this queer bohemia serves as a necessary retort in which the narrator is processed until he is ready to embrace a new sort of blackness or Negro identity. It is through his sojourn with the millionaire that the narrator seizes upon (or is seized by) the idea to build a new sort of high "Negro" art that could serve as the basis for a new black national culture that he distinguishes from some more generic "American" art:

My "millionaire" planned, in the midst of the discussion on music, to have me play the "new American music" and astonish everybody present. The result was that I was more astonished than anyone else. I went to the piano and played the most intricate ragtime piece I knew. Before there was time for anybody to express an opinion on what I had done, a big bespectacled, bushy-headed man rushed over, and, shoving me out of the chair, exclaimed, "Get up! Get up!" He seated himself at the piano, and taking the theme of my ragtime, played it through first in straight chords; then varied and developed it through every known musical form. I sat amazed. I had been turning classic music ragtime, a comparatively easy task; and this man had taken ragtime and made it a classic. The thought came across me like a flash. — It can be done, why can't I do it? From that moment my mind was made up. I clearly saw the way of carrying out the ambition I had formed when a boy. (*Writings*, 86)

It is important to note that the narrator's ambition is not simply a musical one. As the millionaire says to the narrator, it would be possible for the narrator to compose music on "Negro themes," a possibility that the millionaire encourages. However, the narrator also has a political agenda, a sort of nation-building agenda in which the "Negro" "high" art based on the culture of the "Negro" masses, both in the city (ragtime) and in the rural South (the spirituals), composed by himself as a public "Negro," so to speak, would form part of the national infrastructure, resembling the visions of the Irish Renaissance and other European nationalist cultural movements in the late nineteenth and early twentieth centuries that much influenced Johnson.[4] This ambition is frustrated by the narrator's inability to face the horror of the Jim Crow South. However, the pattern set here by the narrator's passage through a queer and predominantly, though not entirely, white bohemia to a black nationalist artistic vanguard is one that will be repeated throughout the twentieth century from the Harlem Renaissance to the Black Arts era of the 1960s and 1970s.

If we take sexual freedom and a rebellion against a patriarchal heterosexual intraracial normativity to be a major concern of modernism and bohemia in the United States from the early twentieth century onward, then, as with the representation of divided or fragmented subjectivities, black writers were, because of their peculiar position in the United States, in the vanguard. Though, as Claudia Tate, Mary Helen Washington, and many others have shown, notions of "true womanhood" and what might be thought of as true masculinity long exerted (and continued to exert) a profound influence on literature by black writers, nonetheless, the evil of sexual coercion and the desirability of sexual freedom, including the representation of women's sexual desire and sexual agency in relatively positive lights, were significant features of African American writing, especially narratives, well before the Civil War. In fact, as in Harriet Jacobs's *Incidents in the Life of a Slave Girl*, the problem of negotiating the contradiction between the strictures of "true womanhood" and female sexual desire within the confines of the veil of racism and the racial regime under slavery is often a foregrounded concern of texts by both black women *and* men in the nineteenth century. Given this long history of concern with sexual coercion and sexual freedom, it is not surprising, that authors such as Pauline Hopkins, Paul Laurence Dunbar, and James Weldon Johnson should be among the first U.S. authors also to strain at the limits of normative heterosexuality in U.S.-published works, depicting gay, lesbian, or at the least queer relationships and black, white, and checkerboard queer bohemias in which heterosexuality is no longer the default norm. These writers also questioned the nature of masculinity and femininity and the boundaries of normative gender types. After all, the narrator of *Autobiography of an Ex-Colored Man* considered the millionaire "about all a man could wish to be." Allowing for the fact that the narrator is often unreliable in his judgments, at least the possibility of a gay masculinity as being a "true" masculinity is raised. Even Dunbar's Sadness in *The Sport of the Gods*, though not exactly admirable, presents a black Wildean dandy version of a viable masculinity — or at least more viable, arguably, than any of the other male characters, black or white, in the novel.

As a result, it is not surprising that Gertrude Stein in her seminal text of U.S. modernism, "Melanctha," should transpose the story of white lesbians in the unpublished *Q.E.D.* (and, indeed, in her own life) to what amounts to a queer black bohemia. Again, as discussed earlier, this is not solely or even primarily due to some primitivist notion of lesbian sexuality. After all, as also previously noted, none of the black characters of the story really correspond to any primitivist stereotypes, despite the narrator's frequent recourse to the racist language of such stereotypes. More often than not, such stereotypes are raised so that the reader can be told how the particular black character in question does not conform to them, does not somehow feel easy in the "Negro sunshine." Another possible (and to me more convincing) reason for the story's racial transmogrification is the influence of what might be thought of as the long line of antiprimitivism in black literature, of the divided self being torn apart by resistance to a racial regime that radically constrains black sexual freedom, especially black women's freedom, to say yes or no largely through a recourse to "high" and popular culture images of a chaotic and unrestrained black sexuality.

At the same time that black writers and black expressive culture play a crucial part in the definition and representation of a U.S. modernism and U.S. bohemia that are not basically transplants from Europe, African American artists also imagine a black nationalist bohemia that is distinct from both the predominantly, but not solely, white and appreciably queer bohemia and the predominantly, but not entirely, black and also significantly queer bohemia shown by Dunbar and Johnson in the Banner Bar and the Club. Interestingly, both sorts of integrated or semi-integrated queer bohemias are seen as necessary stepping-stones to a generally far more heterosexual black nationalist bohemia, setting a pattern that will endure for decades with some challenges and variations.

"Our Beautiful White . . ."

By 1919 the symbolic meaning of the East-West and the North-South axes in the United States had changed dramatically. Thousands of black and white U.S. troops had fought on European soil for the first time in World War I. Despite Woodrow Wilson's advocacy of self-determination for European peoples, U.S. imperialism, an issue that had been the source of so much political debate at the turn of the century, was largely a dead letter so far as mainstream U.S. politics was concerned. Not only had the United States maintained control of all the territories (the Philippines, Guam, and Puerto Rico) it had gained from the Spanish-American War and ensuing campaigns of "pacification," but it had also consolidated its hold on Hawaii and added what had previously been the Danish Virgin Islands. There was also a dramatic increase in the number of U.S. military interventions and occupations in the Caribbean and Latin America in the decades after the war between the United States and Spain, including a twenty-year occupation of Nicaragua, an eight-year occupation of the Dominican Republic, a nineteen-year occupation of Haiti, four years of expeditions against Mexican nationalist revolutionaries, and decades of a military presence in Cuba.

While the United States had long been an expansionist nation, the transformation of U.S. manifest destiny to include the domination of territories outside of North America and of populations that would be ruled rather than displaced entailed the rise of new cultural geographies and new anxieties attending those geographies mapped onto the older meanings of the East-West and North-South axes. Economic and industrial changes also began to transform the symbolic meaning of East and West and North and South as the industrial center of the United States moved from the Northeast to the Midwest and, to a lesser degree, the South. While finance capital and the culture industries, with the exception of the burgeoning film industry, remained based largely in the Northeast, especially New York, the new mass production industries (e.g., steel, automobile, and rubber) and the mineral extraction industries (especially iron and coal) other than the electrical industry were increasingly identified with the Midwest and the South. Even the textile industry, which began the U.S. industrial revolution, was rapidly decamping from New England and the Northeast to the South. By the 1920s economic changes seriously altered the cultural valence of the Far West, particularly California, as Los Angeles became the undisputed film capital of the United States and an increasingly important industrial center, especially of the nascent aerospace industry. California also began to pioneer industrial farming to a degree that would make it the heartland of U.S. agricultural labor struggles for the rest of the century.

If, as Raymond Williams claims, modernism and the twentieth-century version of modernity as international formations were significantly enabled by the vast movement of peoples from the agricultural "periphery" of the "South" and "East" to the industrial centers of the "North" and "West," these movements transformed the symbolic geography of the United States in complicated ways. While the Great Migration of African Americans from the South to the urban North and the immigration of millions from eastern and southern Europe and the Middle East, and hundreds of thousands more from East Asia, the Caribbean, and Latin America to the United States left a huge mark on the Northeast, which contained many of the most active ports of entry for immigrants, it was the midwestern industrial hubs, such as Chicago, Detroit, and Cleveland, that were most marked by these movements. These migrations significantly enabled the modern industrial system. After all, the home plant of Fordism, initially at the Ford Motor Company plant in Highland Park, Michigan, and later its River Rouge complex in Dearborn, drew on a work force populated by immigrants from eastern and southern Europe and their children and by black and white migrants from the U.S. South, eventually making the River Rouge plant the largest employer of black industrial workers in the world.

Perhaps unsurprisingly, these migrations caused an enormous increase of racist and nativist anxieties in the United States with the East (including eastern Europe and Asia) and the South (including the U.S. South as well as the south of the Caribbean and Latin America), figuring prominently in the geography of these new anxieties. Some, such as Madison Grant in his widely read *The Passing of the Great Race* (1916), placed more emphasis on the threat to the "Nordic" body politic of the United States created by the "new immigrants" of what might be thought the offwhite "races" of the Mediterranean rim and eastern Europe. Others, such as the similarly influential Lothrop Stoddard in *The Rising Tide of Color* (1920), stressed the increasing threat that the nonwhite peoples of color (in something like the sense that "of color" would be understood today) posed to "civilization," especially U.S. democracy, which relied on a "Nordic" core anchoring other non-"Nordic" "Aryan races" and containing or (ultimately) eliminating nonwhite races.

In short, the East-West axis, like the North-South axis that African American writers had largely introduced into U.S. literature, became significantly caught up with race and racial anxiety. Of course, one might argue that race had always been a symbolic aspect of the East-West axis, which had earlier involved the displacement of non-"white" peoples (primarily Native Americans and Mexicans) by "white" Americans. Increasingly, however, this shift to a vision of "white" or "Nordic" displacement by non-"white" or off-"white" peoples became a feature of the East-West axis, generating fears increasingly resembling those attending the North-South axis (which, too, became even more intensified with the greatly increasing migration of African Americans from the South to the North and from the country to the city with the advent of World War I).

Love and Fret: Racial Anxiety, Modernism, and the Migration Narrative

> Do you realize the fascination the story of the white woman who had twin
> nigger babies has for us? They accused the woman of having had intercourse
> with the apartment's colored elevator boy. Her husband abandoned her at
> once, of course, — charming man. But you know Mendel's law; they discovered
> there had been a darky in *his* family six generations before! There's the
> dénouement for every good American. Be careful whom you marry! Be
> careful for you can NEVER know. Watch, wait, study.
>
> —William Carlos Williams, *In the American Grain*

The first generation of U.S. "high" modernists (e.g., T. S. Eliot, Ezra Pound, William Carlos Williams, Gertrude Stein, and Wallace Stevens) came of age during the successful rise of the first wave of legal Jim Crow and the emergence of the United States as an imperial power. The second generation of U.S. modernists, including Langston Hughes, Hart Crane, Ernest Hemingway, F. Scott Fitzgerald, Countee Cullen, William Faulkner, and Nella Larsen, came of age during the second wave of Jim Crow and the racial segregation of urban space.

As such critics as Aldon Nielsen, Michael North, David Chinitz, Michael Rogin, and Geoffrey Jacques have shown, anxiety over whether one's culture or even one's self is "white" enough even as ventriloquizing or impersonating black voices and bodies (in short, in some way sounding, acting, moving, and dressing "black") as a way of asserting an "American" vanguard identity became a common stance of many older (and some younger) white U.S. modernists. This sort of impersonation was often practiced even by those who, like Eliot and Pound, found a more perfect future in an idealized (and generally racist and anti-Semitic) European past. What is interesting is that this anxiety (or even anguish) and impersonation are not generally linked to the visible physiological or phenotypical signs associated with "race," but with language, culture, movement, and, as we have seen with Stein, even desire. No one thought, for example, that the young T. S. Eliot really looked "Negro" even if he (or so he feared) sounded black or he (or so he hoped, perhaps) danced black.

One way of approaching this anxiety might be found in the old Derridian critique of the binary of "presence" and "absence" in "Western" metaphysics and in Derrida's important, if somewhat nebulous concept of the "trace" and its relation to the privileged side of the binary pair. One of the noted peculiarities of another binary, "Negro" or "black" and "white," as it was conceived legally and, to a considerable extent, socially in the United States during the increasingly rigid racial regime of the early twentieth century, is the asymmetry of presence and absence in that racial binary. That is to say, the presence of "white" blood does not fundamentally change the "black" subject's identity as a "Negro" — even if the ancestry of that subject is overwhelmingly European and even if, as Margo Crawford notes, that subject suffers from some degree of "dilution anxiety" about his or her "blackness" that is linked to shades of skin color (1–14). Conversely, the merest trace of "black" blood, if known or somehow legible in body, speech, or manner, renders the subject a "Negro" with all the attendant legal, social, cultural, and psychic consequences in the Jim Crow United States.

In other cultures, many African American intellectuals and artists pointed out, even in Europe, such a racial logic did not apply. Alexander Dumas (or Colette, for that matter) could be a quintessentially French writer, and Alexander Pushkin could be *the* national Russian poet despite the presence of publicly known African ancestry in a way unimaginable in the United States. Neither did this asymmetry pertain to all other so-called racial mixtures in the United States during the modernist moment. For example, while the pejorative term "half-breed" referring to near equal Native American and white ancestry remained in use, the presence, alleged or real, of some small amount of native "blood" in an otherwise, as far as was known, European parentage did not make one an "Indian" or render one less "white" — as the many white Americans claiming a native great-grandmother, great-great-grandmother, and so on, attested (and attest).

This asymmetry presents some obvious problems for the "white" or would-be "white" subject. One problem long treated by African American authors and raised, too, by white U.S. modernists is that once the phenomenon of "passing" is brought up as either an actuality or a possibility, the binary of "black" and "white" is destabilized because one can never really be certain about one's own "whiteness," much less anyone else's. Another is the Derridian notion that opposing terms in a binary pair are inevitably present in each other as a sort of negative trace that takes on a positive existence. This is particularly true of the privileged term "white," which excludes or represses all that is not "white" and assigns it to "Negro" or "black." Of course, long before Derrida or even Toni Morrison's *Playing in the Dark* was read in the United States, Ralph Ellison famously, and hilariously, represented the presence of this sort of trace in the U.S. metaphysics of race in the Liberty Paint episode of *Invisible Man*. In that episode, it is revealed that a certain number of drops of black are necessary to produce "Optic White" paint. "Optic" there serves as a reminder that, according the racial logic of the United States, this paint was in fact "black," even if it appeared "white," recalling the endless regress of anxiety and uncertainty of racial presence and absence. Ellison also presents such presence and absence in the prologue of the novel, where the preacher in a hallucinatory sermon asserts, "Black will make you . . . or black will un-make you" (10).

Jacques with his notion of white modernists and the "racial imaginary" is particularly useful here. For example, speaking of Wallace Steven's "The Comedian as the Letter C," Jacques observes: "The very evocation of the banjo here, however, reveals the anxiety at the heart of the poem's language. It is not only the natural environment and the people within it which the poem's explorer must conquer; to be truly responsive, the explorer must conquer as well the art forms and instruments of art making, that he finds within that environment as well. He must learn to play the banjo" (37). In short, Jacques claims, he must embrace a stylized "Negro" identity as signified by the minstrel icon of the banjo.

The articulation of anxiety about race by white modernists was strongly connected to journeys along the North-South axis largely introduced by black writers and to the early African American migration narrative. Stevens wrote frequently of the racialized landscapes encountered in his vacations in Florida and travels in the U.S. South. As Jacques convincingly argues, in his 1923 collection *Harmonium*, Stevens is not simply engaged in a rococo travelogue but displays apprehension about the return of the colonialized or semicolonialized repressed in the form of the "Maya sonneteers" of "The Comedian." He also betrays unease about the ways the act of mastery deform the master, deformations that are not due, as in the narratives of Fredrick Douglass, so much to the corrupting influence of power as to the intimate relationship between master and mastered that causes each to take on characteristics perceived as marking the other. This unease and even fear of a "southern" character or way of being taking dominion "everywhere" reflected not only what was probably the apogee of direct U.S. military intervention in the nations of the Americas but also the changes and dislocations of the urban United States caused by the Great Migration and the far more visible presence of racialized urban space as the black communities of the North, including in Stevens's Hartford, Connecticut, grew dramatically during the second wave of Jim Crow.

In the case of T. S. Eliot, racial anxiety and connection to the migration narrative seem more personal. In a 1928 letter to Herbert Read, he sketches a sort of autobiographical migration narrative he wants to write, "I want to write an essay about the point of view of an American who wasn't an American, because he was born in the South and went to school in New England as a small boy with a nigger drawl, but who wasn't a southerner in the South because his people were northerners in a border state and looked down on all southerners and Virginians, and who was never anything anywhere" (Read, 35). He portrays his journey from St. Louis to New England as from South to North rather than from West to East, linking that trip along the North-South axis to race and an ambivalent, though significantly blackened racial and regional identity. As in so many of the early migration narratives, he describes a subject suspended between North and South, black and white, and racial roots and deracination without any real resolution. What could be seen as a sort of sublimated migration narrative underlies much of Eliot's early poetry, particularly "The Love Song of J. Alfred Prufrock" and "The Wasteland." "Prufrock" in particular displays the sort of public spaces of personal alienation found in Dunbar's Banner Bar in *Sport of the Gods*, Johnson's "club" in *Autobiography of an Ex-Colored Man*, and even the black Boston of Hopkins's *Contending Forces*.

Williams Carlos Williams's racial anxieties were of an even more personal nature. Migration along the North-South axis was the story of his family. His friend Ezra Pound liked to remind him that he was not "American" enough and approached the concrete details of U.S. life essentially as an immigrant, a "dago immigrant," in fact (Tapscott, 22). Paul Mariani calls the "Jewish question" "the most sensitive" and "the most complex issue" for Williams in the late 1930s because of his complicated feelings toward his Jewish ancestry through his maternal grandfather and accusations of anti-Semitic language in his stories within the context of a growing Nazi/fascist threat

(411). However, an even more sensitive and complex, though less openly acknowledged, issue was that much of his Puerto Rican mother's ancestry was not (and is not) known in any clear detail despite Williams's description of his maternal grandfather as of "Jewish and Spanish" descent and his maternal grandmother as of French Basque descent via Martinique (William Carlos Williams, *Selected Letters*, 284). While Williams's mother was not "black" or even "mulatta" as it would have been understood in Puerto Rico, there is some considerable chance that either side of his mother's family tree in the Caribbean contained some African branches. That is to say, given the racial asymmetry of the black and white dyad in the United States, Williams could possibly be reclassified as "black" (as in fact some commentators in essence do now, calling Williams "Afro-Latino"). At least his "whiteness" (and hence his "Americanness," as Ezra Pound chided him with equal amounts of criticism and admiration) was in question to a degree even more than his known Jewish or "Spanish" ancestry would have placed it (William Carlos Williams, *Kora in Hell*, 14). Again, this uncertainty, as Williams asserts in his 1925 *In the American Grain*, is true of any "white" person in the United States, but variation between a Puerto Rican understanding of race and racial and national identity and that of the United States left this uncertainty or anxiety open in a different sort of way. Williams had every reason to suspect that he had "a darky in *his* family" (again, as such things were figured in the United States) six generations or so back.

Interestingly, though Williams describes the "inky curse" as descending through the father, racial anxiety in his writing is figured most often through the mother or an alluring, but somewhat monstrous female. This can be seen in what is perhaps the most famous portion of *Spring and All* (with the possible exception of "The Red Wheelbarrow"), "To Elsie." Williams rhetorically links the maid Elsie to the Ramapough people of northern New Jersey and southern New York in the opening of the poem—though he does not actually say that Elsie is from that community. The Ramapoughs, widely known in the area by the pejorative term "Jackson Whites," see themselves primarily as Native Americans. However, to the non-Ramapoughs in New Jersey and New York, the legend that they are the descendants of escaped African slaves, Hessian deserters, and Native Americans (with some Dutch overlay) was the predominant view until quite recently. If I may break into the autobiographical and anecdotal, pretty much everyone I knew as a teenager in North Jersey regarded the "Jackson Whites" ("Ramapough" was unknown to us except in the form of the Ramapo River and the Ramapo Mountains [where the Ramapough community lived for the most part]) as exotic black "hillbillies."

When Williams, then, speaks of "perhaps a dash of Indian blood," it is hard for anyone familiar enough with the Ramapoughs to recognize the reference not to think about the possibility, really the likelihood given the terms in which the "Jackson Whites" were understood, of a dash of Negro blood. Elsie (a "voluptuous water") with her "ungainly hips and flopping breasts" is grotesque (and even monstrous, as she is described), and yet she possesses a sexual attraction for the poem's speaker, which the poem leads one to conclude is a version of Williams. There is a sense of fascinated horror that seems to reside in the dash of blood, the admixture that is the pure product of America (in the hemispheric sense) as well as the sense of potential racial reclassification that is also the pure product of America (in the sense of the United States). It is worth comparing the figure of Elsie to more straight-forwardly "black" women figures in Williams's writing, such as the "Beautiful Thing" section of *Paterson* in which these women exude a sort of beauty and sexual appeal that is perhaps intimidating but not horrifying. Again, it seems to be the possibility of the dash, the trace, the "darky" somewhere back in the family tree that/who is horrific and attractive (and horrifying in its/her attraction). Elsie, the figuration of this dash, then bears witness to the sort of existential suspension and alienation that we have seen is typical of the migration narrative subject.

The unequivocally black male figures in Williams's work, as seen in the "Shoot It, Jimmy" section immediately preceding "To Elsie," embody and vocalize a genuinely American modernity. While it is true, as Barry Ahearn notes, that it is the figures of the black musician and of jazz that are revealed as the models of the modern U.S. artist and U.S. art, it is the speaker's verbal skills that are being showcased, not his musical prowess — much as Williams does more directly in *In the American Grain* (Ahearn, 72):

> Of the colored men and women whom I have known intimately, the most loquacious is M. — who can't eat eggs because it gives him the hives. Language grows in the original from his laughing lips. . . . The relief is never ending, never failing. It is water from a spring to talk to him — it is a quality. I wish I might write a book of his improvisations in slang. I wish I might write a play in collaboration with him. (210–11)

Williams does connect M. (and Jimmy) to black music, especially jazz, which African American intellectuals such as James Weldon Johnson had long advanced as the first (and really still the only) genuine "American" body of music, a proposition that found a considerable resonance among white Americans to whom F. Scott Fitzgerald's coinage of the "Jazz Age" as a rubric for the post–World War I, pre–Great Depression United States seemed apt. The phrase "improvisations in slang" inevitably connotes jazz and the jazz artist. However, instead of arguing that black language is inflected by black music, Williams is positing the black creation of a modern and fecund "American" speech as analogous to the black creation of jazz — though, as Aldon Nielsen points out, Williams ties both black language and music to the types or stereotypes of minstrelsy/vaudeville and the plantation genre (Nielsen, 72–84).

It might be worth recalling here that Williams's early exposure to poetry included marathon readings by his father not only of Shakespeare but also of the poetry of Paul Laurence Dunbar, another of his father's favorite writers (Williams, *Autobiography*, 15). In other words, Williams's earliest sense of poetry was significantly shaped by the work of the leading black poet of the Nadir. Oddly, though perhaps not unreasonably, some commentators have assumed that Williams was referring to Dunbar's dialect poetry. However, Williams himself does not specify which of Dunbar's poems his father read, saying only that he could "to this day repeat many of the refrains he made familiar to me then" (*Autobiography*, 15). Perhaps Williams recalled "We wear the mask" as well as (or even instead of) "Jump back, honey, jump back." In fact, the lines "as if the earth under our feet / were / an excrement of some sky" of "To Elsie" do look remarkably like "the clay is vile / Beneath our feet, and long the mile" in "We Wear the Mask." Again, "We Wear the Mask" was marked by uncertainty, instability, and ambivalence related to the bifurcated legal, political, and cultural location of African Americans during the Nadir. It may be significant, also, that in his invocation of minstrelsy/vaudeville in "The Advent of the Slaves" chapter of *In the American Grain*, Williams references Bert Williams, again with Bert Williams's complicated response to minstrelsy and the advent of the Jim Crow regime, rather than the still numerous white performers who blacked up (Williams, *In the American Grain*, 209). In short, Williams draws on the different strains of minstrelsy and vaudeville, ragtime, jazz, black vernacular speech, and the Jim Crow migration narrative to figure modernist approaches to sexuality, poetic diction, and subjectivity in ways that address his personal racial anxieties and a broader sense of U.S. modernity.

"Who's Passing for Who?": Migration, Passing, and the Aporia of Racial and Sexual Anxiety in Second-Generation Modernism

> We didn't say a thing. We just stood there on the corner in Harlem
> dumbfounded — not knowing now *which* way we'd been fooled. Were they
> really white — passing for colored? Or colored — passing for white?
> Whatever race they were, they had had too much fun at
> our expense — even if they did pay for the drinks.
>
> — Langston Hughes, "Who's Passing for Who?"

The migration narrative never developed among white writers in the manner that it did among African American authors, even though there were ample demographic reasons for such a development. Journeys along the East-West and the North-South axes were a prominent feature of modernist U.S. literature, but these journeys tended to be detached from larger population movements, often even running counter to those movements. Again, though millions of white southerners moved from the rural and small-town South and Southwest to the urban North and West, southern white writers such as Wolfe and Faulkner generally featured isolated individuals, often intellectuals or would-be intellectuals such as Ben Gant or Quentin Compson, traveling North without any real contact with the millions leaving the South, rather than showing them to be part of a larger social phenomenon.

Still, these isolated modernist migrants bear more than a little resemblance to the protagonists of the early black migration narratives. Faulkner's *Light in August* features several journeys. One is Lucas Burch's flight from the pregnant Lena Grove, a flight that, as their names suggest, seeks to evade his natural destiny. Another is Grove's pursuit of Burch, attempting to heal that rupture. Burch's flight is ultimately successful as he, like many protagonists of the African American migration narrative, damns himself to perpetual rootless motion when he jumps on a freight train to escape Grove. Still another is that of Byron Bunch, a sort of white southern everyman, who replaces Burch, joining Grove and her newly born baby on a democratic American journey.

The story of the possibly mixed-race Joe Christmas is quite literally a black migration narrative. (The other major character, Gail Hightower, goes nowhere — in fact, he refuses to leave the town of Jefferson despite considerable pressure from the townsfolk to do so.) Unlike the usual black narrative with a "passing" element, neither Christmas nor the reader is absolutely sure he is a "Negro" because the tales of his parentage are told by variously self-interested and/or mad characters, none of whom could be said to be reliable or possess reliable information. Nonetheless, *Light in August* delineates the familiar black migration protagonist's gothic cycle yo-yoing between North (including the newly formed ghettos of the urban North) and South, black and white, without any sort of rest or resolution until Christmas's death by lynching.

In Fitzgerald's *The Great Gatsby*, one encounters journeys along both the North-South and the East-West axes. In many respects, the racialized cast of the North-South migration narrative inflects *Gatsby*'s West-East journeys. As critics have noted, Jimmy Gatz's transmogrification into Jay Gatsby, from a poor, non-WASP, possibly Jewish boy into (to use the gangster Meyer Wolfsheim's phrase), an "Oggsford man," has about it much of the African American passing story.[1] Yet, on the face of it, so to speak, Gatsby's effort seems unusually inept when compared to that of the typical protagonist in the African American passing genre. People from the class into which Gatsby is allegedly trying to pass almost immediately identify him as an outsider. Conversely, a given of the African American "passing" genre is that the person "passing" as "white" must be able to masquerade convincingly for white people, if not always for African Americans. Even the *nouveaux riches* or would be *riches* of East Egg are uncertain about Gatsby, reading into his pose all sorts of histories.

It is the characters whose upper-class white heterosexual status seems to be secure who resemble more traditional protagonists of the passing narrative. The novel is marked by strange sexual and racial aporias. There are hints that Daisy Faye Buchanan and Jordan Baker may not be "white." Tom Buchanan, for instance, hesitates before including his wife in the "Nordic race." Nick Carraway is quite possibly gay or bisexual—a possibility that is raised openly in the narration by the scene where Carraway finds himself in a hotel room in his underwear after going to visit the photographer Mr. McKee. Why, after all, does Carraway accept McKee's homoerotically suggestive invitation, or why, for that matter, does he find Gatsby gorgeous, as he clearly finds the taste and even the intelligence of McKee and Gatsby questionable? Obviously, the attraction is on another level.

New York, then, particularly Manhattan, becomes a place where anything is possible, where one can remake oneself, or perhaps in a certain sense become oneself, reversing the traditional symbolic valences of East and West in the United States and mapping onto them also the meanings of North and South in African American literature. The journey north to freedom and the possibility of a remaking of community, social bonds, and culture along with the attendant problems of isolation, alienation, and the loss of a sense of roots in African American narrative become the journey east; and, like North and South in the black migration narrative, both East and West are unbearable. This notion of the world turned upside down can be most clearly seen in the moment on the Queensboro Bridge when Carraway sees a car in which three black men and black women are being driven by a white chauffeur, marking a boundary past which even Gatsby, or some other version of Nick, is possible.

As with the work of the older white (or offwhite) modernists, *Gatsby* displays much anxiety about racial boundaries, which are closely linked to class and sexuality. There is a suggestion that the "old money" characters in *Gatsby* (who are not from the eastern truly old money, but from midwestern wealth of a more recent vintage) are descended from earlier Gatsbys made good. The Carraway family derives its fortune from Nick's great-uncle, an immigrant who avoided service in the Civil War and began a successful hardware business (quite possibly doing much business with the military). The family story about being descended from the Scottish "Dukes of Buccleuch" is at least as fabulous as Gatsby's own self-invention. Even the description of a painting of the great-uncle as "hard-boiled" resembles Carraway's first impression of Gatsby as an "elegant young roughneck." Though the source of the even greater Buchanan family fortune is not revealed, it is likely that Tom's wealth has a similar pedigree. And, as mentioned previously, Daisy and Jordan are southerners whose intertwinings of black and white socially and perhaps biologically call their status into question. To alter slightly the famous British adage about gentlemen, it apparently takes three generations to make a white man (and maybe less for a white woman). Nick, not unlike the protagonist of *Autobiography of an Ex-Colored Man*, opts for a normative heterosexual upper-class white identity, for the "interminable inquisitions" of the Upper Midwest. Carraway takes this path not in pursuit of love, for either Jay Gatsby or Jordan Baker, but in flight from it.

For Fitzgerald, then, like Faulkner, but unlike Eliot, Stevens, and Williams, the central issue or anxiety is not whether or not one is "white" enough—though Fitzgerald did apparently feel some discomfort about his own family's melding of WASP and "Black Irish" (Goldsmith, 447). Rather, the issue is the anxiety about whiteness (and blackness) and various forms of miscegenation itself. This anxiety is closely tied to an extreme commodification of humans and human emotions (seen perhaps most hilariously and poignantly in the moment where Gatsby articulates his love to Daisy, whose own voice is described as sounding "full of money," by showing her his collection of shirts). After all, much of the novel turns on the coining, valuation, hoarding, and spending of social worth and social status, which is linked as much to race and ethnicity as to property. As Faulkner often posited in his novels, whatever his precise beliefs on racial equality, two great and insane events marked out the trajectory of the United States: the commodification of the land (as it was bought or seized from Native peoples as embodied in Ikkemotubbe in the appendix to *The Sound and the Fury*) and the commodification of people in chattel slavery. These two events resulted in the North-South and East-West axes with all their symbolic meanings mapped onto the green land that the Dutch sailors gaze upon at the end of Fitzgerald's novel.

"Real Fun in the Dark House": Black Bohemians/Black Bohemia

> LULA: (*Laughs at him*) Real fun in the dark house. Hah! Real fun in the dark house, high up above the street and the ignorant cowboys. I lead you in, holding your wet hand gently in my hand . . .
>
> CLAY: Which is not wet?
>
> LULA: Which is dry as ashes.
>
> CLAY: And cold?
>
> LULA: Don't think you'll get out of your responsibility that way. It's not cold at all. You Fascist! Into my dark living room. Where we'll sit and talk endlessly, endlessly.
>
> CLAY: About what?
>
> LULA: About what? About your manhood, what do you think? What do you think we've been talking about all this time?
>
> —Amiri Baraka, *Dutchman*

Interestingly, in the work of many black authors of more or less the same generation as Fitzgerald and Faulkner—and even, in a different modality, later writers such as Amiri Baraka—there is often a sense that interracial homosexuality is a way out of or away from race and that intraracial heterosexuality is a way back into an authentic African American identity. Whether this interracial intersection is an occasion for what Margo Crawford terms "dilution anxiety" or for a sense of liberation from the physical and psychic spaces of Jim Crow (or some combination of the two) varies. In part, this has much to do with the continued development of U.S. bohemia as an interracial and significantly "queer" or "free love" space prominently featuring intellectual, social, and sexual intermingling of black and white.

Following in the pioneering footsteps of Paul Laurence Dunbar, James Weldon Johnson, and Fenton Johnson, the representation of a predominantly black bohemia generally tied to Harlem and a predominantly white bohemia most often linked to Greenwich Village became a recurring feature of such New Negro Renaissance novels as Jean Toomer's *Cane*, Jessie Fauset's *Plum Bun*, Nella Larsen's *Quicksand*, Rudolph Fisher's *Walls of Jericho*, Wallace Thurman's *Infants of the Spring*, and Claude McKay's *Home to Harlem* and *Banjo*. I say predominantly because in almost all these novels, bohemia, whether in Harlem, Chicago's North Side, or Greenwich Village (or Copenhagen), seems to require an interracial presence.

These bohemias also seem to require, more often than not, transgressive interracial and often queer, if not gay, sexual pairings. This is not surprising, not simply because of the much remarked biographical fact that a huge proportion of Harlem Renaissance writers were gay, but also because of the importance of gay networks to the careers of male black writers of era.[2] Much of the cultural interaction between uptown and downtown, which resulted in the publishing of many black authors took place through essentially gay networks that connected those artists with white patrons who supported them financially and/or provided contacts to white-owned publishing companies, to white magazine editors, and to white-run foundations, which provided grants to writers and artists, and so on. For example, within three weeks of meeting Langston Hughes, gay white bohemian novelist, critic, photographer, and raconteur Carl Van Vechten lobbied Alfred Knopf for the publication of Hughes's first book, *The Weary Blues* (1926) (Bernard, 36).

However, with the rise of new visions of black vanguards, black nations, and black internationals under the influence of the Garvey movement and the post–October Revolution Communist movement, for the most part African American writers depict these bohemias as ultimately failing the black artist/intellectual. These depictions often draw on the tropes of the early black migration novels, portraying a protagonist doomed to the perpetual motion or sort of death in life that characterized so many of the earlier works — though a few New Negro Renaissance writers, notably McKay, turn the trope on its head and make perpetual movement a virtue. Those who seem to survive more or less unscathed are more distinctly working-class characters who have befriended the artist-intellectual and devoted themselves to intraracial heterosexuality, as in *Walls of Jericho* and *Home to Harlem* (though McKay would revise this vision in *Banjo*), or those who find some sort of haven outside the United States as in *Plum Bun* or *Banjo*, recalling the ending of Pauline Hopkins's *Contending Forces* and anticipating a long line of African American literature, such as Baraka's *Dutchman*, in which an interracial bohemia as a refuge from the Jim Crow United States is interrogated and found tragically wanting.

The U.S. literary careers of Jean Toomer and Claude McKay both largely emerged out of the more Left currents of Greenwich Village bohemia and New York–based outposts of "new poetry" embodied in such journals as ·Seven Arts and The Liberator (which McKay would later coedit for a time with Mike Gold)—though McKay also corresponded with William Stanley Braithwaite in Boston (Wayne Cooper, 78–102).[3] Both (even Toomer) maintained close connections to black artistic, intellectual, and political groups in the late 1910s and early 1920s, Hubert Harrison and the African Blood Brotherhood in McKay's case and Georgia Douglas Johnson's Washington, D.C.–based salon of black writers in Toomer's (Wayne Cooper, 90–91; Hutchinson, "Jean Toomer and the 'New Negroes' of Washington"). Still, for the most part their early publications and literary reputations issued from downtown bohemia. Both prominently display bohemia, both black and white, in their work, linking bohemia to migration and sexual liminality, if not sexual freedom.

Many scholars have noted that Toomer's Cane (1923), with its multiple journeys to and from the folk motivated by desire, anxiety, alienation, and brutal racial violence, mirrored his extremely complicated relationship to the usual divisions of racial identity in the United States. Structurally it replicated his lifelong search for a physical, mental, and spiritual wholeness that did not reduce simplistically his deeply felt sense of a fragmented and often conflicted social, economic, psychological, and sexual identity. This search led him to a deep if uneasy engagement with various bodies of thought that sought to analyze and make whole this complexly broken identity, including Marxism (he was an early contributing editor of New Masses), psychoanalysis, and Gurdjieff's "Fourth Way." This is not so much to say that Toomer's Cane is essentially autobiographical as that Toomer (not unlike the beat poet Bob Kauffman thirty years later) presented himself in a way that harmonized with his work.

Farah Jasmine Griffin perceptively argues that Toomer takes and deepens James Weldon Johnson's emphasis on threat and execution of lynch violence as an impetus for movement out of the South—and as much of the cause of a state of permanent psychic instability for those remaining in (or returning to) the region (24–28). The problem of the South is compounded by the fact that the capitalism and capitalist alienation associated with the North are seen as migrating south, infecting even the black folk. This infection is shown by the young men who run stills, work on the railroad in big cities, and go to college to bring money to Karintha (a "growing thing ripened too soon," 2) and by the transformation of Barlo from prophet to businessman. A mixed-race, alienated woman like Esther might seek a seer of the southern soil and find a drunken bootlegger, as Barlo has become. In short, as in Du Bois's *Souls*, the South is in the process of being colonized economically and spiritually by the North while maintaining the racial terrorism of Jim Crow.

Still, the North, even bohemia, is not seen as viable solution — though, as Mark Whalan notes, Toomer does seem to display an admiration for the vitality of the new urban working-class black culture seen in "Seventh Street" (77). "Paul and Bona," the last part of the second, urban section of *Cane*, features a sexually and racially indeterminate bohemian triangulation of the mixed-race Paul (variously labeled as a "poet," a "philosopher," and a "gym director"), his white roommate Art (a jazz musician), who has a passionate if not openly sexual attachment to Paul, and a white woman, Bona. Art and Bona both want to know Paul's race and feelings (which are closely tied to a notion of race). Art, for example, muses: "Queer about him. I could stick up for him if he'd only come out, one way or the other, and tell a feller. Besides, a room-mate has a right to know. Thinks I wont understand. Said So. He's got a swell head when it comes to brains, all right. God, he's a good straight feller, though. Only, moony" (75). Both Art and Bona want to know if he's black or if he's white, if he's "cold" or "colored," if he can love or not.

Paul is reluctant to answer those questions, to be forced into those polarities of race and sex. After a passionate dance with Bona in a nightclub that seems to have overcome Bona's doubts about his passion and reservations about his "race," Paul stops to talk with a black doorman with knowing eyes. Paul tells the doorman that he's wrong, presumably that the doorman's assessment of Paul and Bona is incorrect. What is this assessment? It is unclear, but it might be the not unreasonable assumption that Paul is a "Negro" passing as white who has successfully pursued a white woman. Paul assures him that he is not passing, but is in fact truly neither black nor white, but both and more. He intends to gather the rose petals of white faces and the dusk petals of dark faces. However, when he finishes his conversation, really a strange soliloquy, he finds Bona has left. As Geoffrey Jacques argues, the final note of "Paul and Bona" is one of irredeemable loss and rupture as one of the petals Paul has sought to gather to himself is gone — one might add that Art, too, has become another disappearing petal (145–46). This failure of what is seen as a middle-class, or petty-bourgeois if you will, bohemia to square the triangle of Art, Bona, and Paul and allow them all to be human outside of the U.S. racial regime anticipates in a less angry and demonic fashion the failure of bohemia as a liberated space for the black subject in Baraka's *Dutchman* — perhaps accounting at least in part for what might seem to be an unlikely admiration of Toomer's work on Baraka's part in the mid-1960s.

The sense of loss and rupture at the end of "Paul and Bona" set the stage for the following and concluding "Kabnis" section. Again, as many have commented, Ralph Kabnis is a light-skinned "Negro" version of the archetypal modernist protagonist, a *luftmensch* "suspended a few feet above the soil whose touch would resurrect him" (96). Kabnis is a bohemian, a writer-intellectual in flight from northern urban alienation and terrified by the violence-soaked gothic atmosphere of the southern Black Belt to which he has come to teach. A remedy for Kabnis's alienation is proposed: all he has to do is descend a few feet and plant himself in the soil.

However, there seems to be no adequate means for him to travel even those few feet. The soil appears to be currently accessible to only a decreasing number of rural black southerners. Farah Jasmine Griffin reminds us that for Kabnis to gain such access he would have to acknowledge in a deep way the black ancestor embodied by Father John (152–53). Kabnis is not prepared or able to do that — or at least he is not prepared to be black in that way. After all, why should he (or even how could he) be black in that way? He is a mixed-race (American race) intellectual-artist from the North. He is in the process of rejecting Father John and returning to the yo-yoing path of the alienated migration protagonist when stopped by Carrie Kate, a figure both heterosexually romantic and maternal. She is able to arrest his dismissal of Father John and what John embodies while leaving open the possibility that Kabnis will finally reach the soil without a clear resolution. Again, such a planting would require much pruning of Kabnis. *Cane* ends with a dawn in mirror image of the dusk that begins the book, suggesting rebirth, renewal, and infinite hope, but whether, after Franz Kafka's famous comment to Max Brod about hope, it is accessible to Kabnis (or Toomer) in the United States is unclear. Certainly, if *Cane* is in part, as many have argued (including Toomer in "Song of the Son"), an elegy for the disappearing southern black folk spirit and folk culture rooted in the slave era, then one cannot be too sanguine that Kabnis can become rooted in the soil of the old folk. And while it is clear that Kabnis needs to be rooted somehow, it is not clear that a return to the faint song of (some of) his ancestors heard by the "son" is entirely desirable. In this, Toomer's vision resembles that of the early William Blake in which "Experience" eclipses "Innocence" with dire results. However, a return to "Innocence" is not possible except as some form of infantilism; instead, some third state, some transcendence of "Experience" that might be thought of as informed or tested "Innocence" is necessary or, as Griffin says, "a form of balance between Southern spirituality and Northern ingenuity" (66).

Carl Van Vechten in many respects takes up Toomer's (and, by extension, James Weldon Johnson's) vision of migration and middle-class black bohemia in his 1926 *Nigger Heaven*. The novel has a bifurcated character as a travel guide to black Harlem in the 1920s presented by the white would-be insider Van Vechten (and one thinks of Miguel Covarrubias's famous caricature of Van Vechten's future transformation into a "Negro" here) and as a cautionary tale of the dangers of middle-class bohemia and alienation in the urban North. The two chief characters of the novel, the writer Byron Kasson and the librarian Mary Love, are alienated from their vital "Negro" essences, rendering them artistically, intellectually, emotionally, and sexually sterile. They stand in contrast to such characters as the criminal rounder Anatole Longfellow (aka "the Scarlet Creeper") and the sadomasochistic, bondage and domination cokehead, Satanist temptress Lasca Sartoris, who are virtually nothing but vital primitive essences. Love and Kasson are doubly (at least) removed from Toomer's folk spirit in that they are migrants to Harlem not from the rural South but from urban black middle-class families in the black bourgeois strongholds of Philadelphia and Washington, D.C.

One might read the tragic narrative of Byron and Mary as a drag and semi-blackface projection on Van Vechten's part. This reading suggests that, like European modernists (especially visual artists with their well-known engagement with African art), white North American writers (and their middle-class black counterparts) need to get in touch with the vital currents of African American popular and folk cultures, must "black up" a bit, in order to create truly viable American modernism. In other words, Byron and Mary really are "white"; and Creeper and Lasca are not people but monstrous forms of the repressed portion of the white subject that must be engaged. In fact, without real engagement this repressed will return in some monstrous form, as it does with Byron after his seduction by Lasca, recalling Robert Louis Stevenson's Jekyll and Hyde and, as Robert Dowling remarks, Joe after his seduction by Hattie in Dunbar's *The Sport of the Gods* (Dowling, *Slumming*, 146). After all, Van Vechten does not seem to suggest that it is desirable Byron and Mary actually become the Creeper and Lasca — Byron's end as a sort of Creeper manqué is tragic. Rather, he argues that they (like urban white people generally) need to get in more intimate touch with the relatively unrepressed spirit of the black urban masses in order to create a new and powerful art (and perhaps life). In that sense, Van Vechten's position is not far from (and is likely largely derived from) that of Toomer in *Cane*—and Hughes in the "The Negro Artist and the Racial Mountain," for that matter. However, one of the many problems with Van Vechten's novel, besides its almost total lack of historical context despite its various details of Harlem life (especially nightlife), is that its characters are pure types without any capacity of transcending those types, whether the instinctual demi-monde Negro or the clichéd introverted and alienated intellectual unable to act. Even Byron's attempt to kill his replacement in Lasca's affections, such as they are, is ineffectual because the Scarlet Creeper has already killed his rival. All Byron will be able to do is take the blame for the murder and no doubt be executed for the death.

While Claude McKay's first published novel, *Home to Harlem* (1928) was often associated with Van Vechten's novel as a salacious misrepresentation of Harlem life, it was in many respects an answer to *Nigger Heaven*, presenting the black intellectual as capable of connecting with the best in the folk spirit and showing the epitome of that spirit as being far from anti-intellectual and contemplative. *Home to Harlem* and the linked novel *Banjo* (1929) project a vision of a mobile working-class queer black bohemia (in which some potentially or lapsed middle-class artist-intellectuals participate) as the ideal rather than a static black middle-class or would-be black middle-class bohemia as a trap and endless migration as a sort of Ancient Mariner–Flying Dutchman–like doom. Both novels are in some senses morality tales featuring temptations/seductions that undermine the solidarity of McKay's black bohemian ideal: a black middle-class (at least in style and aspiration, if not always in occupation and income) heterosexuality in *Home to Harlem* and a predominantly white queer (or even gay) bohemia in *Banjo*.

Home to Harlem is perhaps the most traditionally "proletarian" of the two in that the chief characters generally have fairly steady jobs as stevedores and Pullman porters, with much of the novel describing workers' socialities, both on and off the job. The most clearly heroic character of the novel, the "natural man" Jake, shows almost instinctive working-class values when he refuses to be a scab in a longshoreman's strike—though he will not join a union because of his experience with racist union practices. It is also one of the earliest novels set in the United States with a sympathetic openly gay character, Billy Biase. In that sense, it is the more overtly "queer" of the two novels in that Biase's homosexuality is accepted without question by his friends Jake and Ray even as they pursue (or fall out of) heterosexual unions throughout the novel. While Jake's closest friend (and the major character appearing in both novels), the Haitian expatriate artist-intellectual Ray, does not marry his girlfriend, Agatha, and ships out on a freighter to Europe, Jake does settle down with his romantic obsession Felice (a prostitute whom Jake meets at the beginning of the novel and seeks off and on through the rest of the narrative). In many respects, the real romantic breakup is not Agatha and Ray, but Jake and Ray.

Ironically, it is meeting Agatha that makes Jake desire a stable, heterosexual relationship with a good woman. Though Agatha, an assistant in a beauty shop, could be seen as a typical working-class Harlem woman, she seems to stand in for middle-class uplift and aspiration, which Ray emphatically rejects in the end. Perhaps even more pointedly, the end of the novel critiques the romance of Harlem and the New Negro Renaissance, particularly Alain Locke's claim that Harlem is the modern capital of the Negro world. As in Nella Larsen's portrait of the race-conscious, yet strangely Eurocentric New Negro circles of Anne Grey and Dr. Robert Anderson in her 1928 novel *Quicksand*, McKay depicts the powerful attraction (and even compulsion) of a middle-class cultural nationalism that in many respects reifies a new artistic version of the old model of the "triangle trade" between Europe, Africa, and the Americas, seeing the relationships of that "Atlantic World" (with one of the vertices, Europe, strangely and impossibly at the center) as necessarily the most significant.

As Gary Holcomb notes, what attracts McKay (and Ray) about Harlem is its identity as a center of diasporan black working-class life and of a blue-collar black queer sensibility in which this version of the triangle trade is not fetishized (91–138). It is telling in this respect that the male workers displayed in the novel are primarily those laboring in various transcontinental and transnational transport industries—railroad workers, longshoremen, and merchant seamen. However, for an intellectual and aspiring artist like Ray, it seems the only future that what McKay sees as Lockean Harlem ultimately holds is a heteronormative, bourgeois (or petty-bourgeois, if you will) complacency for "contented hogs in the pigpen of Harlem" and "slaves of the civilized tradition" (*Home to Harlem*, 263). Ray's only real option is to leave Harlem. It is significant that, even though Ray departs for Europe, he does so traveling west on a freighter via the Pacific and Australia, not east across the Atlantic on, say, the Cunard Line.

After losing Jake to heteronormative marriage, Ray finds his soulmate, Lincoln Agrippa Daily (aka "Banjo"), in the second novel, the 1929 *Banjo*. In many respects, the core of the novel is a gay screwball comedy, a sort of *When Harry Met Sally* of the black diaspora, or a novel of no manners in which lovers meet, are attracted, are split up by a group of "gentlemen bum" white bohemians (and a bohemian white woman) who lure Banjo to follow them to the Riviera, and are ultimately reunited. As is the case in many screwball comedies, relatively little action and a great deal of conversation occurs. The setting of the novel is, for the most part, not the Paris beloved of the Francophile Locke, but the Vieux Port or "the Ditch" of Marseilles, France's largest commercial seaport and perhaps the most important port of the Mediterranean rim in the early twentieth century — as well as a prominent center of early twentieth-century black Europe. Again, it is significant that Banjo, like Ray, reaches the Ditch from the east, sailing on a freighter across the Pacific to New Zealand and Australia and then around the entire coast of Africa.

In other words, Banjo's travels describe a diasporic arc that is global in reach and not simply transatlantic. When the pair, anticipating Humphrey Bogart and Claude Rains at the end of *Casablanca*, begin to "beat it a long ways from here" (326) at the end of the novel, they are headed to unnamed "ports where black men assembled for the great transport lines, loafing after their labors long enough to laugh and love and jazz and fight" (319). These men, like those who form the base of the milieu in which Ray and Banjo immerse themselves in Marseilles, come from all across the black world, from North and South America, the Caribbean, Africa, and even Europe, traveling on the multidirectional circuits of the colonialized world as well as on older routes reaching back into antiquity, particularly of the interlocking Mediterranean and Islamic worlds. As a result, the conversations of the screwball comedy are joined by others that form a modernist composite portrait of a new black working class produced by what V. I. Lenin termed "Imperialism," that is "capitalism . . . grown into a world system of colonial oppression and of the financial strangulation of the overwhelming majority of the population of the world by a handful of 'advanced' countries" (674). It is worth noting, as Holcomb does, that the black proletariat of *Banjo* is not the traditional Marxist one because Banjo, Ray, and their crowd work only when absolutely necessary — and often in trades that would mark them as "lumpen" or declassed by many Marxists. However, Ray (and Holcomb) sees in this refusal to assimilate to the industrial system a particularly effective example of class and racial struggle (Holcomb, 155). The Ditch, then, is not a paradise, but it is a space where sailors, waterfront workers, musicians, prostitutes, dancers, drifters, and petty criminals of many nationalities and ethnicities interact more or less freely. In a sense, this (and zones like it around the world) is for McKay the true international capital of the modern Negro World that Locke claimed Harlem to be.

The beautiful friendship between Banjo and Ray is also a utopian marriage of the proletariat and an alienated and radical black intelligentsia, a new black International. Like Jake in *Home to Harlem*, Banjo is from the U.S. South and has worked as a laborer in many trades. He, too, is a sort of "natural man," irresistible to women, an instinctive leader with an innate decency and an intellectual curiosity seen in his deep respect for Ray's serious engagement with art and "book learning." It is this connection, as Holcomb argues, with a transnational proletarian blackness that grounds Ray, allowing him, ultimately, to avoid the various seductions of identification with the metropole (or metropolitan "white" bohemia) to which the black intellectual is prone, just as Banjo avoids the more working-class pitfalls of narrow nationalism and anti-intellectualism. Both escape the trap of normative heterosexual domesticity, whether in a petty bourgeois or working-class mode.

Even the possibility that women could be a part of this mobile marriage is rejected at the novel's end. Interestingly, it is Ray who regrets that Latnah, Banjo's ethnically and racially ambiguous, but clearly non-European paramour, cannot accompany them; and it is the "natural man" and woman magnet Banjo who forecloses that desire with the somewhat cryptic, "A woman is a conjunction. Gawd fixed her different from us in moh ways than one" (326). In this view, it is not only the "middle-class" (in values and aspirations anyway) Agatha who is left behind by this new black International but even the profoundly transnational, mobile, antibourgeois, and hybrid (though, again, non-European) Latnah. In fact, Jake makes a brief cameo in *Banjo*, seeming a bit frustrated and strangely diminished by his choice of domestic heteronormativity in comparison to Banjo's rejection of it. In short, it is a profoundly masculinist and nationalist radical working-class vision that is as troubling in whom it excludes as it is exhilarating in its celebration of sexual, cultural, and economic liberation.[4]

When considering the African American migration narrative of the Harlem Renaissance and its link to bohemia, it is worth noting that while black women writers of the era in such novels as Nella Larsen's *Quicksand* (1928) and Jessie Fauset's *Plum Bun* (1929) are cognizant of the traditional North-South axis of the genre, they are more concerned with the migration of the artist-intellectual to Harlem from northern cities that are often famous and even iconic centers of black middle-class life, such as Philadelphia, Washington, Boston, and even Chicago, but which have become somewhat provincial with the increasing concentration of the culture industries (other than film) in New York.

The political, intellectual, and artistic movement that we still associate with the community of Harlem in New York was both an actual and symbolic migration. As Sterling Brown commented, few of the leading New Negro Renaissance figures connected to Harlem came from New York (185). For example, Dorothy West and Helene Johnson came from New England; Langston Hughes and Larsen came from the Midwest; Arna Bontemps, Louise Thompson, and Wallace Thurman came from the far West; Alain Locke, Jean Toomer, Bruce Nugent, and Fauset came from the Mid-Atlantic states; and Claude McKay and Eric Walrond came from the Caribbean. But virtually none of these writers came from the South (unless one considers Washington, D.C., to be in the South). Thus, the notion of Harlem as the political and cultural "capital of the Negro World" based both on a literal great migration of black artists and intellectuals from what they generally saw as the cultural provinces outside the South to the black metropole and on a symbolic migration in which artists identified with Harlem without actually living there, as in the case of Alain Locke, a leading black intellectual who played a major role in promoting Harlem as the center of an African American "renaissance" but whose home base was Washington, D.C. One might see in Brown's objection to a "Harlem" renaissance an unease with the interracial gay aspect of that association and the relationship of that aspect to white patronage. However, the vehemence of the objection also reflects a discomfort with (and even moral objection to) the shift of the center of black intellectual and literary life from the older centers of Philadelphia and, especially, Washington, to the relatively new black community of Harlem and of the black cultural center of gravity from the South to the "Negro Capital of the World."

The trips to and from New York described in Nella Larsen's *Quicksand* follow the archetypal black migration inherited by the Harlem Renaissance, but with some significant feminist-inflected revisions. The travels of the protagonist Helga Crane, child of a union between a white mother and black father in Chicago, resemble the yo-yoing of James Weldon Johnson's ex-colored man. Like those of Johnson's protagonist, Crane's journeys begin in medias res: the reader knows that she moved from her native Chicago to attend Fisk University and then went on to a teaching position at a Tuskegee-like institution, Naxos, where the novel opens. From there she travels to Chicago, to Harlem, to Copenhagen, back to Harlem, and finally (and probably fatally) to the rural South. Again, she differs from the ex-colored man in that she is not a southerner by birth (and we do not even know if her father was from the South). Her movements anticipate and perhaps influence those of

Janie Crawford/Killicks/Starks/Woods in Zora Neale Hurston's *Their Eyes Were Watching God* in that each place linked to a certain social and ideological milieu comes with a man who in some senses defines that milieu and limits Crane's choices. Obviously, one difference of which Hurston was no doubt aware is that Crane never truly is on her own in the way Janie is in the end, except in one terrifying moment in Chicago that Crane flees as soon as she is able. And Crane never has the control of the narration that Janie has. One might also add that in Larsen's novel almost every place and every man comes with a gate-keeping woman who either blocks Crane or attempts to channel her in ways she ultimately does not want to go, so that the novel also resembles *Their Eyes* in that it is, for the most part, a feminist or feminist-inflected novel about the individual female subject than rather one about women's solidarity.

The journeys that Helga Crane undertakes are in large part a critique of the intellectual and literary movements of the time, particularly of those bohemian movements as adopted and adapted by African American writers in the early twentieth century, including the elitist, repressed, and essentially self-hating if ironically race-conscious bohemia of Robert Anderson, Ann Gray, and their circle in Harlem, as well as the hedonist, primitivist, predominantly white bohemia of Axel Olsen in Copenhagen. Both bohemias (and middle-class black uplift) fail Crane as a black woman intellectual (and possible artist). Not unlike Jean Rhys's *Quartet*, *Quicksand* shows bohemia, both black and white, as a space in which predatory men can behave badly toward women without serious consequences. This space is prowled not only by hard-core bohemians like Axel Olsen but also by pillars of middle-class uplift, as embodied by Robert Anderson and James Vayle, who like to vacation emotionally and sexually in the more bohemian spheres of Harlem before buttoning themselves back up. And, connecting with the end of "Kabnis," Larsen deflates the utopian vision of a simple return to the folk, as Crane finds herself trapped in a series of pregnancies with a hygienically challenged rural preacher who values her, ironically, much like James Vayle in his uplift persona only for her sophisticated appearance but lacks any passion for her (which is reserved for the "blacker" Clementina Richards). With each pregnancy she has grown weaker, and the likely result seems to be death in childbirth.

Ultimately, the failure of Crane is to find her own voice and speak and write. Though one can say that Crane has the capacity to say no or to reject different identities, she never really learns to forge her own identity. This is not to say that Crane wants to or should completely put herself beyond social identity — while the various versions of blackness presented in the novel are clearly unsatisfactory for Crane, probably the most terrifying and most desperate moments of the novel (with the possible exception of the ending) are those in Chicago where Crane has fallen through the cracks of normative class, racial, gender, and family identity with the result that she is really neither one thing nor the other.

If it is possible to present an optimistic reading of *Quicksand*, it is as a text that interacts with other migration texts and reflects on the value and meaning of literature and literacy. The fact that we are reading this book posits a different sort of ending (an ending that Hurston will in fact write — an ending supported by the way Nella Larsen crafted her biography to correspond to that of Crane). That is a sort of alternate universe where Crane moves beyond the parties of Harlem and beyond Anderson, to find her own voice and tell her own story, to write a novel something like *Quicksand*. What I am suggesting is that what we have here is a sort of narrative about the gaining of literacy along the lines of Frederick Douglass's first and second narratives in which literacy means the ability not simply to read what other people have written but to find one's own voice and to speak from the printed page — and, as in Douglass's second narrative and his struggle to found a journal, to actually control the material production of the text. The difference here is that the success story is not that of Helga Crane but that of Nella Larsen.

Fauset's *Plum Bun* has often and unfairly been described as an overly genteel novel, often by her black male contemporaries, such as Claude McKay and even Langston Hughes (who was usually much more generous to fellow writers), perhaps in part as a result of a skepticism about black women writers' ability to really capture the nitty-gritty of the street, especially in the woman-identified, novel-of-manners form that Fauset often adopted and adapted (combined with other genres, such as the *Bildungsroman* and the *Künstlerroman*), and of a resentment toward the power Fauset held for some years as the literary editor of *The Crisis* (Hutchinson, *Harlem Renaissance in Black and White*, 156–57). It is true that she generally focused on what might be seen as black "middle-class" life — though in the case of the Murray family of *Plum Bun*, it might be more accurate to describe the Murrays as a working-class family living in a respectable but nondescript working-class neighborhood where the parents owned a modest home, which was perhaps their most significant economic achievement.

Still, the romantic novel of manners from its beginning, say in Jane Austen's *Pride and Prejudice*, is a genre much associated with gender relations and gender conflict *and* class relations and class conflict. Austen's novels were often quite bitter in their resentment of the old aristocracy and the new bourgeoisie, even if there was some sort of rapprochement in marriage at the end—and even that rapprochement was pretty bitter in *Mansfield Park*, which featured a more or less working-class (and certainly plebian) protagonist. Thus, as Deborah McDowell suggested in her introduction to the 1990 reprint of *Plum Bun*, it was a form that lent itself to explorations of the intersections and conflict between race, class, and gender in that era of black renaissance and high feminism (McDowell, xxviii–xxix).

Fauset particularly modernizes the novel of manners in *Plum Bun* in a bohemian race- and gender-conscious manner. The novel ends not in marriage but in a romantic-sexual union between two "Negro" artists, Angela Murray and Anthony Cross, who had for a considerable time passed (or at least allowed themselves to be taken) as "white." The union takes place in the Latin Quarter of Paris, the bohemian homeland, not the United States. It also diverges notably from the novel of manners in that Murray out of sexual desire, material ambition, and the desire for a "good" marriage, allows herself to be "kept" by a sort of semibohemian white rake, the wealthy and racist heir Roger Fielding. While Murray breaks off and regrets the relationship with Fielding, she does not feel herself to be in any way ruined. She does not really feel bad about having a sexual relationship outside of marriage (or enjoying sex for that matter) but regrets that she had it with Fielding for such shallow reasons, forcing her to deny her own family and the black community generally. She seems happy enough to pursue sex and romance with Anthony Cross when he appears as an erotic Christmas present without any real guarantee that marriage is in the future. While these sorts of scenes are the stuff of popular romances in our own time, it is hardly accurate to call them "genteel" in any normative "middle-class" manner in the 1920s.

One interesting aspect of Fauset's novel is that she depicts the yo-yoing of the typical migration protagonist largely within the confines of New York City, with Murray moving between the basically white bohemian scene of Greenwich Village, where she passes as "white" and the black bohemian milieu of her sister Virginia in Harlem where she is publicly "Negro" again. Particularly after her break with Fielding, she oscillates between these two zones until she declares herself to be a "Negro" in the Village out of her solidarity with the one publicly identified "Negro" in her downtown art school, the dark-skinned Rachel Powell. Unlike most of the migration novels, one might say that the novel has a clearly happy ending, but like Hopkins's *Contending Forces*, it is not one that seems to be possible within the confines of the United States.

Harlem Renaissance novels often take up with varying degrees of bitterness and/or humor Baudelaire's (and Dunbar's) notion of the bohemian flaneur as someone who appears to be uninterested in commerce but who is really in the business of selling himself or herself as well as others. Like Dunbar's *The Sport of the Gods*, these novels frequently emphasize the unequal racial exchange between black bohemians and white bohemians in which black bohemians like Paul Arabian in Wallace Thurman's *Infants of the Spring* travel downtown to a predominantly white bohemia to sell themselves, vouchsafing the radical nature of that bohemia by their presence, while white bohemians travel uptown to Harlem (like Skaggs did to the Banner Bar in Dunbar's novel) to sell a colorful black counterculture to a white public. Indeed, thinly veiled versions of Carl Van Vechten populate quite a few of these novels with various degrees of humorous or sinister intent:

"No, Con. You're the only fay I know that draws the color line on other fays."

"It's natural. Downtown I'm only passing. These," he waved grandiloquently, "are my people."

"Yea—so you seem to think, the way you sell 'em for cash," said Cornelia.

"They enjoy being sold," returned Con. (Fisher, 117)

The result of this intersection of black and white queer bohemia is frequently seen as disastrous for black artists and intellectuals (and sometimes even white artists and intellectuals). In the end, the protagonist of Thurman's *Infants of the Spring*, Ray, rejects black bohemia and white bohemia. His deep homosocial and possibly homosexual relationship with the white Scandinavian Stephen ends with Stephen's return to Europe because Stephen can no longer stand the insanity of race and the polarities of black and white. Black bohemia in its relation to the large black community is seen as too parochial, encouraging mediocrity, if not praising absolute trash. White U.S. bohemia is too shot through with racial fantasies, fears, fetishes, and deep structures of racial hierarchy to be truly welcoming and nurturing for the black artist. In the end, Ray instead gloomily contemplates some sort of internationalist vision of art that is heavily weighted toward various strands of European modernist and classic literature (and a fairly standard heterosexual marriage) resembling the sort of melancholy conclusion of the Nadir migration novel in which a satisfactory ending in the United States for the black artist is almost unimaginable.

Our Black . . . : African American Literature, Modernity, and Modernism

African American writers of the extended Nadir from the onset of Jim Crow to the beginning of the New Negro Renaissance were in many respects our first modernists—or, at the very least, did much to shape the field in which domestic U.S. modernism would grow. In a way, because of the peculiar political, social, cultural, and one might say spiritual situation in which black people in the United States found themselves with the triumph of Jim Crow, it is not surprising that they would be among the first writers to describe the sort of fragmented subjectivity and urban alienation that became a hallmark of modernism in the United States. They did much to make journeys along the North-South U.S. axis important ur-narratives of U.S. modernist fiction and poetry, narratives that also at least partly recast the racial, ethnic, and class meaning of the iconic transit between East and West.

They were also among the very first to imagine, represent, and promote a U.S. artistic bohemia linked to an "American" new literature (especially a "new poetry"), a bohemia that became increasingly defined by its interracial nature, especially by public interracial heterosexual, gay, lesbian, and bisexual unions. The interracial nature of U.S. bohemia was also tied by these writers to a sense of place, that either stood between "black" spaces and "white" spaces in increasingly hypersegregated cities or involved white journeys into public "black" spaces with varying results. This vision of an interracial bohemia continued to be a defining feature of U.S. culture into the twenty-first century.

Interracial bohemia also became a sort of negative touchstone of black nationalism and nationalist-influenced literature, especially in the second half of the twentieth-century, when this sort of bohemia was often represented as the last, false hope of a racially egalitarian American utopia. Again, perhaps the most powerful and explicit black rejection of the sort of bohemia requiring an interracial presence in the 1960s is Amiri Baraka's 1964 *Dutchman*. Baraka has often described this play as a transitional work as he was moving from downtown bohemia to a Black Arts stance in Harlem. It is literally a transitional document as it describes the end of a dream of bohemia as ideological, aesthetic, and social space that is outside the U.S. racial regime while remaining physically within national boundaries. The play is not so much a rejection of the "mainstream" United States as such—that rejection is a given or starting point of a play in which the protagonist Clay likes to imagine he is a "Black Baudelaire." Neither he nor the white temptress/murderer Lula, in search of "tender, big-eyed prey," are "mainstream" "Americans." They are bohemians, talking about going to a party in Greenwich Village followed by sex in a Greenwich Village or Lower Eastside tenement.

Of course, in the end Lula is a "mainstream" "American," is in fact a white murderer of the "black pumping heart" despite the bohemian cover. Interracial bohemia becomes a new strategy of seduction and destruction of black people, especially black men. So *Dutchman*, in a long line of African American treatments of bohemia, is transitional in that the logical extension of the play is the creation of a new sort of avant garde, a black avant garde that does not require any interracial presence and at least potentially includes the entire black community (or nation).[5]

Notes

Introduction

1. For an account of the neoslavery practiced by southern legal systems and various commercial enterprises, including, ultimately, U.S. Steel, see Blackmon.

2. The classic treatment of Harlem's growth as an African American community is James Weldon Johnson's *Black Manhattan*, 145–59. The pioneering academic study is Gilbert Osofsky's *Harlem: The Making of a Ghetto*. See also Jervis Anderson.

3. For an easily accessible source for "You Can Take Your Trunk and Go to Harlem" (and many other popular songs of the era), see the Brown University Library digital collection, "African American Sheet Music," http://dl.lib.brown.edu/sheetmusic/afam/index.html.

4. Even as late as the 1950s, when large numbers of "nonwhite" people from the Caribbean, Africa, and Asia migrated to the United Kingdom and other European countries to fill labor demands, residential patterns more resembled the urban United States of the nineteenth century. That is to say that while there were communities in which African-descended people clustered, say Moss Side in Manchester, Toxteith in Liverpool, or Brixton in London, many other peoples (e.g., poorer white British, Irish immigrants, and so on) also lived in those communities. It was not until the late twentieth century that something like the large-scale hypersegregation that long characterized urban space in the United States began to really take shape in Europe—as in the tower blocks of public housing in traditionally working-class suburbs surrounding large French cities. Even then, it is worth noting that the people segregated were actually extremely diverse ethnically (and racially, as it would be understood in the United States), united largely by their immigrant status (or immediate ancestry), often from former French colonies, and, to a large extent, some perceived or real connection to Islam, rather than descent from "black" Africa. This, of course, is not to say that some notion of race did not severely limit the ability of racial "outsiders" to become truly native citizens of these metropoles.

5. My use of "queer" in this study refers not so much to an anti-"identity politics" stance or some performative notion of gender and sexual identity as to an institutional, geographical, and/or ideological space in which heterosexuality is to some greater or lesser extent decentered, allowing for the flourishing of relatively open gay and lesbian subcultures in a legally and socially repressive era as far as gay men and lesbians (and African Americans generally) were concerned. Also, while I have found that term "queer" as it is most commonly used in Queer Theory as a counter to heteronormativity to be valuable, I remain uneasy about the ways in which such a usage obscures the historical specificities of gay and lesbian communities in the United States. Consequently, I also employ the terms "gay" and "lesbian" to engage those specificities as distinct from notions of "queer" space. Thus, while I certainly think Claude McKay's novel *Banjo*, which I address in the conclusion, has its "queer" aspects, I believe it is fundamentally a black gay novel.

Chapter 1

1. For example, James wrote in his 1890 classic, *The Principles of Psychology*, "It must be admitted, therefore, that in certain persons, at least, the total possible consciousness may be split into parts which coexist but mutually ignore each other, and share the objects of knowledge between them. More remarkable still, they are complementary. Give an object to one of the consciousnesses, and by that fact you remove it from the other or others. Barring a certain common fund of information, like the command of language, etc., what the upper self knows the under self is ignorant of, and vice versa" (206).

2. It was also included in the 1895 *Majors and Minors*. For a sense of Dunbar's typical repertoire for readings to primarily African American audiences, see the programs in the Paul Laurence Dunbar Papers, Archives and Manuscripts Division, Ohio Historical Society.

3. It is interesting to note that Countee Cullen uses much the same movement of waves of rising emotion and repression of that emotion in his most famous poem, "Heritage" — though in Cullen it is love and sexual desire that threatens to overwhelm the speaker and not resentment and anger. For a discussion of Cullen and Langston Hughes and their relation to Dunbar, see Smethurst, "Lyric Stars."

4. Hughes's poem reads:

> You think
>   It's a happy beat
> Listen to it closely:
> Ain't you heard
> something underneath
> like a—
>   What did I say?
> Sure,
> I'm happy!
> Take it away! (*Collected*, 388)

5. Blount's treatment of "An Ante-Bellum Sermon" is the most extended and sophisticated critical examination of the poem. Interestingly, though Blount suggests that the poem provides an interpretive guide for "translating oral vernacular performance" of the African American preacherly tradition "into black poetic subjectivity" (590) and goes on to argue that the poem "compels us to conceptualize the patterns of representation that resonate throughout this poetic tradition" (590), he does not extend his claim to the larger body of Dunbar's poetry.

6. Dunbar appears to have frequently performed "When Malindy Sings" for predominantly African American audiences, judging from the programs contained in his papers. "The Party" seems to have also been one of the most popular of his dialect pieces with black audiences.

For another discussion of "vernacular masking" as an interpretive guide to reading Dunbar's poetry and short fiction, see Jones, 186–202.

7. Baraka has persistently engaged Dunbar's version of double consciousness. His

"An Agony. As Now" from the 1964 collection, *The Dead Lecturer*, which begins "I am inside someone who hates me," is in many ways a rewriting of "We Wear the Mask" from an incipient Black Arts perspective. The post–Black Arts movement "Masked Angel Costume: The Sayings of Mantan Moreland" collected in *Funk Lore* (1996) also directly invokes Dunbar and his dualistic metaphor.

A similar example of a Black Arts poem positing a "hidden transcript" of African American rage in black music can be found in Sonia Sanchez's "on seeing pharaoh sanders blowing":

> hear
> the
> cowbells
> ring out
> my hate. (23–24)

8. It should also be noted that white authors, particularly in the plantation tradition, too, frequently included notes or forewords that made an appeal for the superior authenticity of their rendering of black speech (and sometimes other sorts of American vernacular speech) to those circulating in popular culture, especially the minstrel stage. One might consider these to be "authenticating documents" (to use Robert Stepto's term) that ultimately relied on the testimony of the white southern author as a sort of "native informant" who is both inside and outside the circle of black culture—who "knew the Negro" as opposed to his northern white counterparts who wrote for the minstrel/vaudeville stage. For example, in his first collection of Uncle Remus tales, *Uncle Remus: His Songs and Sayings* (1881), Joel Chandler Harris claimed, "The dialect, it will be observed, is wholly different from that of the Hon. Pompey Smash and his literary descendants, and different also from the intolerable misrepresentations of the minstrel stage, but it is at least phonetically genuine" (4). Similarly, Thomas Nelson Page, the dean of post-Reconstruction plantation fiction, prefaced his 1887 collection *In Ole Virginia: Marse Chan and Other Stories* with a note explaining some of the syntactical features (as well as his orthographical strategy for notating those features) of the speech of the black folk narrators from the Virginia Tidewater region in whose voices most of the stories are told. Page's move resembles that of Mark Twain in his "Explanatory" to *Huckleberry Finn*, a novel with a complex relationship to both the antebellum slave narrative and the plantation tradition. For a brief discussion of the late nineteenth-century white minstrelsy and plantation fascination with re-creating the "authentic" African American culture of the Old South, ironically often in huge productions or "pageants" that employed black vaudeville performers, see Sundquist, 287–89.

9. Gavin Jones makes something of the same point—though one might question his assumption that if the diction of a dialect poem is not pointedly (and conventionally) "black," then it must be "white" (205–6).

10. For example, David Levering Lewis proclaims Du Bois's formulation of "double consciousness" to be a "revolutionary conception." By "revolutionary," Lewis seems to be emphasizing what he takes to be the novelty of Du Bois's concept as well as its implications for the direction of African American self-conception. However, while pro-

claiming the revolutionary nature of Du Bois's version of double consciousness, Lewis does note that notions of the divided self, including the racially divided subject, were not unique to Du Bois (281–83).

11. As such scholars as Louis Harlan and Shawn Alexander have shown, Washington often preached accommodation with Jim Crow while secretly funding legal and political challenges to segregation through the Afro-American Council and other civil rights organizations. Given that the promotion of industrial education for African Americans considerably antedated the founding of Tuskegee and the ascendancy of Washington, and that all leaders of historically black educational institutions in the South had to come to some sort of understanding with Jim Crow if those institutions were to survive, August Meier's claim that what irked Washington's detractors was not so much his positions as his increasing intolerance of criticism of those positions (and his ability to punish his critics through his influence on the funding of African American projects and institutions and his control of much of the black press) seems plausible. Harlan, *Booker T. Washington: The Wizard of Tuskegee*, 238–65; Alexander, "Afro-American Council," 21–22; Meier, 110–16.

12. There has been some contestation of Harlan's notion of Webber's incompetence in more recent scholarship. For a relatively early demurral that claims Washington's objection to Webber's work was more a question of political expediency than of competency (and that the first autobiography is in fact superior to the second in many respects), see Fitzgerald.

13. Douglass was an early patron of the young poet, hiring him as an assistant clerk at the Haitian exhibit of the 1893 World Columbian Exhibit in Chicago and paying him out of his own pocket. Dunbar as the foremost black writer of his day also had a publicly cordial relationship with Washington. Despite public reservations about Tuskegee's policy of industrial education — and, at times, private concerns about Washington's motivations, Dunbar was a fairly frequent visitor to the school as well as the librettist for "The Tuskegee Song." Booker T. Washington, *Booker T. Washington Papers*, 4:456, 6:380–81; Brawley, 32–33; Dunbar, *Dunbar Reader*, 453.

14. For two essays comparing Washington's second autobiography unfavorably to his first, see Bresnahan and Charlotte Fitzgerald.

15. Sundquist points out, for example, that Frederick Douglass drew on *Uncle Tom's Cabin* in *My Bondage and My Freedom*, despite his public reservations about the representation of African Americans in Stowe's novel (101–2).

16. For an excellent survey of the impact of *Uncle Tom's Cabin*, especially on film and drama, see the website on Stowe's novel sponsored by the University of Virginia and the Harriet Beecher Stowe Center at http://www.iath.virginia.edu/utc/onstage/films/fihp.html. The film clips of silent-era movie adaptations of *Uncle Tom's Cabin*, and of such direct and indirect responses to those adaptations as D. W. Griffith's 1915 *Birth of a Nation*, are particularly fascinating.

17. For an incisive study of the struggle over the meaning and memory of the Civil War and Reconstruction, and the consequences of this struggle that resulted in the victory of those forces, North and South, that opposed Reconstruction and its ideals, see Blight, *Race and Reunion*.

18. As Robert Weimann points out, in the English dramatic tradition, one could

go back to at least the medieval mystery plays, such as *Mankind*, to find a sort of pointed comedy that turned on linguistic difference, invoking class and ethnic conflict (116–18).

19. Both poems were first collected by Dunbar, ironically, in the 1903 *Lyrics of Love and Laughter*.

20. Johnson, *Book of American Negro Poetry*, 42–3.

21. For an essay that convincingly links Johnson's account of Wetmore in his 1933 autobiography *Along This Way* (in which Wetmore is named only as "D——") to the narrator of *Autobiography*, see Skerrett.

22. This bitterness can still be seen years later in his actual autobiography *Along This Way* (1933) when he speaks of his decision to leave Florida for New York in 1901 as being significantly motivated by the rise and triumph of Jim Crow in Jacksonville at the end of the nineteenth and the beginning of the twentieth centuries after a relatively halcyon period for African Americans during his youth. Johnson describes the culminating event in his decision as a terrifying and life-threatening encounter with members of the local militia (the city was more or less under martial law immediately after the great fire of 1901) who saw him talking to a very light-skinned African American woman whom they took to be white (165–70).

23. Harrison gave one of his earliest public lectures on Dunbar and organized a memorial for Dunbar at the St. Marks Lyceum in New York after Dunbar's death in February 1906. See William Dean Howells's February 28, 1906 letter to Harrison sending his regrets about not being able to attend the memorial (box 2, folder 45, Hubert Harrison Papers, Rare Book and Manuscript Library, Butler Library, Columbia University).

It is worth noting that Harrison admired Dunbar's dialect poetry (notably "When Malindy Sings") as well as his exhortatory political work (e.g., "Ode to Ethiopia") and "high" literary verse (e.g., "When Sleep Comes Down") (395).

Chapter 2

1. Nora is generally concerned with a unitary notion of "nation" and is relatively insensitive to the problem of minority groups and the management of memory. That is to say that minority groups, whether African Americans or Native Americans in the United States or Bretons or North Africans in France, long had to deal with memory crises of language, culture, religion, and history, legally and quasi-legally enforced by the state.

2. As noted elsewhere in this book, there has been considerable work in recent years by such scholars as Matthew Jacobson and Noel Ignatiev about the complicated processes by which immigrants from various regions of Europe in the nineteenth and early twentieth centuries were socially and, through the passage of restrictive immigration laws in the 1920s, legally distinguished from and eventually included in the category of "white." Less attention has been paid to the anxieties about the process of becoming "white" "Americans" expressed in such "ethnic" literary works as Abraham Cahan's *The Rise of David Levinsky* (1917) and Samuel Ornitz's *Haunch, Paunch, and Jowl* (1923).

3. Blight writes, "But memories and understandings of great events, especially apocalyptic wars, live in our consciousness like monuments in the mind. The aging Douglass's rhetoric was an eloquent attempt to forge a place on that monument for those he deemed the principal characters in the drama of emancipation: the abolitionist, the black soldier, and the freed people (Blight, "Something Beyond the Battlefield," 1176).

4. Du Bois, for example, writes in *The Souls of Black Folk*: "The history of the American Negro is the history of this strife, — this longing to attain self-conscious manhood" (11). Later in the same chapter he names the special gifts of African Americans to the United States as faith, humility, good humor, and spiritual strivings. Of course, black authors such as Du Bois tend to emphasize black agency and desire as well as the equality of the exchange between black and white in ways that white authors rarely did.

5. While Harper's is the only poem by a black author mentioning the Fifty-fourth published during the war that I have discovered, Joshua McCarter Simpson's "Let the Banner Wave" in *The Emancipation Car* features a subtitle indicating that it was written shortly after Lee's surrender at Appomattox.

6. For a relatively easily accessible text of Harper's poem (which originally appeared in the October 10, 1863, issue of the New York *Weekly Anglo-African*), see Yacovone, 105–6.

7. I have been able to discover only two poems mentioning Shaw and the Fifty-fourth written by white authors between the end of the war and the dedication of the memorial. One is John Hay's "The Advance Guard," which first appeared in *Harpers* in 1871. The other is Thomas Wentworth Higginson's "Memorial Ode" which was read at a Boston Memorial Day ceremony in 1881. In both relatively long poems, which are primarily about other (white) martyrs of the Civil War, there are just brief mentions of Shaw and the Fifty-fourth. For a copy of Higginson's poem, see Long.

8. For a short sketch of Bell, who achieved a certain fame for his dramatic public readings of his epics, and a brief analysis of his poetry, see Sherman, 80–87.

9. As noted elsewhere, the subtitle of "Let the Banner Proudly Wave" makes the claim that the poem was written shortly after Lee's surrender, placing the composition of the poem in the very late Civil War era or the very early Reconstruction period. However, I have chosen to deal with this poem as part of the cultural conversation of the mid-1870s when the poem was first published (so far as I can tell). Whatever the precise date of composition, the author certainly felt that the poem was germane enough to the moment of the mid-1870s to warrant its inclusion in the collection. Certainly the readers of the poem interpreted it within the framework of Reconstruction and its debates rather than that of the rather uncertain period at the end of the Civil War.

10. For a history of the Fifty-fourth by a former officer of the regiment, a history that was itself a monument of the sort that David Blight describes, see Emilio.

11. One might see a feminist counterpart to these poems in Frances E. W. Harper's "Aunt Chloe" poems that she wrote initially for use in southern literacy classes for freed men and women and which were collected in the 1872 *Sketches of Southern Life*. These poems, such as the frequently anthologized "Aunt Chloe's Politics" and

"Learning to Read," are notable in the first place because they represent one of the first literary attempts to create a distinctly African American literature drawing on black vernacular language that would not be confused with minstrelsy or plantation literature. Harper, though, was not averse to using plantation stereotypes against themselves, as she did in "Aunt Chloe's Politics," where Aunt Chloe (an older former slave) announces that she doesn't know much about politics and then demonstrates that she knows everything worth knowing about politics. Chloe serves as not only a defense of the franchise for black males but also an argument for the extension of that franchise to women. In these poems, while literacy is shown to be of enormous use to black political, social, and economic citizenship, an undivided African American self-consciousness and the capacity for citizenship are posited as anteceding emancipation.

12. One possible ending could be when the last black southern congressman before the post–Civil Rights era, George White of North Carolina, left office in 1901.

13. For a brief discussion of Whitman's poem, see Sherman, 117–21.

14. For example, Martha Perry Lowe in an 1864 poem, "The Picture of Colonel Shaw in Boston," that appeared in both the *Boston Daily Advertiser* and *The Liberator* wrote after seeing a picture of Shaw: "Look upon him, Nation of the free! / Surely this will cure thee of thy meanness" (192).

15. Why there were few, if any, poems about the black soldier in the 1880s when the Jim Crow system began to take shape is hard to answer. Certainly, African American intellectuals and political leaders used the black soldier in their attacks on the new segregation and the curtailment of black civil rights. However, it may be that the sheer accumulation of Jim Crow laws and practices as the 1880s wore on provoked a return to the powerful figure of the African American veteran. It is worth noting that there was also an increase in the use of the veteran by other sorts of black writers besides poets in the late 1880s and early 1890s. Frances Harper's novel *Iola Leroy* is mentioned elsewhere in this chapter. One could also cite the appearance of historian George Washington Williams's *History of the Negro Troops in the Rebellion* (1888) and Luis Emilio's *A Brave Black Regiment: History of the Fifty-Fourth Regiment of Massachusetts Volunteer Infantry, 1863–1865* (1969). Both Williams and Emilio were themselves Civil War veterans.

16. Rowe also included in the same collection a poem, "The Reason Why," about a standard-bearer of the First Louisiana Regiment, United States Colored Troops, who died defending the regimental colors in the 1863 assault on Port Hudson, Louisiana.

Because Rowe's text is virtually unavailable in print form, it (and the works of the other African American writers discussed here with the exception of Harper and Dunbar) is most easily accessible to readers through the Chadwyck-Healey Literature Online (Lion) service's *African American Poetry (1750–1900)*.

17. For example, Dunbar, along with Simpson, was one of the few writers to allude to the broader, distinguished career of the Fifty-fourth beyond the suicidal, if heroic, attack on Battery Wagner, mentioning, for example, the 1864 battle of Olustee, Florida, at which the bravery and discipline of the Fifty-fourth and other black regiments saved a Union army from complete rout.

18. All page citations of Dunbar's poetry in this chapter refer to *The Complete Poems*.

19. It is worth noting that this era featured not only the institution of Jim Crow and the practical disenfranchisement of African Americans in most of the South but also an increasingly intense debate about the relationship between race in a broad sense and citizenship. The new intensity of this discussion was fueled largely by the immigration of millions from southern and eastern Europe and featured a rhetoric that spoke of the "Hibernian race," the "Teutonic race," the "Jewish" or "Semitic race," the "Syrian race," and so on. Ultimately, this debate led to the establishment of immigration laws in the 1920s that severely limited the ability of southern and eastern Europeans (and others) to enter the United States. Thus, the issue of race, blood, and citizenship was one that dominated the thinking of Americans in the North as well as in the South. For an incisive study of this debate, see Jacobson.

20. Dunbar, like many African Americans, was ambivalent about American participation in the Spanish-American War. On the one hand, he wrote poems praising Theodore Roosevelt and, especially, the black soldiers who fought in the war. On the other, he criticized what he called a "new attitude" engendered by the war in which white Americans were perfectly willing to let black soldiers fight and die but not vote or exercise the other prerogatives of full citizenship. It is worth noting that in both cases, Dunbar used the figure of the black soldier in much the same way that he always had, suggesting that he would have resisted any move to shift the meaning of that figure. For a brief discussion of Dunbar's attitude towards the war, see Gatewood, 110.

21. These poems appeared most frequently, though not exclusively, in Boston-based magazines and journals such as the *Atlantic Monthly* and the *Boston Journal*.

22. Probably the most famous literary example of this nationalist or nationalist-influenced rhetoric of manhood in the early twentieth century is Claude McKay's 1919 poem "If We Die," which concludes with the couplet, "Like men we'll face the murderous, cowardly pack, / Pressed to the wall, dying, but fighting back!" However, even a casual glance at the poetry published in *Negro World*, the mass weekly newspaper founded by nationalist leader Marcus Garvey in 1918, will confirm that McKay's conflation of manhood and racial self-assertion was part of a much larger literary (and political) phenomenon.

23. "The Unsung Heroes" was first collected along with "Robert Gould Shaw," "Douglass," "The Haunted Oak," and "To the South" in the 1903 volume *Lyrics of Love and Laughter*.

24. This trope of forgotten and unsung heroes or martyrs would reappear in later African American poetry, perhaps most directly in Countee Cullen's 1935 "Scottsboro, Too, Is Worth Its Song."

25. It is also unclear when Ray actually wrote her sonnet-elegy to Shaw. She was of an earlier generation than Brawley, with a poetic career dating back to the 1870s. Her first book was published in 1893. The 1910 *Poems* (in which "Robert G. Shaw" appeared) was her second and last collection. In short, it is quite possible that Ray wrote the piece during the flurry of poems about Shaw in the last years of the nineteenth century.

26. Fiction by black authors was far more likely to utilize the figure of the black veteran of past wars, but even there, as in Ralph Ellison's *Invisible Man* and Toni Morri-

son's *Sula* and *Song of Solomon*, the World War I veteran was given much more play than his Civil War counterpart.

27. Aptheker was a Communist Party member when he wrote his pioneering works on African American slave revolts and black participation in the American Revolution and the Civil War in the late 1930s and early 1940s. Du Bois had a more troubled relationship with the Communist Party when *Black Reconstruction* appeared in the early 1930s—though he would become associated with the Communist Left in the 1940s. Indeed, the Communist Party and its newspapers and journal were severely critical of Du Bois's work. However, Du Bois's study is clearly marked by a Marxist influence that derived in no small part from the new prominence of the Communist Left in the early years of the Great Depression.

28. It could be argued that Lowell through his relationship to Shaw (whose family intermarried with the Lowells) and his investment in family history in the Civil Rights era engaged the earlier literary tradition. Still even in this case, it was a retrospective engagement rather than a contemporary one.

Chapter 3

1. As Gregory points out, southern white authors frequently wrote about the regional expatriation of individual southern white artists-intellectuals (or would-be artists-intellectuals), such as William Faulkner's Quentin Compson or Thomas Wolfe's Eugene Gant. These representations often mirrored the authors' own short- or longterm migration from the South in search of greater professional, social, and/or political possibilities even if, like Robert Penn Warren, they were in many respects "professional Southerners" whose careers centered on representing, explicating, and even personally embodying the South (183–92).

2. For an insightful look at narratives of the "Okie" migration, particularly the racial dynamics of those narratives, in literature, photography, and film, see Michael Denning, 259–82. See also Vials, xviii–xxiii.

3. The first part of Martin Delaney's novel *Blake*, serialized in the late 1850s and early 1860s, did picture black as a country with a sort of secret government of semi-African conjure men hidden in the Great Dismal Swamp. However, the novel was never published in its entirety and perhaps never completed.

4. For a discussion of *Contending Forces* and melodrama, see McCann.

5. Charles Chesnutt's 1905 *The Colonel's Dream*, too, moves back and forth, between North Carolina and New York, with only a nominally happy resolution. Like the mood of *Contending Forces* (and *The Souls of Black Folk*) before it and *Autobiography of an Ex-Colored Man* after it, its dominant tone is one of a somewhat gloomy consolation and uncertain possibility within the United States—a possibility that has largely passed the characters of the novels by. The novel is somewhat anomalous in that a Confederate war hero and son of a ruined white planter, Colonel French, who has succeeded in the business world of the North while retaining a nostalgic attachment to a vision of a genteel Old South, stands in for the typical black migration protagonist. In the novel, Chesnutt mixes the tropes of the plantation tradition (including the return of the white Confederate officer to his ruined home) with the Horatio

Alger story and the emerging migration tale so as to undermine plantation tradition — and the interpretations of Reconstruction (which, in turn, heavily relied on a pastoral and romantically feudal vision of the slave South) linked to that tradition.

6. Of course, one might say that this notion of being melancholically uncomfortably between is inherent in the origin of the term *mulatta/o*, suggesting a sterile union between two species. And certainly, such a view, no doubt influenced by black literature and thought of the Nadir, became a staple of modern U.S. sociology, particularly that of the Chicago School of Sociology. Robert Park, for example, considered the "Mulatto in the United States," along with the "Eurasian in Asia," to be the archetypal "marginal man" who "lives in two worlds, in both of which he is more or less a stranger" (893).

7. My use of "melancholy" here draws on the Freudian sense of "melancholia" as a cyclical sort of grief or sense of loss that, unlike "mourning," one is unable to transcend. For an interesting study of "racial melancholia," see Cheng.

Chapter 4

1. Pound did promote the poetry of Amy Lowell in the United States and H. D. in London, but that was as a sort of patron and guide. He had far more trouble when Lowell began to assume a position of authority in the "new poetry" scene of the United States.

As Shari Benstock has demonstrated, expatriate women such as Natalie Barney did make a considerable mark on European bohemia, but, until the 1920s, it was primarily through the hosting of salons rather than as editors, publishers, theorists, or even artists. Gertrude Stein was an exception, of course, but she had relatively little contact with Parisian bohemians other than Pablo Picasso (Benstock, 16–17). Expatriate women came to play a more important role in bohemian cultural institutions and as artists in Paris with some, notably Margaret Anderson and her *Little Review*, essentially moving an already extant institution. In many cases, these women were lesbians or bisexuals who were able to live more freely in Paris than they had in the United States, even in Greenwich Village or Harlem.

2. For two useful scholarly considerations of Fenton Johnson and his impact on the "new poetry," see Thomas, 11–44, and Kenny Williams.

3. For an account of the origins of the term and concept of the "New Negro," see Gates.

4. The *Oxford English Dictionary* credits Thackeray with introducing into the English language "bohemian" in the social sense as meaning, in Thackeray's works, "an artist or littérateur who, consciously or unconsciously, secedes from conventionality in life and in art." However, Thackeray makes clear in the cited passage that he is using "a very commonly accepted" term.

5. For a brilliant discussion of the Roma, "exoticism," and "theatrical authenticity" in the creation of bohemian personae in the early European avant garde (with a resulting impact on subsequent bohemias), see Sell.

6. For a useful account of the continuing popular and literary (and popular literary) association of bohemia with Europe well into the twentieth century, see Soto, 99–104.

7. For scholarly descriptions of the actual black bohemia, see Sotiropoulos, 52–62, and James Weldon Johnson, *Black Manhattan*, 74–124.

8. For accounts of the Chicago's North Side bohemia, see Rosemont, introduction to *Hobohemia*, and Rosemont, *The Rise and Fall of the Dil Pickle*, 7–42.

9. For a discussion of Johnson's politics as well as an incisive analysis of his work as an editor and poet, see Thomas, 11–44.

10. A *Defender* review of Johnson's *Visions of the Dusk* declared, "Chicago may well be proud of this young man who, in his youth, has become a writer of such prominence as well as his aunt, Mrs. E. J. Binga, who gives him every encouragement" ("Authors and Books," 6).

11. Letter from Fenton Johnson to William Stanley Braithwaite, September 5, 1916; letter from Fenton Johnson to William Stanley Braithwaite, July 22, 1918, William Stanley Braithwaite Papers, Houghton Library, Harvard University.

12. It is worth noting that Rexroth's account is not entirely reliable and is certainly very loose as to the timing of events. However, as the preeminent historian of the North Side bohemia, Franklin Rosemont, said to me in conversation, Rexroth's narrative is almost always basically faithful to the facts (or his sense of them) even if his chronology is shaky.

13. For an account of this struggle and transition, see Eisinger.

14. Braithwaite emphasized the *Transcript*'s Brahmin base: "It went to all the universities, was the preferred paper in the Back Bay, Brookline, and on Beacon Hill" (Braithwaite Oral History, 15).

15. Braithwaite did join after Higginson and Julia Ward Howe apparently threatened to quit the club and start a new club if Braithwaite were denied membership (Braithwaite Oral History, 80).

16. Letter from James Weldon Johnson to William Stanley Braithwaite, July 21, 1911, and letter from Fenton Johnson to William Stanley Braithwaite, July 22, 1918, William Stanley Braithwaite Papers, Houghton Library, Harvard University; letter from William Stanley Braithwaite to James Weldon Johnson, September 3, 1917, James Weldon Johnson Papers, Special Collections, Woodruff Library, Emory University.

17. For the best account of the dispute between Braithwaite and Monroe, see Thomas, 45–73. Braithwaite attributed Frost's hostility as emanating from jealousy over Braithwaite's praise of E. A. Robinson as "our greatest poet" (Braithwaite Oral History, 134–35).

18. For an account of the turn-of-the-century Beacon Hill bohemia focusing on the Brahmin architect Ralph Adams Cram, see Shand-Tucci.

19. Interestingly, though, later when Braithwaite was a professor at Atlanta University, he pushed for the study of African American life and culture: "I began to think, after all, there's a terrible neglect here. You have a Negro institution. It's accredited, and it can give Masters' degrees, and yet there has been no thesis written on a Negro theme. I thought at least one out of the eight, ten, or twelve Masters theses that were being worked on, — one at least should be on a Negro theme, in a Negro institution" (Braithwaite Oral History, 220).

20. Johnson encouraged Braithwaite to go forward with the anthology in a Janu-

ary 15, 1919, letter. William Stanley Braithwaite Papers, Houghton Library, Harvard University.

21. Braithwaite was also an early fan of Johnson's *Autobiography of an Ex-Colored Man*, calling it a "fine piece of work." He included the novel as one of the year's best books in his annual literary round up in the *Boston Evening Transcript*. (Letter from William Stanley Braithwaite to James Weldon Johnson, March 13, 1913, box 3, folder 53, James Weldon Johnson Papers (Correspondence), Beinecke Library, Yale University.

22. For an account of the New Negro Renaissance in Washington, see Hutchinson, "Jean Toomer and the 'New Negroes' of Washington."

23. Both McKay and Cullen eventually fell out with Braithwaite to some extent, but to get a glimpse into their early relationships, see McKay's September 29, 1918, letter thanking Braithwaite for his interest in McKay's work and giving him permission to use "A Negro Dancer" and "The Little Peoples" in the 1919 anthology; and Cullen's February 1921 letter in which he introduces himself as "a young colored lad interested in poetry to such an extent that it means more to me than anything else. For the last four years your anthology has inspired me and my greatest ambition is that some day I shall have a poem worthy of a place there," William Stanley Braithwaite Papers, Houghton Library, Harvard University.

24. For two articles extolling Braithwaite and his role in the poetry revival in a major black newspaper, the *Baltimore Afro-American*, see "William Stanley Braithwaite" and "W. S. Braithwaite."

Chapter 5

1. For an example of the seriousness with which African American organizations took these laws, see the front-page *Chicago Defender* article about the 1913 passage of a "Marriage Act" by the U.S. House of Representatives prohibiting interracial marriage in Washington, D.C., "Equal Rights League Opposes Marriage Act."

2. Since Stein so often repeats the descriptive tags, I will not provide page citations except for more lengthy quotes.

3. It is worth noting that Jaime Hovey does in fact make this argument in her valuable essay, "Sapphic Primitivism in Gertrude Stein's *Q.E.D.*"

4. For a study of the impact of the Irish Renaissance and its relation to African American writers, see Mishkin.

Conclusion

1. For one reading of *Gatsby* as a passing story, see Goldsmith.

2. For discussions of the gay subcultures and networks in Harlem during the New Negro Renaissance, see Chauncey, 244–67; Wirth, 20–30; and A. B. Christa Schwarz.

3. For a discussion of *Seven Arts* and its significance to the inception of the New Negro Renaissance, see Hutchinson, *The Harlem Renaissance in Black and White*, 93–96. I say U.S. careers because McKay had some considerable foreground as a vernacular poet in Jamaica before his first move to the United States.

4. For a fascinating view into McKay's mixing of Marxism and black nationalism

in the immediate post–World War I period, see his 1919 letter to Marcus Garvey. In that letter, McKay argues that black radicals and white radicals should join together on common ground. He says, "I don't mean that we should accept them unreservedly and put our cause into their hands. No: they are fighting their own battle and so are we; but at present we meet on common ground against the common enemy. We have a great wall to batter down and while we work on one side we should hail those who are willing on the other. We need have no fear if, as a race, we have ability to safeguard our own peculiar rights." He concludes the letter, "Yours for an awakened Negro race" (box 2, folder 66, Hubert Harrison Papers, Rare Book and Manuscript Library, Butler Library, Columbia University).

5. For a discussion of Baraka and the Black Arts movement and the notion of a popular avant garde, see Smethurst, *The Black Arts Movement*, 58–76.

Bibliography

Archival Sources

Amherst, Massachusetts
  University of Massachusetts–Amherst, W. E. B. Du Bois Library,
    Special Collections
    W. E. B. Du Bois Papers
Atlanta, Georgia
  Emory University, Woodruff Library, Special Collections
    James Weldon Johnson Papers
Cambridge, Massachusetts
  Harvard University, Houghton Library
    William Stanley Braithwaite Papers
    Howells Family Papers
Columbus, Ohio
  Ohio Historical Society, Archives and Manuscripts Division
    Paul Laurence Dunbar Papers
New Haven, Connecticut
  Yale University, Beinecke Library
    James Weldon Johnson Papers
New York, New York
  Columbia University, Butler Library, Oral History Research Office
    William Stanley Braithwaite Oral History
  Columbia University, Butler Library, Rare Book and Manuscript Library
    Hubert Harrison Papers
  New York Public Library
    Henry W. and Albert A. Berg Collection of English and American Literature
  Schomburg Center for Research in Black Culture
    William Stanley Braithwaite Papers
    Paul Laurence Dunbar Letters
    Andy Razaf Papers
    Arthur A. Schomburg Papers
Providence, Rhode Island
  Brown University, John Hay Library
    Harris Poetry Collection
    Hay Broadsides Collection
Washington, D.C.
  Howard University, Moorland-Spingarn Research Center
    Anna Julia Cooper Papers
    Andy Razaf Papers

Books, Chapters, Essays, Articles, Broadsides, Pamphlets, and Dissertations

Abrahams, Edward. *The Lyrical Left: Randolph Bourne, Alfred Stieglitz and the Origins of Cultural Radicalism in America.* Charlottesville: University of Virginia Press, 1986.

"African American Sheet Music." http://dl.lib.brown.edu/sheetmusic/afam/index.html.

Ahearn, Barry. *William Carlos Williams and Alterity: The Early Poetry.* New York: Cambridge University Press, 1994.

Aldrich, Thomas Bailey. *The Poems of Thomas Bailey Aldrich.* Boston: Houghton, Mifflin, 1907.

Alexander, Shawn Leigh. "The Afro-American Council and Its Challenge of Louisiana's Grandfather Clause." In *Radicalism in the South since Reconstruction,* edited by Chris Green, Rachel Rubin, and James Smethurst, 13–36. New York: Palgrave Macmillan, 2006.

———. "'We Know Our Rights and Have the Courage to Defend Them': The Spirit of Agitation in the Age of Accommodation, 1883–1909." Ph.D. dissertation, University of Massachusetts, 2004.

Allen, Cleveland G. "Fenton Johnson Makes Hit East." *Chicago Defender,* November 28, 1914, 4.

———. "Young Songster of Rare Talent." *Baltimore Afro American,* December 5, 1914, 2.

Allen, Ernest, Jr. "Du Boisian Double Consciousness: The Unsustainable Argument." *Massachusetts Review* 43.2 (Summer 2002): 217–53.

Alter, Robert. *Imagined Cities: Urban Experience and the Language of the Novel.* New York: New York University Press, 2005.

Anderson, Jervis. *This Was Harlem: A Cultural Portrait, 1900–1950.* New York: Farrar, Straus, and Giroux, 1982.

Andrews, William. *The Literary Career of Charles Chesnutt.* Baton Rouge: Louisiana State University Press, 1980.

———. *To Tell a Free Story: The First Century of African American Autobiography, 1760–1865.* Urbana: University of Illinois Press, 1986.

"Authors and Books." *Chicago Defender,* July 24, 1915, 6.

Baker, Houston. *Long Black Song: Essays in Black Literature and Culture.* Charlottesville: University of Virginia Press, 1972.

———. *Modernism and the Harlem Renaissance.* Chicago: University of Chicago Press, 1987.

———. *Turning South Again: Rethinking Modernism/Rethinking Booker T. Washington.* Durham: Duke University Press, 2001.

Baraka, Amiri (LeRoi Jones). *The Dead Lecturer.* New York: Grove Press, 1964.

———. *Funk Lore.* Los Angeles: Littoral Press, 1996.

———. *Home: Social Essays.* New York: Morrow, 1966.

———. *Selected Plays and Prose of Amiri Baraka/LeRoi Jones.* New York: Morrow, 1979.

"Beatrice." *Champion Magazine* 1.1 (September 1916): 37.

Bell, James Madison. *Poetical Works of James Madison Bell*. Freeport: Books for Libraries Press, 1970.

Benjamin, Walter. *Charles Baudelaire, a Lyric Poet in the Era of High Capitalism*. London: NLB, 1973.

————. *Illuminations*. Edited by Hannah Arendt. New York: Schocken Books, 1968.

Benstock, Shari. *Women of the Left Bank*. Austin: University of Texas Press, 1987.

Berlin, Ira. *The Making of African America: The Four Great Migrations*. New York: Viking, 2010.

Bernard, Emily. "The Renaissance and the Vogue." In *The Cambridge Companion to the Harlem Renaissance*, edited by George Hutchinson, 28–40. New York: Cambridge University Press, 2007.

Bernstein, Charles. "Poetics of the Americas." *Modernism/Modernity* 3.3 (1996): 1–23.

Blackmer, Corrine. "African Masks and the Arts of Passing in Gertrude Stein's 'Melanctha' and Nella Larsen's *Passing*." *Journal of the History of Sexuality* 4.2 (October 1993): 230–63.

Blackmon, Douglas A. *Slavery by Another Name: The Re-Enslavement of Black People in America from the Civil War to World War II*. New York: Doubleday, 2008.

Bland, James. "Carry Me Back to Old Virginny." Boston: John F. Perry, 1878.

Blight, David. "'For Something beyond the Battlefield': Frederick Douglass and the Struggle for the Memory of the Civil War." *Journal of American History* 75.4 (March 1989): 1156–78.

————. *Race and Reunion: The Civil War in American Memory*. Cambridge: Harvard University Press, 2001.

Blount, Marcellus. "The Preacherly Text: African American Poetry and Vernacular Performance." *PMLA* 107.3 (May 1992): 582–93.

Boyd, Melba Joyce. *Discarded Legacy: Politics and Poetics in the Life of Frances E. W. Harper, 1825–1911*. Detroit: Wayne State University Press, 1994.

Braithwaite, William Stanley. *House of Falling Leaves*. Boston: John W. Luce, 1908.

————. "The House under Arcturus: An Autobiography." *Phylon* 2.1 (1941): 9–26.

————. "The House under Arcturus: An Autobiography; Second Installment." *Phylon* 2.2 (1941): 119–36.

————. "The House under Arcturus: An Autobiography, Part III." *Phylon* 2.3 (1941): 220, 250–59.

————. "The House under Arcturus: An Autobiography, Part IV." *Phylon* 3.1 (1942): 31–45.

————. "The House under Arcturus: An Autobiography, Part V." *Phylon* 3.2 (1942): 183–95.

————. *Lyrics of Love and Life*. Boston: Herbert Turner, 1904.

"Braithwaite's 'Poetry Review.'" *Champion Magazine* 1.1 (September 1916): 12.

Brawley, Benjamin Griffith. *Paul Laurence Dunbar: Poet of His People*. Chapel Hill: University of North Carolina Press, 1936.

Breitweiser, Mitchell. "Jazz Fractures: F. Scott Fitzgerald and Epochal Representation." *American Literary History* 12.3 (Autumn 2000): 359–81.

Bresnahan, Roger J. "The Implied Readers of Booker T. Washington's Autobiographies." *Black American Literature Forum* 14.1 (Spring 1980): 15–20.

Bridgeman, Richard. *Gertrude Stein in Pieces*. New York: Oxford University Press, 1970.

Brinnin, John Malcolm. *The Third Rose: Gertrude Stein and Her World*. Boston: Little, Brown, 1959.

Brooks, Tim. *Lost Sounds: Blacks and the Birth of the Recording Industry, 1890–1919*. Urbana: University of Illinois Press, 2004.

Brown, Sterling. *A Son's Return: Selected Essays of Sterling A. Brown*. Boston: Northeastern University Press, 1996.

Bruce, Dickson D., Jr. *Black Writing from the Nadir: The Evolution of a Literary Tradition, 1877–1915*. Baton Rouge: Louisiana State University Press, 1989.

———. "James Corrothers Reads a Book; or, the Lives of Sandy Jenkins." *African American Review* 26.4 (Winter 1992): 665–73.

Carby, Hazel. *Reconstructing Womanhood: The Emergence of the Afro-American Woman Novelist*. New York: Oxford University Press, 1987.

"The Champion Magazine." *Champion Magazine* 1.1 (September 1916): 1.

Chauncey, George. *Gay New York: Gender, Urban Culture, and the Makings of the Gay Male World, 1890–1940*. New York: Basic Books, 1991.

Cheng, Anne Anlin. *The Melancholy of Race: Psychoanalysis, Assimilation, and Hidden Grief*. New York: Oxford University Press, 2000.

Chesnutt, Charles. *The Colonel's Dream*. 1905. New Milford, Conn.: Toby Press, 2004.

———. *The Conjure Woman and Other Conjure Tales*. 1898. Durham: Duke University Press, 1993.

———. *Essays and Speeches*. Edited by Joseph R. McElrath Jr., Robert C. Leitz III, and Jesse S. Crisler. Palo Alto: Stanford University Press, 1999.

———. *The Marrow of Tradition*. Boston: Houghton Mifflin, 1901.

———. *Stories, Novels, and Essays*. New York: Library of America, 2002.

Chude-Sokei, Louis. *The Last "Darky": Bert Williams, Black-on-Black Minstrelsy and the African Diaspora*. Durham: Duke University Press, 2006.

Churchill, Suzanne W. *The Little Magazine Others and the Renovation of Modern American Poetry*. Burlington, Vt.: Ashgate, 2006.

———. "Making Space for *Others*: A History of a Modernist Literary Magazine." *Journal of Modern Literature* 22.1 (Fall 1996): 47–62.

Cooper, James Fenimore. *The Last of the Mohicans*. 1826. New York: Oxford University Press, 1990.

Cooper, Wayne. *Claude McKay: Rebel Sojourner in the Harlem Renaissance*. New York: Schocken Books, 1987.

Crawford, Margo Natalie. *Dilution Anxiety and the Black Phallus*. Columbus: Ohio State University Press, 2008.

Crooks, James B. *Jacksonville after the Fire, 1901–1919: A New South City*. Gainesville: University Press of Florida, 1991.

Crunden, Robert M. *American Salons: Encounters with European Modernism, 1885–1917*. New York: Oxford University Press, 1993.

Cullen, Countee. *My Soul's High Song: The Collected Writings of Countee Cullen.*
New York: Anchor Books, 1991.

———, ed. *Caroling Dusk: An Anthology of Verse by Negro Poets.* New York:
Harper and Brothers, 1927.

Cunningham, Virginia. *Paul Laurence Dunbar and His Song.* New York: Dodd,
Mead, 1947.

De Jongh, James. *Vicious Modernism: Black Harlem and the Literary Imagination.*
New York: Cambridge University Press, 1990.

Delany, Martin. *Blake; or, the Huts of America.* Boston: Beacon Press, 1970.

Denning, Michael. *The Cultural Front: The Laboring of American Culture in the
Twentieth Century.* New York: Verso, 1996.

Dodson, N. Barnett. "Chicago's Young Business Men." *Baltimore Afro-American,*
August 26, 1916, 15.

Dormon, James F. "Shaping the Popular Image of Post-Reconstruction Blacks: The
'Coon Song' Phenomena of the Gilded Age." *American Quarterly* 40.4 (December
1988): 450–71.

Douglas, Ann. *Terrible Honesty: Mongrel Manhattan in the 1920s.* New York: Farrar,
Straus, and Giroux, 1995.

Douglass, Frederick. *Autobiographies.* New York: Library of America, 1996.

———. *Life and Times of Frederick Douglass.* Boston: De Wolfe & Fiske, 1892.

———. "The United States Cannot Remain Half-Slave and Half-Free." In
Frederick Douglass: Selected Speeches and Writings, edited by Philip S. Foner,
656–68. Chicago: Lawrence Hill, 1999.

Dowling, Robert M. "A Marginal Man in Black Bohemia: James Weldon Johnson
in the New York Tenderloin." In *Post-Bellum, Pre-Harlem: African American
Literature and Culture, 1877–1919,* edited by Barbara McCaskill and Caroline
Gebhard, 117–32. New York: New York University Press, 2006.

———. *Slumming in New York: From the Waterfront to Mythic Harlem.* Urbana:
University of Illinois Press, 2007.

Doyle, Laura. "The Flat, the Round, and Gertrude Stein: Race and the Shape of
Modern(ist) History." *Modernism/Modernity* 7.2 (April 2000): 249–71.

———. *Freedom's Empire: Race and the Rise of the Novel in Atlantic Modernity,
1640–1940.* Durham: Duke University Press, 2008.

Du Bois, W. E. B. *Black Reconstruction in America: An Essay toward a History of
the Part Which Black Folk Played in the Attempt to Reconstruct Democracy in
America, 1860–1880.* 1935. New York: Oxford University Press, 2007.

———. *The Souls of Black Folk.* 1903. New York: Norton, 1999.

Dunbar, Paul Laurence. *The Collected Poetry of Paul Laurence Dunbar.* Edited by
Joanne Braxton. Charlottesville: University of Virginia Press, 1993.

———. *The Complete Poems of Paul Laurence Dunbar.* New York: Dodd, Mead,
1913.

———. *The Heart of Happy Hollow.* 1904. New York: Harlem Moon, 2005.

———. *In His Own Voice: The Dramatic and Other Uncollected Works of Paul
Laurence Dunbar.* Edited by Herbert Woodward Martin and Ronald Primeau.
Athens: Ohio University Press, 2002.

———. *Lyrics of Love and Laughter*. New York: Dodd, Mead, 1903.

———. *Lyrics of Lowly Life*. New York: Dodd, Mead, 1896.

———. *Lyrics of the Hearthside*. New York: Dodd, Mead, 1899.

———. *Majors and Minors*. Toledo: Hadley and Hadley, 1895.

———. *Paul Laurence Dunbar Reader*. Edited by Jay Martin and Gossie H. Hudson. New York: Dodd, Mead, 1975.

———. *The Sport of the Gods and Other Essential Writings*. Edited by Shelley Fisher Fishkin and David Bradley. 1902. New York: Modern Library, 2005.

Edwards, Brent Hayes. *The Practice of Diaspora: Literature, Translation and the Rise of Black Internationalism*. Cambridge: Harvard University Press, 2003.

Eisinger, Peter K. "Ethnic Political Transition in Boston, 1884–1933: Some Lessons for Contemporary Cities." *Political Science Quarterly* 93.2 (Summer 1978): 217–39.

Eliot, T. S. *The Collected Poems, 1909–1962*. New York: Harcourt, Brace, 1970.

———. *Inventions of the March Hare*. Edited by Christopher Ricks. New York: Harcourt, Brace, 1996.

Ellison, Ralph. *Invisible Man*. 1952. New York: Random House, 1989.

Emerson, Ralph Waldo. *Poems*. Boston: Houghton, Mifflin, 1886.

Emilio, Luis. *A Brave Black Regiment: History of the Fifty-fourth Regiment of Massachusetts Volunteer Infantry, 1863–1865*. 1891. New York: Arno Press, 1969.

English, Daylanne. "Gertrude Stein and the Politics of Literary-Medical Experimentation." *Literature and Medicine* 16.2 (Fall 1997): 188–209.

"Equal Rights League Opposes Marriage Act." *Chicago Defender*, January 16, 1913, 1.

Evans, Brad. *Before Cultures: The Ethnographic Imagination in American Literature, 1865–1920*. Chicago: University of Chicago Press, 2005.

Fauset, Jessie. *Plum Bun: A Novel with a Moral*. 1929. Boston: Beacon Press, 1999.

"Fenton Johnson Makes Hit East." *Chicago Defender*, November 28, 1914, 4.

"Fenton Johnson Publishes Great Magazine." *Chicago Defender*, August 10, 1918, 10.

"Fenton Johnson Triumphs." *Chicago Defender*, December 25, 1915, 5.

Fisher, Rudolph. *The Walls of Jericho*. New York: Knopf, 1928.

Fishkin, Shelley Fisher. *Was Huck Black? Mark Twain and African-American Voices*. New York: Oxford University Press, 1993.

Fitzgerald, Charlotte. "*The Story of My Life and Work*: Booker T. Washington's Other Autobiography." *Black Scholar* 21.4 (Fall 1991): 35–40.

Fitzgerald, F. Scott. *The Great Gatsby*. 1925. New York: Simon & Schuster, 1992.

———. *Trimalchio: An Early Version of the Great Gatsby*. Edited by James L. W. West III. New York: Cambridge University Press, 2000.

Foley, Barbara. *Spectres of 1919: Class and Nation in the Making of the New Negro*. Urbana: University of Illinois Press, 2003.

Foner, Eric. *Reconstruction: America's Unfinished Revolution, 1863–1877*. New York: Harper & Row, 1988.

Forbes, Camille F. *Introducing Bert Williams: Burnt Cork, Broadway, and the Story of America's First Black Star*. New York: Basic, 2008.

Fortune, T. Thomas. "Characteristics of Afro-American Literature." *Los Angeles Times*, August 30, 1896, 23.

Gaines, Kevin. "Assimilationist Minstrelsy as Racial Uplift Ideology: James D. Corrothers's Literary Quest for Black Leadership." *American Quarterly* 45.3 (September 1993): 341–69.

———. *Uplifting the Race: Black Leadership, Politics, and Culture in the Twentieth Century*. Chapel Hill: University of North Carolina Press, 1996.

Gates, Henry Louis, Jr. "The Trope of a New Negro and the Reconstruction of the Image of the Black." *Representations* 24 (Autumn 1988): 129–55.

Gates, Henry Louis, Jr., and Gene Andrew Jarrett, eds. *The New Negro: Race, Representation, and African American Culture, 1892–1938*. Princeton: Princeton University Press, 2007.

Gatewood, Willard B., Jr. *Black Americans and the White Man's Burden, 1898–1903*. Urbana: University of Illinois Press, 1975.

Gayle, Addison, Jr. *Oak and Ivy: A Biography of Paul Laurence Dunbar*. Garden City, N.Y.: Doubleday, 1971.

Gebhard, Caroline. "Inventing a 'Negro Literature': Race, Dialect, and Gender in the Early Works of Paul Laurence Dunbar, James Weldon Johnson, and Alice Dunbar-Nelson." In *Post-Bellum, Pre-Harlem: African American Literature and Culture, 1877–1919*, edited by Barbara McCaskill and Caroline Gebhard, 162–78. New York: New York University Press, 2006.

Giddings, Paula J. *Ida: A Sword among Lions*. New York: Amistad, 2008.

Gilder, Richard Watson. *The Poems of Richard Watson Gilder*. Boston: Houghton, Mifflin, 1908.

Gilmore, Al-Tony. "Jack Johnson and White Women: The National Impact." *Journal of Negro History* 58.1 (January 1973): 18–38.

Gilroy, Paul. *The Black Atlantic: Modernity and Double Consciousness*. Cambridge: Harvard University Press, 1993.

Glick, Elisa F. "Harlem's Queer Dandy." *MFS Modern Fiction Studies* 49.3 (Fall 2003): 414–42.

Goldsmith, Meredith. "White Skin, White Mask: Passing, Posing, and Performance in *The Great Gatsby*." *Modern Fiction Studies* 49.3 (Fall 2003): 443–68.

Gregory, James N. *The Southern Diaspora: How the Great Migration of Black and White Southerners Transformed America*. Chapel Hill: University of North Carolina Press, 2005.

Griffin, Farah Jasmine. *"Who Set You Flowin'?": The African-American Migration Narrative*. New York: Oxford University Press, 1995.

Haller, Mark. "Policy Gambling, Entertainment, and the Emergence of Black Politics: Chicago from 1900 to 1940." *Journal of Social History* 24.4 (Summer 1991): 719–39.

Handy, W. C. *Father of the Blues*. New York: Collier, 1970.

Hargrove, Hondon B. *Black Union Soldiers in the Civil War*. Jefferson, N.C.: McFarland, 1988.

Harlan, Louis. *Booker T. Washington: The Making of a Black Leader, 1856–1901*. New York: Oxford University Press, 1972.

———. *Booker T. Washington: The Wizard of Tuskegee, 1901–1915*. New York: Oxford University Press, 1983.

———. "*Up From Slavery* as History and Biography." In *Booker T. Washington and Black Progress: Up from Slavery 100 Years Later*, edited by W. Fitzhugh Brundage, 19–37. Tallahassee: University Press of Florida, 2003.

Harper, Frances E. W. *Iola Leroy; or, Shadows Uplifted*. 1892. Boston: Beacon Press, 1987.

———. *Sketches of Southern Life*. Philadelphia: Merrihew, 1872.

Harris, Joel Chandler. *Uncle Remus: His Songs and Sayings; the Folk-Lore of the Old Plantation*. New York: D. Appleton, 1881.

Harrison, Hubert H. *A Hubert Harrison Reader*. Edited by Jeffrey Perry. Middletown: Wesleyan University Press, 2001.

Hart, Joseph. "You Can Take Your Trunk and Go to Harlem." New York: T. B. Harms, 1899.

Hay, John. *The Complete Poetical Works of John Hay*. Boston: Houghton, Mifflin, 1917.

Haywood, Harry. *Black Bolshevik: The Autobiography of an Afro-American Communist*. Chicago: Liberator Press, 1978.

Holcomb, Gary Edward. *Claude McKay, Code Name Sasha: Queer Marxism and the Harlem Renaissance*. Gainesville: University Press of Florida, 2007.

Hopkins, Pauline. *Contending Forces: A Romance Illustrative of Negro Life North and South*. Boston: Colored Cooperative Publishing Company, 1900.

Hovey, Jaime. "Sapphic Primitivism in Gertrude Stein's *Q.E.D.*" *Modern Fiction Studies* 42.3 (Fall 1996): 547–68.

Hughes, Langston. *The Big Sea*. 1940. New York: Thunder's Mouth Press, 1986.

———. *The Collected Poems of Langston Hughes*. Edited by Arnold Rampersad and David Roessel. New York: Knopf, 1994.

Hutchinson, George B. *The Harlem Renaissance in Black and White*. Cambridge: Harvard University Press, 1995.

———. "Jean Toomer and the 'New Negroes' of Washington." *American Literature* 63.4 (December 1991): 683–92.

Huyssen, Andreas. *After the Great Divide: Modernism, Mass Culture, Postmodernism*. Bloomington: Indiana University Press, 1986.

Ignatiev, Noel. *How the Irish Became White*. New York: Routledge, 1995.

Jacobs, Harriet. *Incidents in the Life of a Slave Girl*. Boston: Published for the Author, 1860.

Jacobson, Matthew Frye. *Whiteness of a Different Color: European Immigrants and the Alchemy of Race*. Cambridge: Harvard University Press, 1998.

Jacques, Geoffrey. *A Change in the Weather: Modernist Imagination, African American Imaginary*. Amherst: University of Massachusetts Press, 2009.

James, Jennifer C. *A Freedom Bought with Blood: African American War Literature from the Civil War to World War II*. Chapel Hill: University of North Carolina Press, 2007.

James, William. *Memories and Studies*. New York: Longmans, Green, 1911.

———. *The Principles of Psychology*. New York: Henry Holt, 1890.

———. *Selected Writings*. New York: Book of the Month Club, 1997.

Jarrett, Gene Andrew. *Deans and Truants: Race and Realism in African American Literature*. Philadelphia: University of Pennsylvania Press, 2006.

Johnson, Fenton. *A Little Dreaming*. N.p., 1913.

———. *Songs of the Soil*. 1916. New York: AMS Press, 1975.

———. *Visions of the Dusk*. 1915. Freeport, N.Y.: Books for Libraries Press, 1971.

Johnson, James Weldon. *Along This Way: The Autobiography of James Weldon Johnson*. 1933. New York: Da Capo Press, 1973.

———. *Autobiography of an Ex-Colored Man*. 1912. In *Three Negro Classics*. New York: Avon, 1965.

———. *Black Manhattan*. New York: Knopf, 1930.

———. *Fifty Years and Other Poems*. Boston: Cornhill, 1917.

———. *God's Trombones: Seven Negro Sermons in Verse*. New York: Viking Press, 1927.

———. *The Selected Writings of James Weldon Johnson*. Vol. 2, *Social, Political, and Literary Essays*. Edited by Sondra Kathryn Wilson. New York: Oxford University Press, 1995.

———. *Writings*. New York: Library of America, 2004.

———, ed. *Book of American Negro Poetry*. New York: Harcourt, Brace, 1922, 1931.

Jones, Gavin. *Strange Talk: The Politics of Dialect Literature in Gilded Age America*. Berkeley: University of California Press, 1999.

Kaplan, Sidney. *American Studies in Black and White: Selected Essays*. Amherst: University of Massachusetts Press, 1991.

Keckley, Elizabeth. *Behind the Scenes; or, Thirty Years a Slave in the White House*. 1868. New York: Penguin, 2005.

Kersten, Holger. "The Creative Potential of Dialect Writing in Later-Nineteenth Century America." *Nineteenth-Century Literature* 55.1 (June 2000): 92–117.

Knupfer, Anne Meis. "If You Can't Push, Pull, If You Can't Pull, Get Out of the Way: The Phillis Wheatley Club and Home in Chicago, 1896 to 1920." *Journal of Negro History* 82.2 (Spring 1997): 221–31.

Kreymborg, Alfred. "Red Chant." *Crisis* 17 (November 1918): 31.

———. *Troubadour: An Autobiography*. New York: Boni and Liveright, 1925.

Kusmer, Kenneth L. *A Ghetto Takes Shape: Black Cleveland, 1870–1930*. Urbana: University of Illinois Press, 1976.

Lamothe, Daphne. *Inventing the New Negro: Narrative, Culture, and Ethnography*. Philadelphia: University of Pennsylvania Press, 2008.

Larsen, Nella. *Quicksand and Passing*. New Brunswick: Rutgers University Press, 1986.

"Late Literary News." *Baltimore Afro-American*, September 16, 1916, 4.

Lenin, V. I. *Selected Works*. Moscow: Progress Publishers, 1970.

Lewis, David Levering. *W. E. B. Du Bois: Biography of a Race*. New York: Henry Holt, 1993.

Lhamon, W. T. *Raising Cain: Black Face Performance from Jim Crow to Hip Hop*. Cambridge: Harvard University Press, 1998.

"'A Little Dreaming' by Fenton Johnson." *Baltimore Afro-American*, August 2, 1913, 1.

Logan, Rayford W. *The Betrayal of the Negro, from Rutherford B. Hayes to Woodrow Wilson*. New York: Collier, 1965.

Long, John Davis. *Memorial Day: Oration by Gov. John D. Long; Ode by Thomas W. Higginson*. Boston: Lockwood, Brooks, 1881.

Lott, Eric. *Love and Theft: Blackface Minstrelsy and the American Working Class*. New York: Oxford University Press, 1993.

Lowe, Martha Perry. "The Picture of Colonel Shaw in Boston." *The Liberator*, November 25, 1864, 192.

Lowell, Robert. *Selected Poems*. New York: Farrar, Straus and Giroux, 1976.

Mariani, Paul. *William Carlos Williams: A Naked New World*. New York: McGraw-Hill, 1981.

Martin, Waldo. "In Search of Booker T. Washington: *Up from Slavery*, History, and Legend." In *Booker T. Washington and Black Progress: Up from Slavery 100 Years Later*, edited by W. Fitzhugh Brundage, 38–57. Tallahassee: University Press of Florida, 2003.

Marx, Karl, and Friedrich Engels. *The Communist Manifesto*. New York: International, 1948.

Maxwell, William J. "Dunbar's Bohemian Gallery: Foreign Color and Fin-de-Siècle Modernism." *African American Review* 41.2 (Summer 2007): 341–46.

McCann, Sean. "Pauline Hopkins and the Work of Melodrama." *ELH* 64.3 (Fall 1997): 789–822.

McDowell, Deborah. Introduction to *Plum Bun: A Novel with a Moral*, by Jessie Fauset, ix–xxxiii. Boston: Beacon Press, 1999.

McFarland, Gerald W. *Inside Greenwich Village: A New York City Neighborhood, 1898–1918*. Amherst: University of Massachusetts Press, 2001.

McKay, Claude. *Banjo, a Story without a Plot*. New York: Harper & Brothers, 1929.

———. *Complete Poems*. Edited by William J. Maxwell. Urbana: University of Illinois Press, 2004.

———. *Home to Harlem*. New York: Harper & Brothers, 1928.

———. *A Long Way from Home*. 1937. New York: Arno Press, 1969.

Meier, August. *Negro Thought in American, 1880–1915: Racial Ideologies in the Age of Booker T. Washington*. Ann Arbor: University of Michigan Press, 1963.

Mellow, James R. *Charmed Circle: Gertrude Stein & Company*. New York: Praeger, 1974.

Melnick, Jeffrey. *A Right to Sing the Blues: African Americans, Jews, and American Popular Song*. Cambridge: Harvard University Press, 1999.

Miller, Monica L. "The Black Dandy as Bad Modernist." In *Bad Modernisms*, edited by Douglas Mao and Rebecca Walkowitz, 179–205. Durham: Duke University Press, 2006.

Miller, Rosalind S., ed. *Gertrude Stein: Form and Intelligibility, Containing the Radcliffe Themes*. New York: Exposition Press, 1949.

Minnick, Lisa Cohen. *Dialect and Dichotomy: Literary Representations of African American Speech*. Tuscaloosa: University of Alabama Press, 2004.

Mishkin, Tracy. *The Harlem and Irish Renaissances: Language, Identity, and Representation*. Gainesville: University Press of Florida, 1998.

Monroe, Harriet, and Alice Corbin Henderson, eds. *The New Poetry: An Anthology*. New York: Macmillan, 1917.

Moody, William Vaughn. *The Poems and Plays of William Vaughn Moody*. Vol. 1.
Boston: Houghton, Mifflin, 1912.

Morrison, Toni. *Playing in the Dark: Whiteness and the Literary Imagination*.
Cambridge: Harvard University Press, 1992.

Moses, Wilson. "The Lost World of the Negro, 1895–1919: Black Literary and
Intellectual Life before the 'Renaissance.'" *Black American Literature Forum*
21.1/2 (Summer 1987): 1–84.

Mumford, Kevin J. *Interzones: Black/White Sex Districts in Chicago and New York in
the Early Twentieth Century*. New York: Columbia University Press, 1997.

Newcomb, John Timberman. *Would Poetry Disappear? American Verse and the
Crisis of Modernity*. Columbus: Ohio State University Press, 2004.

Nielsen, Aldon. *Reading Race: White American Poets and the Racial Discourse in the
Twentieth Century*. Athens: University of Georgia Press, 1988.

Nora, Pierre, and Laurence Kriztman, eds. *Realms of Memory: Rethinking the
French Past*. Vol. 1. New York: Columbia University Press, 1996.

North, Michael. *The Dialect of Modernism: Race, Language, and Twentieth-Century
Literature*. New York: Oxford University Press, 1994.

Nugent, Richard Bruce. *Gay Rebel of the Harlem Renaissance: Selections from the
Work of Richard Bruce Nugent*. Edited by Thomas H. Wirth. Durham: Duke
University Press, 2002.

Osofsky, Gilbert. *Harlem: The Making of a Ghetto*. New York: Harper & Row, 1966.

Page, Thomas Nelson. *In Ole Virginia: Marse Chan and Other Stories*. New York:
Scribner, 1887.

Park, Robert. "Human Migration and the Marginal Man." *American Journal of
Sociology* 33.6 (May 1928): 881–93.

Perry, Jeffrey B. *Hubert Harrison: The Voice of Harlem Radicalism, 1883–1918*. New
York: Columbia University Press, 2009.

Peterson, Carla L. "Commemorative Ceremonies and Invented Traditions:
History, Modernity, and Memory in the 'New Negro' Novel of the Nadir." In
Post-Bellum, Pre-Harlem: African American Literature and Culture, 1877–1919,
edited by Barbara McCaskill and Caroline Gebhard, 34–56. New York: New York
University Press, 2006.

———. "The Remaking of Americans: Gertrude Stein's 'Melanctha' and African
American Musical Traditions." In *Criticism and the Color Line*, edited by
Henry B. Wonham, 140–57. New Brunswick: Rutgers University Press, 1996.

"Phyllis Wheatley Club." *Chicago Defender*, October 18, 1913, 5.

"The Phyllis Wheatley Club." *Chicago Defender*, October 7, 1911, 1.

"Pleasant Sunday Afternoon Enjoyed at Bethel." *Chicago Defender*, May 4, 1918, 12.

"Praise for Braithwaite." *Baltimore Afro-American*, December 4, 1915, 1.

Rampersad, Arnold. *The Life of Langston Hughes*. New York: Oxford University
Press, 1986–88.

Ray, Cordelia. *Poems*. New York: Grafton, 1910.

Read, Herbert. "TSE: A Memoir." *Sewanee Review* 74 (Winter 1966): 31–57.

"Reconciliation Committee Meets." *Chicago Defender*, July 31, 1920, 3.

Reed, Adolph. *Stirrings in the Jug: Black Politics in the Post-Segregation Era.*
Minneapolis: University of Minnesota Press, 1999.

Rexroth, Kenneth. *An Autobiographical Novel.* Garden City, N.Y.: Doubleday, 1966.

Ridgely, J. V. *Nineteenth Century Southern Literature.* Lexington: University Press
of Kentucky, 1988.

Riis, Jacob W. *How the Other Half Lives.* 1901. New York: Penguin Books, 1997.

Roediger, David. *Working toward Whiteness: How America's Immigrants Became
White.* New York: Basic Books, 2005.

Rosemont, Franklin. Introduction to *Hobohemia* by Frank Beck. Chicago: Charles
Kerr, 2000.

———, ed. *The Rise and Fall of the Dil Pickle.* Chicago: Charles Kerr, 2003.

Rowe, George Clinton. *Our Heroes: Patriotic Poems on Men, Women and Sayings of
the Negro Race.* Charleston, S.C.: Walker, Evans & Cogswell, 1890.

Rowe, John Carlos. "Naming What Is Inside: Gertrude Stein's Use of Names in
Three Lives." *Novel: A Forum on Fiction* 36.2 (Spring 2003): 219–43.

Ruotolo, Christine. "James Weldon Johnson and the Autobiography of an Ex-
Colored Musician." *American Literature* 72.2 (June 2000): 249–74.

Sacks, Marcy S. *Before Harlem: The Black Experience in New York City before World
War I.* Philadelphia: University of Pennsylvania Press, 2006.

Saldivar-Hull, Sonia. "Wrestling Your Ally: Stein, Racism, and Feminist Critical
Practice." In *Women's Writing in Exile,* edited by Mary Lynn Broe and
Angela Ingram, 181–98. Chapel Hill: University of North Carolina Press, 1989.

Sanchez, Sonia. *Homecoming.* Detroit: Broadside Press, 1969.

Sargent, Epes. "Colonel Shaw: On Hearing That the Rebels Had Buried His Body
under a Pile of Twenty-five Negroes." *Boston Evening Transcript,* August 4, 1863, 2.

Schneider, Mark R. *Boston Confronts Jim Crow, 1890–1920.* Boston: Northeastern
University Press, 1997.

Schocket, Eric. *Vanishing Moments: Class and American Literature.* Ann Arbor:
University of Michigan Press, 2006.

Schwarz, A. B. Christa. *Gay Voices of the Harlem Renaissance.* Bloomington: Indiana
University Press, 2003.

Schwarz, Judith. *The Radical Feminists of Heterodoxy: Greenwich Village, 1912–
1940.* Norwich, Vt.: New Victoria Publishers, 1986.

Scruggs, Charles. *Sweet Home: Invisible Cities in the Afro-American Novel.*
Baltimore: Johns Hopkins University Press, 1993.

Sell, Mike. "Bohemianism, the Cultural Turn of the Avantgarde, and the Forgetting
of the Roma." *TDR* 51.2 (Summer 2007): 41–59.

Shand-Tucci, Douglass. *Boston Bohemia, 1881–1900: Ralph Adams Cram; Life and
Architecture.* Amherst: University of Massachusetts Press, 1995.

Sherman, Joan R. *Invisible Poets: Afro-Americans of the Nineteenth Century.*
Urbana: University of Illinois Press, 1974.

Simpson, Joshua McCarter. *The Emancipation Car.* 1874. Miami, Fla., Mnemosyne
Publishing, 1969.

Sinfield, Alan. *The Wilde Century: Effeminacy, Oscar Wilde, and the Queer Moment.*
New York: Columbia University Press, 1994.

Skerrett, Joseph T., Jr. "Irony and Symbolic Action in James Weldon Johnson's *The Autobiography of an Ex-Coloured Man*." *American Quarterly* 32 (Winter 1980): 540–58.

Smedman, Lorna J. "'Cousin to Cooning': Relation, Difference, and Racialized Language in Stein's Nonrepresentational Texts." *Modern Fiction Studies* 42.3 (1996): 569–88.

Smethurst, James. *The Black Arts Movement*. Chapel Hill: University of North Carolina Press, 2005.

———. "Lyric Stars: Countee Cullen and Langston Hughes." In *The Cambridge Companion to the Harlem Renaissance*, edited by George Hutchinson, 112–25. New York: Cambridge University Press, 2007.

Sollors, Werner. *Ethnic Modernism*. Cambridge: Harvard University Press, 2008.

Somerville, Siobhan. "Passing through the Closet in Pauline E. Hopkins's *Contending Forces*." *American Literature* 69.1 (March 1997): 139–66.

———. *Queering the Color Line: Race and the Invention of Homosexuality in American Culture*. Durham: Duke University Press, 1999.

Sotiropoulos, Karen. *Staging Race: Black Performers in Turn of the Century America*. Cambridge: Harvard University Press, 2006.

Soto, Michael. *The Modernist Nation: Generation, Renaissance, and Twentieth-Century American Literature*. Tuscaloosa: University of Alabama Press, 2004.

Southern, Eileen. *The Music of Black Americans*. New York: W. W. Norton, 1983.

Spear, Allan H. *Black Chicago: The Making of a Negro Ghetto*. Chicago: University of Chicago Press, 1967.

Stansell, Christine. *American Moderns: Bohemian New York and the Creation of a New Century*. New York: Metropolitan Books, 2000.

Stein, Gertrude. *The Autobiography of Alice B. Toklas*. 1933. New York: Vintage, 1960.

———. *Three Lives*. 1909. New York: Pocket Books, 2003.

Stepto, Robert. *From Behind the Veil: A Study of Afro-American Narrative*. Urbana: University of Illinois Press, 1991.

Stowe, Harriet Beecher. *Uncle Tom's Cabin*. 1852. New York: Oxford University Press, 2002.

Sundquist, Eric. *To Wake the Nations: Race in the Making of American Literature*. Cambridge: Harvard University Press, 1993.

Szefel, Lisa. "Beauty and William Braithwaite." *Callaloo* 29.2 (2006): 560–86.

———. "Encouraging Verse: William S. Braithwaite and the Poetics of Race." *New England Quarterly* 74.1 (March 2001): 32–61.

Tapscott, Stephen. *American Beauty: William Carlos Williams and the Modernist Whitman*. New York: Columbia University Press, 1984.

Tate, Claudia. *Domestic Allegories of Political Desire*. New York: Oxford University Press, 1996.

Terdiman, Richard. *Past and Present: Modernity and the Memory Crisis*. Ithaca: Cornell University Press, 1993.

Thomas, Lorenzo. *Extraordinary Measures: Afrocentric Modernism and Twentieth-Century American Poetry*. Tuscaloosa: University of Alabama Press, 2000.

Thoreau, Henry David. *A Week on the Concord and Merrimack Rivers.* 1849. Mineola, N.Y.: Dover, 2001.

Thurman, Wallace. *Infants of the Spring.* 1932. Boston: Northeastern University Press, 1992.

Toomer, Jean. *Cane.* 1923. New York: Liveright, 1993.

Turner, Joyce Moore. *Caribbean Crusaders and the Harlem Renaissance.* Urbana: University of Illinois Press, 2005.

Twain, Mark. *The Adventures of Huckleberry Finn.* 1885. New York: Oxford University Press, 1996.

Van Vechten, Carl. *Nigger Heaven.* New York: Knopf, 1926.

Vials, Chris. *Realism for the Masses: Aesthetics, Popular Front Pluralism, and U.S. Culture, 1935–1947.* Jackson: University Press of Mississippi, 2009.

"W. S. Braithwaite Literary Critic." *Baltimore Afro-American,* April 22, 1916, 1.

Wagner, Jean. *Black Poets of the United States: From Paul Laurence Dunbar to Langston Hughes.* Urbana: University of Illinois Press, 1973.

Wagner-Martin, Linda. *"Favored Strangers": Gertrude Stein and Her Family.* New Brunswick: Rutgers University Press, 1995.

Washington, Booker T. "The Awakening of the Negro." *Atlantic Monthly* 78 (September 1896): 322–28.

———. *Booker T. Washington Papers.* 14 vols. Edited by Louis R. Harlan. Urbana: University of Illinois Press, 1972–89.

———. *My Larger Education: Being Chapters from My Experience.* Garden City, N.Y.: Doubleday, Page, 1911.

———. *The Story of My Life and Work: An Autobiography.* Napierville: J. L. Nichols, 1901.

———. *Up From Slavery.* New York: Doubleday, 1901.

Washington, Salim. "Of Black Bards, Known and Unknown: Music as Racial Metaphor in James Weldon Johnson's *The Autobiography of an Ex-Colored Man.*" *Callaloo* 25.1 (2002): 233–56.

Webb, Barbara. "The Black Dandyism of George Walker: A Case Study in Genealogical Method." *TDR* 45.4 (Winter 2001): 7–24.

Weimann, Robert. *Shakespeare and the Popular Tradition in the Theatre.* Baltimore: Johns Hopkins University Press, 1978.

Weiss, M. Lynn. "Among Negroes: Gertrude Stein and African America." In *Race and the Modern Artist,* edited by Heather Hathaway, Josef Jarab, and Jeffrey Melnick, 115–25. New York: Oxford University Press, 2003.

Whalan, Mark. "Jean Toomer and the Avant-Garde." In *The Cambridge Companion to the Harlem Renaissance,* edited by George Hutchinson, 71–80. New York: Cambridge University Press, 2007.

Whitman, Albery. *Not a Man and Yet a Man.* 1877. Upper Saddle River, N.J.: Gregg Press, 1970.

"William Stanley Braithwaite." *Baltimore Afro-American,* May 10, 1918, 4.

Williams, George Washington. *History of the Negro Troops in the Rebellion.* New York: Harper & Bros., 1888.

Williams, Kenny J. "An Invisible Partnership and an Unlikely Relationship:

William Stanley Braithwaite and Harriet Monroe." *Callaloo* 32 (Summer 1987): 516–50.

Williams, Raymond. *The Politics of Modernists: Against the New Conformists*. New York: Verso, 1996.

Williams, William Carlos. *The Autobiography of William Carlos Williams*. New York: New Directions, 1951.

——. *The Collected Poems of William Carlos Williams*. Vol. 1, *1909–1939*. New York: New Directions, 1986.

——. *In the American Grain*. 1925. New York: New Directions, 1956.

——. *Kora in Hell: Improvisations*. Boston: Four Seas, 1920.

——. *The Selected Letters of William Carlos Williams*. Edited by John C. Thirwell. New York: New Directions, 1957.

Wilson, Harriet. *Our Nig; or, Sketches from the Life of a Free Black*. 1859. New York: Vintage Books, 1983.

Wineapple, Brenda. *Sister Brother: Gertrude and Leo Stein*. New York: G. P. Putnam & Sons, 1996.

Wirth, Thomas H. Introduction to *Gay Rebel of the Harlem Renaissance: Selections from the Work of Richard Bruce Nugent*, edited by Thomas H. Wirth, 1–61. Durham: Duke University Press, 2002.

Wooley, Lisa. *American Voices of the Chicago Renaissance*. Dekalb: University of Northern Illinois Press, 2000.

Work, John W. *American Negro Songs and Spirituals*. New York: Crown Publishers, 1940.

Wright, Richard. *Early Works*. New York: Library of America, 1991.

Yacovone, Donald. "Sacred Land Regained: Frances Ellen Watkins Harper and 'The Massachusetts Fifty-fourth,' a Lost Poem." *Pennsylvania History* 62.1 (Winter 1995): 90–110.

Index